To Wendy,

Congratulations!

It is all by God's
wonderful grace!

Barb Orlowski

Spiritual Abuse Recovery

Spiritual Abuse Recovery

Dynamic Research on Finding a Place of Wholeness

BARBARA M. ORLOWSKI

WIPF & STOCK · Eugene, Oregon

SPIRITUAL ABUSE RECOVERY
Dynamic Research on Finding a Place of Wholeness

Wipf & Stock
An Imprint of Wipf and Stock Publishers
199 W. 8th Ave., Suite 3
Eugene, OR 97401

www. wipfandstock.com

ISBN 13: 978-1-60608-967-5

Manufactured in the U.S.A.

Unless otherwise stated, Scripture quotations are from the New International
Version.

To Jim

My Best Friend and Confidant

Contents

Illustrations

Acknowledgements

I AM GRATEFUL TO my husband Jim for his steady encouragement and faithful support on this unique journey through uncharted waters, and for our adult children, Jessica and Ben. I would like to thank my advisor, Dr. Larry Perkins, who motivated me to deeply research my theological ideas.

I am particularly thankful to the many website hosts who posted the information for this doctoral research so that I could find participants. Without their willing help, I could not have done it with such gusto!

I am also grateful to the participants who were willing to share the details of their experience with me. Their answers, comments, suggestions, book recommendations, website links, and other observations during the research process were appreciated. Learning about the grace of God working in the lives of the participants has made me a richer person. I appreciate those who were cheerleaders for this study, those who informed others, those who offered words of encouragement, and those who offered to pray for me during the course of this project.

Finally, my thanksgiving goes to our Great God—the Father, the Lord Jesus, and the Holy Spirit. I appreciate heaven's faithful oversight in gently guiding a curious young woman into the delightful and fulfilling realms of theology and biblical studies and ultimately helping her to complete this project for him. My cup continually overflows!

The following are the website hosts that the researcher initially used or those who later confirmed that they had heard about this study from others and were also posting the information on their sites. Apologies for any that the researcher has inadvertently excluded:

Emerging Grace: http://emerging grace; blogspot.com

Kingdom Grace: http://kingdomgrace.wordpress.com

Paul Sue: http://batteredsheep.com

Barry and Jennifer Pendergast: http://bleatinglambs.org (site now discontinued)

Brother Maynard: http://subversive influence.com

Christians For Biblical Equality: http://www.cbeinternational.org

SmuloSpace: http://www.johnsmulo.com

Prodigal Kiwis: http://prodigal.typepad.com

Mary: http://one-thing-is-needed.blogspot.com

Decompressing Faith: erinword.com

Jason Clark: http://jasonclark.ws/tag/leadership

Benjamin Potter: http://loomnwheel.wordpress.com

A Former Leader's Journey: http://retrofited.blogspot.com

Wayne Jacobsen: Lifestream.org

Elizabeth: messychristian.com

Makeesha Fisher: http://www.swingingfromthevine.com

Len Hjalmarson: http://www.nextreformation.com

Darryl Dash: http://www.dashhouse.com

Because It Matters: http://dannimoss.wordpress.com

My True Self: http://mytrueself.typepad.com

Radical Reversal: radicalreversal.org

Alan Knox: http://assembling.blogspot.com

A School Without Walls: http://paulwhiting.blogspot.com

Rick Meigs: http://www.blindbeggar.org

Kevin Bussey: http://kevinbussey.wordpress.com

Alan Hirsch: http://www.theforgottenways.org

Tyler Watson: http://spacebetween.blogsome.com

Ron Cole: http://thewearypilgrim.typepad.com

Cindy Bryan: http://cindybryan.blogspot.com

The researcher appreciated being interviewed and this study referenced in the Winnipeg Free Press by Brenda Suderman, January 27, 2008.

Preface

SPIRITUAL ABUSE, THE MISUSE of spiritual authority to maltreat followers in the Christian church, is a complex issue. This study focused on how people processed their grief after experiencing spiritual abuse in their local church and how they rediscovered spiritual harmony.

The goal of this research was not to open old wounds, but to allow those who healed over time the opportunity to give voice to their previous suffering as well as to gain understanding as to how they recovered. The Christian community needs to recognize that these distressing situations exist. We need to grieve and heal together.

This book aims to help people who have been wounded by spiritual abuse. It can also function as a resource for pastors, denominational leaders, seminary and Bible college instructors, church consultants, and Christians in general to better understand, and thus prevent, this complex issue.

What's Going On?

E VERY YEAR DEDICATED CHRISTIANS[1] leave churches because of spiritual maltreatment at the hands of clergy. What factors cause dedicated believers in Christ, who have been active in serving in their local church for a number of years, to be spiritually abused, pushed outside the church, and reduced to an exiting statistic? This book is based on the doctoral research of Barb Orlowski who traced the process of spiritual recovery among church congregants who were compelled to make the decision to leave their home church.

Spiritual abuse is a complex issue and the devastating emotional toll upon exiting active church attendants beckons consideration. The concept of spiritual abuse may not be a familiar one to church leaders. Many issues demand the time and energy of pastoral and other church leaders; therefore, spiritual abuse and the recovery of abused believers may remain at the periphery of their attention and interest. This book aims to bring spiritual abuse to the center of clergy's attention, invites them to consider this very real dysfunction in the Church today, and asks them to decide whether they and their church community can be part of the solution to this malady, rather than part of the problem. Participants in this study describe how they went from a point of emotional woundedness to a place of spiritual recovery. Learning what factors helped in their recovery will aid church ministry leaders in how they and their congregations can minister more effectively in this area of need in the Church.

---

1. In the context of this discussion, the term "Christian" can be defined as those who personally believe that Jesus Christ is the Son of God, (fully God, fully man) and that by believing in his finished work on the cross and his Lordship from heaven, that they have his indwelling presence by his Holy Spirit. Christians have the hope of eternal life with God after this life.

The following excerpt, "Shattered Illusions," is from a popular Internet website.[2] Along with this website host's description of spiritual abuse are selected comments by those who replied to the post. This shows an immediate and parallel response to the host's understanding of the issue by others.

> A large number of people who leave churches have experienced spiritual abuse. One of the reasons I want to talk about this is because it is a reality in the lives of many who are a part of the emerging church conversation. Spiritual abuse is trauma. The three characteristics of trauma are: 1. An external cause—Someone does it to you. 2. Violation—You are violated by an unwelcome intrusion. 3. Loss of control—It is unexpected and beyond your control. The result is a shattering of the basic assumptions the person held about their world. For me, the shattering was the realization that things within the church are not always as they should be, and truth and justice do not always prevail. Evil within the world doesn't surprise me. Mistakes and misunderstandings in relationships don't shock me. I have always believed that conflicts between Christians can be worked through when both parties submit their will to God. Intentional, malicious action against me by a church leader blew me away. The unwillingness of others involved to challenge the leader's actions, but instead look the other way in denial, preserving their positions, shattered my trust in church leadership.
>
> The tendency of those who have not experienced spiritual abuse is to minimize the experience. Honestly, it is something you do not truly understand unless you have experienced it. Those who leave churches are often portrayed as overly sensitive, embittered, and difficult to get along with. While they may be reactionary immediately following their abuse, most recover and grow beyond that. Their experience is a contributing factor in forming different expectations of what the church should be.

Selected excerpts from online comments about this article:

> Like yourself, I have experienced this, and it was a life-altering event. The loneliness, the second-guessing, the longing to be vindicated, resisting the urge to strike out, etc.

---

2. Kingdom Grace. "Shattered Illusions." Spiritual Abuse Series. no. 1. No pages. Online: http://kingdomgrace.wordpress.com/2005/09/11/shattered-illusions/. September 11, 2005 (accessed March 2006).

My first pastorate ended in a way that is eerily similar to what you have described here. The abuse, the lies, the manipulations, the cowardice of the other leaders who looked the other way, and the gullibility of the congregation that bought the whole spin-doctoring—hook, line and sinker. I was a total mess for a year at least. The biggest casualty was my trust in other leaders and "mature" Christians. . . . It's far too prevalent. But God is merciful and gracious, and brings healing to those who have been through these dark waters. I can also bear witness to His restorative power in my life.

I've written about this too. . . . It's a story of my personal path to what, where, and why I am today. Painful curves, but still, God knows how to make good things happen out of the bad, too.

Your post has begun a powerful conversation here. Thanks for being willing to open yourself up. I know from personal experience that there's fear in doing that, even among friends, for a long time. I was hurt by manipulative lay leaders. It's been ten years—and it took most of those ten years to get past it. We settled in a church where God clearly led us for healing. They are loving people, who cared for us, and mostly didn't hurt us.

A friend of mine points out that there is a culture of silence in many churches to not confront hypocrisy or injustice in leadership. When someone does speak out, [they are] tarred and feathered and characterized as rebellious or bitter. It is good that you are bringing this out into the open Grace.

This selected account and the responses given on this website provide a snapshot of this multifaceted and widespread problem in the Church today and illustrate the nature of the issue. It also shows that recovery and spiritual restoration are possible.

CHURCH ISSUE AND MINISTRY PROBLEM

People who experience spiritual abuse report that they arrive at a point in their Christian journey where grief and disappointment with previous church leadership and disenchantment with their previously held beliefs overwhelms them. They experience grief, distress, and dissatisfaction with their former church community, and specifically, its leadership. As a result, they encounter a personal dilemma regarding the entire concept of Church.

In seeking solutions to their abusive situation many thoughts flood their mind. Some of the questions these bruised participants asked were: Why should I continue to go to church? Why should I attend church at all if I have been wounded by church leadership? Why can't I just be a Christian and not bother to go to church? I believe that I need to find a healthier church—where can I find a caring church family?[3]

As a result of this experience, numerous Christians have opted for other forms of church community. These may include house churches, coffee shop fellowships, or simply meeting with other believers on a regular basis at an agreed upon location. Some church attenders have given up on the institutional church and have developed their own coping mechanisms apart from church buildings and traditional formats for Christian meetings. Alan Jamieson designates these individuals and groups as post-church.[4] Post-church individuals and couples find themselves faced with a situation of spiritual dissonance as well as emotional inequilibrium. It has been observed by researchers, authors, and website hosts interested in this topic that, over time, individuals can make positive steps toward spiritual harmony. Towards that end, these questions arise: How have Christians worked through their pain and disillusionment with their church and church leadership, and how have they eventually come to a place of spiritual harmony? What have been the significant factors that have sustained and encouraged spiritual growth in their Christian life after being wounded?

THE CONTEXT OF THIS STUDY

This study centers on the suffering of individuals as a result of unexpected hurtful situations in their home church, something that happens in many places.[5] These Christians have not stayed in a state of grief and disillusionment, but successfully processed their negative church experience to find renewed spiritual harmony.

My interest in this topic was undeveloped until my husband and I, along with our adult son, were in the middle of a difficult and unexpected church situation. The charismatic church that we had attended

3. These sentiments are representative of those who have posted comments on various websites as well as by the participants in this study. Various authors allude to these questions as well.

4. Jamieson et al., *Church Leavers*, 13.

5. See Enroth, Johnson and VanVonderen, Blue, Farnsworth, Jamieson, and Cudmore.

for sixteen years had become a place of spiritual anxiety, discouragement, and a hindrance to fruitful Christian ministry. As active members, we began to realize that the spiritual and theological health of the church under the leadership at the time was in jeopardy. Observing the disconcerting behavior of leadership over a period of time raised many questions. We, along with other involved members, made the decision to leave our home church. As church companions, we witnessed the end of an era, the end of our hopes and dreams for our home church, and the fracturing of a fellowship that was previously known for its hospitality and Christian heritage.

The experience left us perplexed, frustrated, angry, and disillusioned with the church leadership. Those who had raised concerns were seen as agitators against how the leadership had felt that the Holy Spirit was leading. To the leadership, it probably seemed that withdrawal of active members from the fellowship was a sure affirmation that these congregants were not willing to walk with the Holy Spirit—consequently those congregants were marginalized. From the perspective of those who left, it appeared that the Holy Spirit was leading them away from a system that did not place discerning whether certain teachings were biblical truth or not and caring for the active members as priorities. Each individual multiplied the losses experienced by those who left. It was a time now to seek God through this season of disappointment and grief in order to make sense of and process this untimely experience in fruitful ways.

This experience motivated me to understand the issue of spiritual abuse. Equal interest was generated to understand how people could heal after this perplexing condition. What was unanticipated yet reassuring was reading the numerous Internet websites and blogs that highlighted this church ministry issue. Our family's negative church experience was shared by many in the mainstream of Christendom. Ronald Enroth confirms that from the people interviewed he has discovered that the types of churches and denominational streams they represent include a wide range of groups located almost anywhere. This is not just a North American occurrence but can be found in Christian faith communities almost any place in the world. Although there are many healthy churches, there are no perfect churches to emulate.[6]

---

6. Enroth, *Recovering from Churches*, 17.

My personal church crisis became the catalyst for deeper research into this complex and sensitive topic. I began to examine recognizable consistencies among the many experiences of those injured as well as indicators that pointed to a wholesome recovery. There seemed to be a recovery process that individuals went through in order to understand and deal with their situation. This process of restoration and spiritual recovery became part of our family's experience and mirrored what many others had found to be helpful.

Jeff VanVonderen and David Johnson's book on spiritual abuse, published in 1991, is still widely circulated. To the question, "I guess the problem hasn't gone away?" VanVonderen replied, "Usually a book will be out there for a couple of years and then go out of print. But people keep finding *The Subtle Power of Spiritual Abuse* as if it's a new book. The stories I hear from people haven't gotten any nicer over the last decade either."[7] VanVonderen brings out what other authors have uncovered as well. This church ministry issue appears to be ongoing and recognizable in many areas of the Christian Church. Therefore, it needs to be acknowledged and understood by church leaders so that they may be involved as part of the solution.

This book aims to demonstrate a path forward to greater freedom in Christ and spiritual harmony after a debilitating season of disillusionment. Spiritual recovery from woundedness and disillusionment can be defined in the following ways:

1. Christians have become reoriented after their negative experience.

2. Christians have a greater appreciation for the work of God's grace in their lives.

3. Christians have forgiven the offending leaders.

4. Christians are able to articulate their experience clearly without resentment.

5. Christians are able to reflect positively on what they have learned through this experience.

---

7. VanVonderen, http://www.spiritualabuse.com/?page_id=58, lines 8–11. VanVonderen is an author, a speaker, and the executive director of Spiritual Abuse Recovery Resources, a ministry of Christian Recovery International. This interview first appeared in 2000 in STEPS magazine, a publication of the National Association for Christian Recovery.

6. Christians are available to humbly serve and minister to others with wisdom and gentleness.

7. Christians can look to the future with optimism.

PURPOSE AND RESEARCH QUESTION

The purpose of this book is to show how Christians may transcend a devastating experience in a local church setting to achieve a state or condition of spiritual harmony. It aims to demonstrate how people who experienced grief and loss in their Christian lives at the hands of church leaders worked through a purposeful spiritual process and regained a measure of spiritual equilibrium. Their spiritual journey can instruct those who are facing similar losses. This book can also help church ministry leaders understand spiritual abuse.

The research question was: How have Christians recovered after experiencing perceived spiritual abuse in a local congregation? I hypothesized that:

1. Subjects need confidants—mature Christians, such as good friends, relatives, or church leaders from other fellowships—to help them process their negative experience. Subjects need time to tell their story. These confidants would include two categories of people:

   a) Those who have been in this type of church experience and have come through it wisely. (These ought to be able to minister without bitterness or resentment in their attempt to help those presently dismayed.)

   b) Those who know and understand God's grace, have a mature understanding of the Scriptures, and can empathize with the unsettling situation.

2. Subjects may discover a range of resources that offer practical insights:

   c) They may use the Internet to connect with people via websites or blog interactions to receive immediate support and feedback.

   d) They may find books that give insights into the roots of spiritual abuse and the factors that contribute to abusive leadership styles.

e) Some churches may offer support groups that can help.

Realizing that this unsettling but valid dilemma in the Christian Church is found in many sectors helps people understand their own situation from a broader perspective. They begin to understand that they are not alone since they recognize that many others have gone through a similar experience.

3. Subjects are pressed in their desire to get closer to God through a deepening faith experience. Subjects realize that they need time to heal spiritually and emotionally.

    a) They are enabled by the Spirit to grow deeper in the Lord through this crisis as he can provide comfort, give wisdom, renew, refresh, stir-up the need to forgive, create compassion for those caught up in error, and finally, guide them in a renewed and healthier spiritual direction.

    b) They are enabled by the Spirit to experience God's grace in fresh and revitalizing ways.

    c) They are enabled by the Spirit to be renewed in body, mind, and spirit in order to understand the Kingdom of God in new and innovative ways.

4. Subjects may find that pastors are able to provide insights that they have gained from ministering to others who have come to them for similar help.

OVERVIEW OF THE LITERATURE REVIEW

The literature review, outlined in chapter 2, considers research studies and books that demonstrate the widespread incidence of people leaving their home church because of negative and hurtful experiences. The literature paints a picture of an occurrence more widely spread than initially thought. The fact that there are various layers to spiritual abuse makes this issue a complex one, and a number of topics and categories related to Church and Christian ministry converge and interconnect with it. Deviant theologies and questionable ministry practices create varied yet predictable affects in the lives of individual Christians. In order for church consultants, church leaders, professional counselors, or concerned Christians to have a comprehensive understanding of this church ministry issue, they will need to be familiar with the multifaceted nature of this issue as well as the types of literature that are available for study and reflection.

Four main steps have been identified to aid in healing from spiritual abuse:

1. Allow sufficient time to grieve.

2. Forgive and release the situation to God.

3. Find a suitable faith community.

4. Move forward in Christ with the help of the Holy Spirit.

The need to help rebuild a solid theological foundation in people becomes the task of caring helpers in healthy spiritual communities.

OVERVIEW OF THE THEOLOGICAL AND BIBLICAL FOUNDATIONS

This study has considered the theological and biblical foundations that proceed from the research question. Some specific areas of Christian belief and understanding have been distorted in abused people—these misshapen beliefs need to be discerned and set straight so that spiritual life might be revitalized. Distortions in understanding the Christian faith include:

1. Not understanding salvation and sanctification by grace.

2. Not understanding sound hermeneutical principles to interpret God's Word.

3. Not understanding how to discern whether certain teachings are biblical truth or not.

4. Not differentiating a flawed leadership model from a legitimate biblical leadership model.

5. Not experiencing authentic Christian community.

6. Not experiencing appropriate treatment by leaders of God's people.

People who have come from abusive churches must wrestle with the theological inaccuracy of legalism. The hierarchical and authoritarian model of leadership will be described and critiqued. In the context of the contemporary Christian church, a deficient Old Testament leadership style can easily be developed by the fusion of a Mosaic model with that of the Aaronic/Levitical priesthood. The New Testament model of leadership, which was taught and demonstrated by Christ, demonstrates an egalitarian servant leadership model.[8] To hold that a servant leadership model is solely a New Testament model of leadership may be a common assumption. The Old Testament gives an understandable portrayal of servant leadership that needs to be revisited. Various New Testament passages that address the topic of godly leadership will be considered. The ideals of both a valid Old Testament view as well as understanding New Testament beliefs and practices provides a better foundation for a healthy model of Christian leadership. Spiritual recovery after spiritual abuse is multifaceted, but understanding a suitable process can help church leaders in future ministry to others. The biblical and theological foundations ought to establish this study and provide a better understanding of these related issues.

The primary focus of this research is to understand how believers recover spiritual harmony, that is, to understand how believers go from a devastating experience with their church leadership in their local church setting to a state or condition of renewed spiritual harmony. I have attempted to reconstruct the subjects' realities and provide insight into their distinct narratives. This study contains the accounts of people who were injured by church leadership. There has been no attempt to verify the accuracy of these accounts.

HOW PARTICIPANTS WERE RECRUITED

Some potential local participants were contacted by telephone but most were contacted via email. I made contact with various website hosts to gain assistance in posting information about this research project on their websites, along with an appeal for participants. Website hosts welcomed the opportunity to post the information and encouraged involvement among their readership. Internet contacts recommended other websites or forwarded the material to associates. Some who saw the postings informed family and friends about this research. The Internet provided a

---

8. A comprehensive study of this issue brings me to conclude that in order for believers to recover successfully they need to adopt this perspective.

broad base for soliciting potential participants from Canada, the United States, the United Kingdom, Australia, New Zealand, and elsewhere.

The covering letter sent to enquirers provided simple guidelines for answering the questionnaire. Participation was voluntary. The information given by those participating would be kept confidential. The questionnaire for pastors would enquire regarding a pastor's experience in counseling people who had faced this distress in a previous home church.[9]

The people sample was taken from those who had Internet access; those who hosted certain websites or blogsites and/or those who read about the information; those who fit the criteria; and those who were willing to share their story with others. The people sample was taken mainly from those who live in Canada and the United States. There was interest from people who are Canadian and American but live as expatriates in the Middle East. There was equal individual interest from people who live in the United Kingdom, New Zealand, Australia, Malaysia, and the Philippines.

During the period the project information was posted, there were over 230 individual email enquiry contacts; people who expressed interest, would tell others, had something to share, etc., but may not have fit the criteria and/or did not complete a survey but had great interest in this research. One hundred ten people actually completed a survey: one hundred who totally fit the criteria and ten who did not fully fit the criteria. The final number of participants was fifteen local and eighty-five from Internet contacts, for a total of one hundred. The seven pastors that completed surveys were from Canada or the United States.

There were many who were interested in participating in this study but found that they could not at this time. The approximate number of those who formally declined active participation was over twenty. Many of them expressed their frustration and genuine regret at not being able to follow through with their intention to participate and add their voice to this issue.

This study has not focused on any one group or denomination. It was broadly based in the Evangelical, Pentecostal, and Charismatic (EPC) streams. Face-to-face interviews were not done due to time and

9. A list of counselors available in various locations was forwarded to pastors. This list of counselors could be a helpful resource for pastors who may feel that some people under their care could benefit by the help of a professional counselor.

distance constraints. Contact through the Internet seemed the most effective means of soliciting participants, which meant that reliance was mainly on the descriptive written accounts given to the survey questions.[10] There have been opportunities to meet personally with or talk on the telephone with some participants. This has been a valued dynamic of this process.

My role as a researcher was to interpret the accounts given; this was inevitably done through the filter of my own experience. In this regard, I have gained an understanding of various church denominations in these three main streams by being an active member as well as by taking courses that examined the history and theological distinctives of each group. These combining factors have given me an understanding of and appreciation for the Christian heritage of these groups.

It may be a distinct advantage in this study for subjects to feel comfortable in sharing information with a researcher who is not an ordained pastor. Also, since I am not a pastor, the insights understood from the viewpoint of "the other side of the pulpit" may also have some advantage when delving into this rather sensitive topic.

People's diverse understanding of the term "spiritual abuse" is especially a restrictive weakness in this study. Nevertheless, the safeguards built into this project include a clear presentation of the criteria defined for participants which was posted on various websites;[11] thoughtful reflection questions for the potential participants; if the individuals themselves felt that they fit the criteria; and availability of the researcher if participants had any unanswered questions about the study. A further verification of the suitability of a participant was achieved when each returned questionnaire was read and validated that this participant survey fit the criteria for this study.

---

10. As stated earlier, many participants emailed more detail about their situation as an introduction to them and their experience. Other participants simply completed the survey.

11. 1. Christians who have experienced emotional and spiritual distress under authoritarian and controlling church leaders and who have ceased to be associated with those congregations; 2. Christians who subsequently recognized and processed their spiritual grief and pain and have experienced spiritual recovery; 3. Christians who are willing to share how they have processed their negative experience and have recovered spiritual harmony; those who can share what has happened since this painful episode. Christians who can answer this question: What factors have helped you to restore your confidence in God and his people?

In this study, the term "spiritual abuse" is used in a very specific sense. Enroth defines spiritual and pastoral abuse this way: "Spiritual abuse takes place when leaders to whom people look for guidance and spiritual nurture use their positions of authority to manipulate, control, and dominate."[12] When the sacred trust between a church leader and a congregant has been violated and ecclesiastical power is used instead to control and manipulate the flock, spiritual abuse is the behavior that brings devastating results.[13]

In his book *Healing Spiritual Abuse*, Ken Blue compares other types of abuse with spiritual abuse:

> Abuse of any type occurs when someone has power over another and uses that power to hurt. Physical abuse means that someone exercises physical power over another, causing physical wounds. Sexual abuse means that someone exercises sexual power over another, resulting in sexual wounds. And spiritual abuse happens when a leader with spiritual authority uses that authority to coerce, control or exploit a follower, thus causing spiritual wounds.[14]

Many people have borrowed the definition of the term spiritual abuse found in the book *The Subtle Power of Spiritual Abuse* by David Johnson and Jeff VanVonderen:

> Spiritual abuse is the mistreatment of a person who is in need of help, support or greater spiritual empowerment, with the result of weakening, undermining or decreasing that person's spiritual empowerment.[15]

These authors go on to refine this definition:

> Spiritual abuse can occur when a leader uses his or her *spiritual position* to control or dominate another person. It often involves overriding the feelings and opinions of another, without regard to what will result in the other person's state of living, emotions or well-being. In this application, power is used to bolster the position or needs of a leader over and above one who comes to them in need. Spiritual abuse can also occur when *spirituality* is used to make others live up to a "spiritual standard." This pro-

12. Enroth, *Recovering from Churches*, 7.
13. Enroth, *Churches That Abuse*, 30.
14. Blue, *Healing Spiritual Abuse*, 12.
15. Johnson and VanVonderen, *Subtle Power*, 20–21.

motes external "spiritual performance," also without regard to an individual's actual well-being, or is used as a means of "proving" a person's spirituality.[16]

On the website *Spiritual Abuse Recovery Resources*, Jeff VanVonderen summarizes the term spiritual abuse in the introduction by stating:

> Spiritual abuse occurs when someone in a position of spiritual authority, the purpose of which is to "come underneath" and serve, build, equip and make God's people more free, misuses that authority placing themselves over God's people to control, coerce or manipulate them for seemingly godly purposes which are really their own.[17]

In an interview with VanVonderen about spiritual abuse he confirmed that:

> Spiritual abuse is always a power issue. In order for abuse to happen, by definition, it has to come from a place of higher power to a place of lesser power. People in low-power positions can't abuse people in high power.[18]

Therefore, spiritual abuse involves using one's spiritual authority inappropriately and thereby violating the sacred trust of a spiritual shepherd. The misuse of ecclesiastical power to control and manipulate congregants ultimately results in damage.

Not all exercise of spiritual authority by church leadership is abusive. Furthermore, Johnson and VanVonderen emphasize in their books that it is not always easy to figure out who has the power in a dysfunctional system. If someone takes exception to the way the authority is leading, the behavior of the leader does not necessarily indicate that it is spiritual abuse. Or, if a person in a position of authority does something to hurt someone else, either intentionally or unintentionally, this is not classed as spiritual abuse either.[19] It is imperative to understand what spiritual abuse is in order to make an appropriate assessment. Enroth does not want people to make a mistake in judgment but to be aware: "Whatever label we apply, spiritual abuse is an issue the Christian community must

---

16. Ibid. Italics in original.

17. VanVonderen, http://www.spiritualabuse.com, lines 9–13.

18. Idea credited to Jeff VanVonderen in a 2000 interview for STEPS magazine, a publication of the National Association for Christian Recovery.

19. Ibid.

acknowledge and confront. It is far more prevalent and much closer to the evangelical mainstream than many are willing to admit."[20]

Paul's analogy about the body in the First Corinthian passage is fitting here: "If one part suffers, every part suffers with it . . ."[21] Therefore, it is important for Christian leaders to correctly understand spiritual abuse. The severity of the emotional and spiritual repercussions of spiritual abuse necessitates a recovery process in order to restore and rebuild what has been damaged.

It is impossible to examine the many reasons why people choose to leave their home church. This study has considered those who have left for the reason of spiritual abuse. The recovery process for participants who have experienced spiritual abuse under authoritarian and controlling leadership has been carefully considered, yet it will not be exhaustive. This study has considered the main factors identified by these participants which has led to their personal recovery and has established their spiritual restoration in the Christian faith.

INTERNET FACTOR

There was a significant dynamic in this study that may be nonexistent, unavailable, or not factored into previous studies. This dynamic is Internet activity engaged in by a large number of Christian people. The Internet has made information, opinions, and personal experiences readily available for immediate expression with the invitation to comment by others. It provides instant and accessible opportunities for online submissions and the interchange of ideas. This study has benefited from the opportunity to consider information from reputable websites where people interact on the subject of church abuse. While no attempt was made to ensure the accuracy of the postings (anyone can say what they want on a site) the assumption stands that most of the postings actually represent real people facing real issues of personal spiritual abuse.

People who contribute online may include those who are personally interested in this topic—students, scholars, and researchers of Christian leadership and ecclesial issues. The virtual Christian community is often the first line of help available to devastated and hurting Christians. The

---

20. Enroth, *Churches That Abuse*, 109–10.
21. 1 Cor 12:26a.

Internet provides an immediate oasis of consolation for church attenders who find themselves disfellowshiped.

Although online contributors would not be considered experts on the topic of Christian leadership or the complex issues involved in effective church ministry, many are knowledgeable, well read, and are keen to examine subjects of concern in the Church today. They also attend conferences and seminars of authors and church leaders who speak on important and compelling church matters. Information access, such as book reviews from a variety of viewpoints, can have an immediate audience. People can read and make comments regarding the same book via websites, forums, or blogs to affirm a particular author's work, challenge assumptions, or expose weak aspects of the author's argument.

Online readers will often buy the particular book that has been reviewed positively, which further spreads the insights highlighted by a certain author. On the other hand, there may be a descriptive list of reasons given by those who question the author's findings or the author's personal slant. The strengths or weaknesses of the author's argument are invited, entertained, stimulated, and documented for immediate review by many.

In the book *Missio Dei*, this recognition of the value of the blogging community's online contributions is brought to the forefront. In an online book review of Peatross's book, the website host notes that:

> Peatross took blogging seriously as part of the change happening in the Christian landscape. I largely agree with Peatross when he writes, "If you think you can go to the bookstore and check out the most recent book and find out what's going on, you'll miss 90 percent of the conversation, which is essentially a grassroots, democratic, electronic, and interpersonal conversation."[22]

Recurring spiritual abuse among Christians has led to using the Internet in new ways to communicate ideas. Website and blog activity has arisen as many Christians have begun to process their disheartening church stories and to write their thoughts down, which is therapeutic as well as informative. What ultimately happens is that a host of other Christians who have had disheartening church experiences respond and express their common debilitating and disappointing experience of

22. Smulo, review of *Missio Dei*, http://johnsmulo.com/Books/missio-dei-book-review.html.

church life. This single factor adds exponentially to the magnitude of this ministry dilemma.

The questioning Internet reader, one who is familiar with the works of various authors who have written about the incidence of spiritual abuse, notices parallel patterns about people's unfortunate experiences of church life. They observe that the following are the major issues that have brought each of them to this same point of cynicism with their former church: hierarchical leadership styles, simply recognized as power and control; insincerity, hypocrisy, and kingdom building among leaders (rather than people building and pastoral care); church leadership's inability to deal with criticism; church leadership's heavy handed ways of dealing with believers who oppose or question the leader's direction; and the feeling of having no voice in that congregation, especially regarding issues of injustice. These multiple yet interrelated factors have led Christians into a season of depression, frustration, helplessness, and isolation. The virtual Christian community has, for many, been a significant bridge to the road to recovery.

The challenge for pastors reading this book, as well as other church leaders, will be to try to set aside preconceived ideas of why they feel that people have left churches and to consider what issues this research is trying to address. This study should dispel preconceived ideas about the personality type of the participants, the integrity of their character, if they have truly forgiven those leaders, or if they yet remain unhealed and vindictive against them.

The reader of this book should ask these questions: Do the participants in this study portray an exaggerated view of their previous church situation and thus need to be discounted? Are they simply a group that is made up of discontented complainers who may never be happy anywhere? Do these participants characterize those who are "overly sensitive, embittered, and difficult to get along with?"[23] Conversely, do these participant accounts portray a valid picture of many church situations? Basically, does this study characterize a fair representation of a condition that exists in the Church today and of the ways in which people have recovered from it? The critical question for the reader, then, is this: How can I aim to be a positive agent of change?

23. Kingdom Grace. "Shattered Illusions." Spiritual Abuse Series. no. 1. No pages. Online: http://kingdomgrace.wordpress.com/2005/09/11/shattered-illusions/. September 11, 2005 (accessed March 2006).

As the reader reflects on the various participant comments regarding their personal journeys from severe distress to spiritual harmony, it is hoped that the word pictures, multiplied by each account, will slowly paint a broader picture of recovery from this type of problem. Through each survey question, every participant shows another facet of their experience. Many times, though unknown to each other through distance and varied locations, differences in church denomination, or differences in size or structure of a congregation, commonalities are identified. There have been virtual echoes of what others have experienced as well as specific details of each person's particular circumstance. The writer's expectation is that there will be a better understanding of the complex nature of participant suffering and recovery.

The best way to understand this church dilemma and the recovery process which has worked for this company of participants is to allow those who have experienced it the opportunity to inform and to instruct; to allow their individual and corporate wisdom to be heard, to be valued as reasonable witnesses of this situation, and to allow this wisdom to be a catalyst for change and renewal in how we do church.

2

What Do Other People Say?

THE STATISTICS REGARDING PEOPLE leaving their home church because of a negative and hurtful experience reveal that this is a widespread occurrence. Yet the fact that there are various layers to this ministry problem makes this issue a complex one. Several topics related to church and Christian ministry converge and interconnect with this subject matter. Deviant theologies and questionable ministry practices affect individual Christians. In order for church consultants, church leaders, or concerned Christians to have a comprehensive understanding of this church ministry issue, they will need to be familiar with its multifaceted nature. The complexity of the issue complicates categorization of the literature, but the literature falls into the following broad categories:

1. Literature that deals with abusive church leadership/spiritual abuse, biblical church leadership, and the reasons why Christians leave churches. The literature in this section includes several research studies. Book titles include: *Church Leavers, Emerging Churches, Leadership Next, The Younger Evangelicals, The Subtle Power of Spiritual Abuse, Healing Spiritual Abuse, Churches That Abuse, Recovering from Churches That Abuse, Wounded Workers, The Love of Power or the Power of Love, In the Name of Jesus, Twisted Scriptures,* and *Toxic Faith.*

2. Literature that provides theological foundations regarding God's grace, reading God's Word, one's identity in Christ, and healthy life in community. This literature gives insight into the divine nature of the Church and how members of a Christian community can connect with one another in order to give and receive spiritual and emotional healing. Healthy church life is egalitarian

in nature and is inclusive of women in ministry. The literature in this section includes these books: *The Transforming Power of Grace; Paul, the Spirit, and the People of God; Community 101; Women in the Church; Churches That Heal; Connecting;* and *The Emotionally Healthy Church.*

3. Literature which focuses on Pentecostal, Charismatic, Vineyard, and Word Faith issues, particularly aberrant theologies and practices in the movement. The literature in this section includes: *The Love of Power or the Power of Love* and *What Happened to the Fire?*

CHURCH LEADERSHIP AND SPIRITUAL ABUSE

People have always left churches—a fact well documented in Church history—but the reasons why many Christians have recently left institutional churches has caught the attention of scholars and researchers who have made it their goal to understand current leaving patterns. Their aim is to bring these observations to the attention of those who teach and train future church leaders. In 1998, Alan Jamieson's PhD thesis looked into the range of reasons why people left Evangelical, Pentecostal, and Charismatic (EPC) churches in New Zealand.[1] The University of Bielefeld, under Heinz Streib, documented the habits of Christians and church attendance in Germany and the United States. These "deconversion" studies[2] give a comprehensive understanding of the many reasons why people left the church or changed their beliefs. Jamieson's research reveals two basic trajectories for Christians who had left churches in New Zealand: those who returned to the institutional church and those who did not.

Marilyn Cudmore researched the experience of victim suffering and perception of leadership abuse in Christian organizations.[3] This research focused on people who experienced a serious spiritual setback because of harmful authoritarian leaders. It examined the characteristics and structures from the perspective of abuse victims. After processing their suffering, they eventually came to a state of spiritual recovery.

---

1. Jamieson, "A Churchless Faith."
2. Streib, "Bielefeld-Based Cross-Cultural Research."
3. Cudmore, "Victim Suffering." Cudmore references Trevor Brewer's thesis, "Religious Legalism and Psychopathology."

Current literature describes the many reasons why Christians are leaving the church but there has been no clear description of the process that brings them a measure of resolution and spiritual healing. Different works provide prescriptions for recovery but there has been little testing whether such prescriptions work for individuals who have experienced wounding in their local church. This research seeks to fill this gap and will provide an understanding of the processes by which people discovered a positive path through their spiritual difficulty.

There are a number of Internet websites which investigate the occurrence of exiting from the local church, the problem of authoritarian and controlling leaders, how to cope after such an occurrence, and aspects of healthy recovery. Compassionate remarks from those who have had a similar experience abound. Websites provide information regarding how to recognize erroneous teachings in the Church, how to recognize leadership maltreatment and spiritual abuse, how to recognize the components of godly leadership, cult awareness, and support for those who have walked away from a cult. Articles provide insights regarding counseling the spiritually and emotionally abused and how to ground Christians in the knowledge of God's grace towards them and their spiritual identity in Christ.

Websites provide opportunities for those who had damaging and hurtful church experiences to freely share their personal stories without condemnation. Website hosts are often the first to share their own experiences online. The majority of people choose to remain anonymous yet some choose to identify themselves. Commonalities can be observed from these accounts. It is pertinent to recognize the virtual army of participants who are addressing this common, yet multifaceted situation. Internet sites have become a suitable resource to aid people during their recovery process.

SPIRITUAL ABUSE AND LEAVING THE CHURCH

Literature that deals with abusive church leadership and the reasons why Christians leave churches are the primary topics in this section. Literature that defines healthy church leadership will provide a contrast to abusive leadership.

Jamieson's PhD thesis looked into the reasons why people left Evangelical, Pentecostal, and Charismatic (EPC) churches in New Zealand during the 1990s. The title of the thesis, "A Churchless Faith" and later a book[4] with the same name may stimulate a question in the reader's mind: What does Jamieson mean by a *churchless faith*? His research uncovered the observable fact that although Christians had left churches, they had not left their faith. In summarizing this study there are three key interconnecting factors: personal faith stage transitions, EPC church theology and structures, and the shift from modernism to postmodernism.

His research was based on interviews with 108 church leavers. Through personal interviews, the faith journey of those who participated in this study were documented and categorized. This sociological research investigated a "hole in the bucket" effect—where people leaving was an indication of a problem that needed to be fixed—in the New Zealand church. Jamieson's original hypothesis—why he thought people left the church—was adjusted through the process of his research findings. The findings showed that those who were involved as core leaders in the church ministry[5] and were active in church body life were those who had now exited from the local church scene. This singular fact caused him to further reflect on the causes and the implications of this serious condition which had obviously been unfolding in his country. Another key factor that Jamieson discovered was that the majority of those who were interviewed did not leave their church suddenly. In fact, the majority of leavers indicated a gradual process of reflection, questioning, and withdrawal, which lasted a considerable number of months or years prior to their decision to leave.[6]

His research design also included fifty-four church leaders and informed insiders. These participating church leaders suggested four categories that influenced church exiting: societal factors, individual factors, church leadership factors, and faith concerns.[7] It is relevant to note that the reasons that church leaders and informed insiders gave for people leaving churches in New Zealand was decidedly different from the reasons that the church leavers themselves gave. This discrepancy provides an insight into the lack of mutual understanding of this church

4. Jamieson, *A Churchless Faith*. Other books by Jamieson include: *Called Again* and *Journeying In Faith*; Jamieson et al, *Church Leavers*.

5. Ninety-four percent of study participants had been involved in a significant area of church leadership.

6. See Jamieson, "A Churchless Faith," section 5.5, 101.

7. Ibid., 5.3, 93.

situation and demonstrates an evident disconnect between the church leaders and the congregants.

These interviews revealed that pastors generally felt that people left the church because they were backsliding because of *worldly* temptations, disappointment with the church, or a general abandonment of faith. Yet the face-to-face interviews revealed that although people were leaving the church, they were not leaving their faith. Only one of the interviewees left with the intention of abandoning Christian faith altogether. The vast majority of interviewees indicated that while they were leaving church, they were not leaving their faith in the decision to leave the church.

It is helpful to track the breakdown of reasons, given by church leaders and informed insiders regarding why people left Evangelical, Pentecostal, or Charismatic Churches, by looking at the following table. The items listed in the column containing "Church Leadership Factors" (in italics) are relevant to this study.

TABLE 1: Reasons Provided by Church Leaders and Informed Insiders as to Why People Leave EPC Churches.[8]

Societal Factors	Individual Factors	Church/Leadership Factors	Faith Factors
1. Other time pressures • work • leisure activities • Sunday shopping • television	1. Backsliding • giving up faith	1. *Leadership* • *dictatorial, authoritarian styles* • *lack of women leaders* • *sexual/spiritual abusive leadership* • *change of leadership* • *leaders demise (falling)* • *lack of relationship with leader*	1. Lack of personal grounding in faith • lack of clear conversion experience
2. Changes in societal attitudes • reduced loyalty • lack of resilience	2. Stage of life issues • demands of work or family	2. *Unable to find a place of service or role in church*	2. Crisis of faith

8. Jamieson, "A Churchless Faith," table 5.1, 5.3.1, 94.

Societal Factors	Individual Factors	Church/Leadership Factors	Faith Factors
	3. Become comfortable with lifestyle and give less energy to church/faith	3. *Hurt, bitter, disenchanted, or disillusioned by church decisions, direction, or vision*	3. Lack of theological framework within which to make sense of pain and difficulties of life
	4. Focus on financial security and job	4. *Church no longer relevant to life concerns of people leaving*	4. Demonic oppression
	5. Hurt or burnt-out people	5. *Lack of space to raise concerns about church direction, decisions*	
	6. Unrealistic expectations of church	6. *Legalism within church teaching and practice*	
	7. Leave through personal moral "failing"	7. *Lack of theological and intellectual depth*	
	8. Children wanting to stop going to church		
	9. Get out of touch with the church		

One of the disturbing results of the research was that the majority of those leading and pastoring in the EPC churches lacked an understanding as to what alienates people from church structures. This unfortunately underscores the relative isolation of the pastors within the EPC churches at that time.[9] Although "disillusionment with leaders or church structure was a consistent theme identified by pastors,"[10] the doubting process, described by the majority of interviewees, indicated a broader

9. Ibid., 5.3.4, 97.
10. Ibid., 5.6.1, 104.

issue: disenchantment with the whole package of church.[11] Even if a final factor could be given as to why people may have left, there was also a lack of serious investigation into the composite underlying reasons that led to the certainty of church leaving. It may be that it was easier for pastors to point to a singular incident rather than pursue any underlying reasons among leavers.[12]

Essential aspects of the church leaving process provide foundational core data for this study. Since over a decade has passed, there is a need to revisit the findings of his study as well as to establish commonalities in why people continue to leave the church currently. The issues that Jamieson discovered in New Zealand complement the issues that can now be identified in American and Canadian churches as well as in other countries. Jamieson, along with other authors, have established that church leaving does not just happen randomly in obscure places, but rather across the denominational spectrum. Although his study gave a number of insights into how people processed their grief after leaving the church, this new study probes aspects of the recovery process in a deeper way.

Church Leavers: Faith Journeys Five Years On[13] is a sequel to the book *A Churchless Faith* and tracks the spiritual journey of Jamieson's original study participants in New Zealand after five years. This complementary investigation considers whether these individuals reconnected with a local church or whether they formed or found other meaningful faith groups. It considered their current beliefs and practices such as views on prayer, mission, church, human nature, leadership, the Bible, and God. The sequel also describes the development of Spirited Exchanges, an initiative to support church leavers.[14] Those involved in the previous study were searched out. Of the original 108 participants, thirty-six could not be located. Of those located forty-seven completed interviews. This represents 66 percent of those located (or 43.5 percent of the original 108), a high return rate since the interview required a substantial amount of each respondent's time and thought.

11. Ibid.
12. Ibid., 5.6.3, 109.
13. Jamieson et al, *Church Leavers*.
14. A Spirited Exchanges group has also been initiated in the United Kingdom.

The following are some of the pertinent findings of the second enquiry.[15]

1. People who left an EPC church are unlikely to rejoin one. Only four people who left an EPC church went back to regular participation in any form of established Christian church during the last five years. Taken together these results indicate that:

   1. Having left, very few people will return to regular involvement in any form of established church within five years.

   2. Many who are apparently on the edge of leaving an EPC church may in fact not leave.

   3. Few "wayfinders" (those with an integrated, mature faith) having left church go on to reconnect with established forms of church.

2. There was a consistent concern about church. All the respondents expressed reservations, significant concerns, or clear aversion to established churches. For most, church was simply irrelevant to their faith and life. Considering the deep and long-term commitment these people had previously made to their churches (on average being adult committed members for fifteen and eight-tenths years) this raises serious concerns for those responsible for shaping churches today.

3. People across all faith categories raised significant concerns with regard to leadership in faith and church groups. Universally, the leavers looked primarily for character strengths including integrity, vulnerability, and willingness to express weakness. The wayfinders especially pointed to the need for theological and pastoral training, spiritual and psychological maturity, and the deep personal skills of empathy and listening.

It was discerned that over this five-year period the majority of respondents showed stability in their faith position. Furthermore, most did not move a faith category in that period.[16] This fact challenges the prevailing presumption that there is a connection between leaving church and a loss of faith. The results of this study would not support

15. Jamieson et al, *Church Leavers*, 78–83.
16. Ibid., 81.

this presumption. "The faith stability of the Wayfinders (90%) across the five-year period while most (77%) have no connection to any form of church raises questions for church leaders who see their own structures as essential to an ongoing maturing of Christian faith."[17] These conclusions suggest "new glimpses in an area where anecdotal evidence and hunches have previously dominated."[18]

These authors agree that the findings from the "Five Years On" study reinforce the need for groups like Spirited Exchanges. They base this on the fact that there is a need for people to have a place to express their own doubts without feeling that they are being judged or of destabilizing the faith of others.[19] Furthermore, it is important for the Church to listen to leavers. Intentional listening to those who are reconsidering their faith or those who are considering leaving a church is necessary because it is allows those interested in understanding these issues the opportunity to be more aware of these people's position by examining their feelings with them. Such listening is not only helpful but it also can provide healing on someone's spiritual journey.[20]

From this follow-up study there are two areas needed for future church leadership participation. Post-church groups need to include church leaders since it is one thing for those who have had negative church experiences to talk among themselves and it is another thing to be able to talk directly to someone who is still an active participant in church life. People have experienced so much misuse of Scriptures that they need positive input from someone who teaches with clarity on a regular basis. As church leaders listen, then there is opportunity for change. It is in the nonjudgmental and even painful listening that the Spirit of God can be heard through this purposeful exercise.[21]

Church leaders should not be wary of church leavers but should engage them. Leaders need to toughen up, to be prepared to dig deeper, and to be prepared to hear criticisms. This can turn out to be an opportune moment to gain knowledge and grow in order to better understand the issues and to be an informed change agent. This exchange of ideas can have a positive outcome in the lives of spiritual leaders. They can

17. Ibid., 81–82.
18. Ibid., 83.
19. Ibid., 96.
20. Ibid., 109.
21. Ibid., 112.

be more resolute in their efforts to bring change as well as to have a greater capacity for compassion and personal honesty.[22] Jamieson and coauthors Jenny McIntosh and Adrienne Thompson provide a valuable resource for the Christian community. Their insights provide relevant information that complements Jamieson's original study and establishes spiritual priorities through the faith journeys of these Christians. *Church Leavers* adds important data to this study.

Heinz Streib documented the habits of Christians and their church attendance patterns in both Germany and the United States and noted a significant shift in the paradigm of conversion based on the sudden change of beliefs. The prototype was the conversion model of the Apostle Paul, which was replaced by a new paradigm by the second half of the twentieth century. Conversion became characterized by meaning making and appeared to be a gradual and rational process.[23]

Streib's findings confirm that: "More than half of the deconverts whom we have interviewed leave the field of organized religion altogether and refrain from affiliation with a new religious organization."[24] People identified themselves as spiritual rather than religious. These findings complement the fact that although many participants in this study left the institutional church, they have not left their faith. Some switched denominations while others withdrew from institutional church attendance in order to pursue other forms of Christian fellowship, ministry, and service.

Marilyn Cudmore's work[25] in the Canadian context complements and supports Jamieson's research. Cudmore interviewed individuals who felt that they had experienced leadership abuse in various Christian organizations. Their personal struggles, coping efforts, and suffering were explored. The leadership characteristics and structures were examined from the perspective of abuse victims.[26] Her study adds to the mounting literature that abusive leadership can be found in Christian

22. Ibid., 116.

23. Streib, "Bielefeld-Based Cross-Cultural Research," 8.

24. Ibid., 63.

25. I appreciated an opportunity to meet with Marilyn Cudmore since we are located near each other. From the perspective of her research and her present vantage point, one of the questions that she posed was: "What happens to those Christians who do not heal and consequently do not return to any church?" This is a sobering question, indeed.

26. Cudmore, "Victim Suffering," 2.

organizations. Her goal was to expose what so often has remained hidden within the Christian culture. It is necessary to understand the contributing factors of leadership abuse in order to aid in prevention.[27] It is mandatory for Christians to be alerted in order to recognize the consequences of abusive leadership tactics. The conspiracy of silence in the Church may be an invitation for narcissistic leaders to be emboldened to continue their abusive practices.[28] It is imperative that church leaders identify and prevent leadership abuse in order to heal and strengthen Christian organizations.[29] Since abuse can be covert in nature, victims are not always aware of the inevitable crises ahead.

It is necessary to consider how devastating the violation of trust can be in any human relationship. This fact is maximized when the spiritual dimension is added to that trust. Since the trust level between a congregant and a spiritual leader is unique, the depth of vulnerability increases. When there is abuse of this vulnerability there is a betrayal in the very setting that should have provided security, faith, and restoration. Deep distress is generated in the individual that deteriorates trust of leadership and even of God, to the point of severe spiritual "woundedness."[30]

Abusive leadership across the centuries has been called "clergy malfeasance." The influence of the Roman Catholic Church hierarchy from the fourth century to the sixteenth century was substantial and there would be implications in the Reformation period.[31] Calvin affirmed that this movement was not a new religion but a return to the genuine and original faith of the Bible. However, there appears to be a problem with that logic. It has also been reasoned that "Although many theologians acclaim Calvin's democratic approach to church leadership, some have evaluated the Protestant Reformation movement as a breeding ground for authoritarian, controlling leadership."[32] It is not the fact that man is controlled by a higher power outside himself but the idea of authoritarian theistic thinking found in Calvin's theology. There is the feeling

27. Ibid., 5–6.
28. Ibid., 6.
29. Ibid., 6–7.
30. Ibid., 1.
31. Ibid., 15.
32. Ibid., 17.

of *entitled* obedience, reverence, and worship.[33] Although different denominations may have varying acceptance levels for authoritarianism it
appears that ultra-fundamentalists may be more inclined to emphasize
biblical passages that refer to submission to church leadership be adhered
to.[34] Followers are more easily positioned to feel compelled to obey the
rules and regulations of their religious culture since their good behavior
will earn favor with God, other Christians, and maybe even themselves.[35]
Although some Protestants may think that leadership abuse exists outside of their sphere, this fact needs to be more thoroughly examined
since it would be more accurate to conclude that leadership abuse affects
all churches. Consequently, any attempt to simply identify it with one
religious group will dilute the need for vigilance by everyone.[36]

One might enquire: What perpetuates anomalies such as extremes
of obedience? It could be agreed that obedience to authority is necessary,
to some degree, for a stable society, but when leadership goes beyond
"giving direction" to "imposing upon" others certain factors must exist
that preclude high degrees of obedience.[37] Personal characteristics may
give insights into how a leader handles authority and responsibility.
The reviewed literature considered authoritarianism, legalism, rigidity,
insecurity, charisma, neuroticism, and narcissism.[38] It is important to remember that parental authority is the first legitimate authority for children and that secondary authority figures also play a role.[39] Childhood
discipline affects later adult authoritarian stances. The outcome of childhood abuse can be summed up this way: "It is the sense of individual
weakness and loss of control that 'ignites an internal rage that weakness
is contemptible and that rules and prejudice provide a security.'"[40]

It is mandatory that narcissism in leaders be recognized earlier on.
Narcissism is a defense against internal negative feelings; it is motivated
by excessive self-love and is self-centered.[41] Leaders with narcissistic

33. Ibid.
34. Ibid., 19.
35. Ibid.
36. Ibid., 22.
37. Ibid., 19–20.
38. Ibid., 30–44.
39. Ibid., 32.
40. Ibid., 33.
41. Ibid., 38.

traits have achievement-based orientations requiring constant approval in order to maintain self-image.[42] It has been ascertained that narcissism is a complex and difficult problem because leaders of this personality type can use creative façades in how they present themselves publicly to their organizations.[43] These leaders may feel threatened by criticism and competition. It appears that not challenging such a leader will keep things in check; otherwise an unwarranted catalyst will upset things in significant ways.

> As long as no one criticizes, competes, or attempts to share their glory, they can be encouraging, supportive, and fun to work with and for. However, if this unwritten agreement is breached, they can react with vengefulness. Finally, they can function effectively in the mentor role provided that those under their tutelage are perceived as loyal and noncompetitive.[44]

What predisposes leaders to take advantage of their influence on others? A leader's psychological nature is a critical factor, especially if charismatic and narcissistic tendencies are evident, because charismatic leaders have a heightened symbolic power that makes followers more susceptible to their influences and a narcissistic leader is inclined to abuse symbolic status. The end result is that this type of leader manipulates relationship with followers for their own personal gain at the expense of their follower's psychological well-being.[45] The problem is that the pretense of authoritarianism in Christian organizations may disguise the inadequacies of leaders who believe they must take control of situations.[46] Since many Christians are not cognizant of how genuine faith systems operate, they place themselves in danger by not recognizing abusive leadership.[47]

A recurring factor in Christian organizations has begun to gain prominence. There has been increased attention in literature on dys-

---

42. Ibid., 40–41.

43. Ibid., 40.

44. Cudmore, p. 43, quotes Sperry and where his line of thinking is found. See Len Sperry, "Leadership Dynamics: Character and Character Structure in Executives," *Consulting Psychology Journal: Practice and Research* 49 (1997): 268–80.

45. Cudmore, "Victim Suffering," 43–44.

46. Ibid., 44.

47. Ibid., 45.

functional leaders in the last decade.[48] It is essential that careful assessment of leadership be factored into the inner workings of Christian organizations in order to ensure ongoing health of the organization. It is important to recognize that spiritual abuse may not always be obvious to spot and assessing it is not always easy.[49] Therefore, it is important for congregations, college faculties, church boards, and staff to be aware of what healthy leadership is.[50] It is crucial to understand that in Christian organizations influence is earned through hard work and gained by respect from others not by the title or position held.[51]

Nine participants were interviewed for this study. Five questions were developed for semi-structured interviews:

1. How did you experience leadership in the organization?

2. What caused you to recognize that you were feeling abused?

3. What incident can you describe that would suggest abuse?

4. What has been the impact on your life? How have you coped with this experience?

5. How would you describe the characteristics of leadership of the organization?[52]

Participants were from six Protestant denominations and equally represented female and male perspectives. Six were employees of a Christian organization with four being members of the church in which they were employed. The participants were among those who had faithful and voluntary involvement in the church ministry.[53] This factor also complemented the participant involvement statistic in this study.

There was therapeutic value for the participants to be able to disclose their painful story, in its entirety, without blame or critique of their stature as a Christian.[54] This was also characteristic of the experience of many who participated in this study. A "powerful tool of understanding was the specific language that the participant used in the interview

48. Ibid., 47.
49. Ibid., 51.
50. Ibid.
51. Ibid., 52.
52. Ibid., 173.
53. Ibid., 68–72.
54. Ibid., 60.

process, as each word conveyed considerable meaning."[55] An understanding of the victim's perception of events was established and themes were traced. The meaning units were categorized into fourteen themes. Theme twelve was of particular interest since it covered the participant's descriptors of their leaders, which were similar to those found in this research study and included the following: "authoritative, a rigid thinker, controlling, manipulative, resistant to opinions, demanding respect and submissiveness to the leadership, [and] claiming the leader's authority as holy and accountable only to God."[56] Cudmore's study also suggested that intervention should come sooner after this type of trauma.[57]

The counseling implications included that empathy is a critical skill required at the outset of therapeutic intervention with victims of abusive leadership. Since connections and assumptions have been utterly shattered and since these Christians received much judgmental criticism, safety and reassurance should be the initial focus of caring counselors. Individual counseling as well as a group therapy component would address the need to belong and the need to replace lost friendships as much as possible. Because the experience of betrayal came from someone they trusted, the counselor would need to respect ambivalence and make efforts not to surprise the client with changes to schedules or demands.[58]

The seven individuals and the one couple who told eight stories were traumatized by the abuse of trust issue. That the place Christians had connected spiritually with God would become the place of abuse that would cripple their Christianity was unacceptable.[59] Cudmore's research gives another voice to the depth of victim loss and alerts the Body of Christ that religious conviction does not give Christian leaders entitlement to make others suffer.[60] Cudmore's thesis has a direct correlation with many of the findings of this study.

55. Ibid., 62.
56. Ibid., 112.
57. Ibid., 147.
58. Ibid., 149.
59. Ibid., 151.
60. Ibid.

THE EMERGENT CHURCH

Literature on the Emergent Church also includes the exiting factor of many from the institutional church. This will not be an extensive look at the Emergent Church but will consider books that intersect with this topic of study.

Emerging Churches by Eddie Gibbs and Ryan Bolger, along with Gibbs's book *Leadership Next*, offer numerous insights into Christian church leadership issues and how leaders of the emergent churches in the United States and the United Kingdom view the model of leadership from a modernist perspective. The under-thirty-five age group does not look upon the established model of church practice as relevant or effective for their generation. This reality stimulates creativity to reconfigure the concept of church. Yet, the desire for change in the church is not relegated only to those under thirty-five. The need for change has been recognized by many in church leadership and among those who previously participated in institutional church settings. The need to reconsider all aspects of the role and practices of the Church has stimulated serious reckoning with the biblical text in today's world in order to "do church" more effectively.

Leadership Next gives the reader a composite view of leadership from a number of vantage points. Leadership is redefined in light of the current cultural context of rapid change and the need for present leaders to discern the signs of the times. Older leaders are challenged to question their assumptions about leadership, adopt new attitudes, and learn new skills.[61] Leadership roles and styles must change because it is a necessity, not an option.

Churches need to move from a hierarchical and highly controlling style of leadership to a decentralized relational model since "Leadership is about connecting, not controlling."[62] Seeing a congregation not as "a crowd of people but a federation of teams" would be an innovative change. This change in style necessitates developing and sustaining teams. Gibbs concedes that this would be a complex, rather than a simple endeavor.[63]

---

61. Gibbs, *Leadership Next*, 16.
62. Ibid., 106.
63. Ibid., 106–36.

Leadership Next focuses on traits, activities, and attitudes modeled by many younger leaders. The cost of leadership is examined in light of the present cultural climate as well as costs that may arise out of misunderstandings within the Church.

Guidelines are given to identify and equip new leaders for ministry in the twenty-first century. Innovative approaches in the United Kingdom, North America, and Australia are presented. These vital aspects of leadership now and for the future can give insights into areas that can strengthen Christian leadership in positive ways and provide guidelines for building bridges and ensuring opportunities for a meaningful exchange of ideas, expectations, and life experiences.

Robert Webber's book *The Younger Evangelicals* looks at the new evangelical awakening that is introduced by an emerging generation of leaders. Their thinking regarding ministry and how it often differs from how their elders in the ministry practice church is described. Younger leaders are thinking through many beliefs and practices theologically and are not reticent to implement their findings—which seem to be appropriate in a postmodern context. Most people would grant that the question of leadership has been an issue in the local church from the very beginning of Christianity.[64] The Apostle Paul described three functions of ministry—oversight, teaching, and service. Looking at a historical overview of church leadership up to the present considers the difference between the modern form of CEO leadership and the emergence of the servant model of leadership. Leadership beliefs among Reformation churches and megachurches are decidedly different. The former regard leadership in the church to be a matter of doctrine, the latter consider the organization of leadership within the church as a pragmatic matter. In the midst of both is the question about the place of the laity. "Do they have a calling to ministry, or are they primarily the sheep led by clerics?"[65] Webber concedes that there has been no end of this discussion, the books written, or the suggested models to follow.[66]

Webber cites E. Glenn Wagner, author of *Escape from Church, Inc.*,[67] who writes about his concern for the "growing number of 'drop out Christians' who have been hurt and abused in churches that seem to see

64. Webber, *Younger Evangelicals*, 147.

65. Ibid.

66. Ibid.

67. Ibid., 148. Wagner, *Escape from Church*, 10.

people as objects" and expresses concern for the "numbers of pastors being dismissed because they don't fit the corporate model now in vogue."[68]
Webber notes that Wagner firmly believes that: "Ministry is not task but
relationship." Wagner concedes that the answer does not lie in sociological, psychological, or managerial expertise but in the simple act of being
a shepherd to God's people.[69]

Among the younger evangelical ministers there is a resurgence of
servant leadership in the Church that is defined by its missional nature.
Although many have been mentored under caring pastors who followed
a valid servant model, many have not. The local church is no longer
viewed as just a saving station, but is regarded as a place for spiritual formation, healing, and being a countercultural influence in a local community. Incarnational living that demonstrates mutual servanthood, rather
than power, and where God's *shalom* rests, is a viable witness to the reign
of the Lord Jesus Christ.[70] It shows that Christ's lordship influences all
relationships and structures not just one's personal salvation. It calls for
a life that endeavors to follow what Jesus modeled. Younger evangelicals
want to turn away from business models of leadership and return to
biblical principles.[71] Webber's email questionnaire asked, "What is the
leadership style of your pastor?" The most frequent response was a negative view of boomer leadership.[72]

Webber cites Len Hjalmarson who claims that "the priesthood of all
God's people, first introduced by Luther, was lost as the Church quickly
returned to hierarchical structures of leadership.[73] Therefore, these critical insights must be reckoned with.

68. Webber, *Younger Evangelicals*, 148. Webber quotes Wagner: "Why is it, he asks,
that the only continent in the world where the church is not growing is North America?
His answer: 'because we have bought into gimmicks and programs, the razzle dazzle Las
Vegas syndrome of Christianity, all flesh and lights and gaudiness. But we have forgotten what it means to be the church and do ministry.'"

69. Webber, *Younger Evangelicals*, 148.

70. Ibid., 148–49.

71. Ibid., 149. Webber gives a response from Leroy Armstrong, pastor of a church
in Kentucky: "that the megachurch movement of the last twenty years has been led by
'superstar' pastors who are now 'dying out or burned out' without having mobilized lay
people for ministry. As a result, the church, which should be an army, 'still looks like an
audience.'"

72. Webber, *Younger Evangelicals*, 149.

73. Ibid., 150. The researcher is acquainted with Len Hjalmarson through the
Doctor of Ministry program at A.C.T.S., The Associated Christian Theological Schools

The challenge we face in restoring the priesthood of all God's people is (1) current leaders are accustomed to control; (2) leaders fear disorder if they are not in control; (3) a sense of "professional" leadership has crept into the church, which means pastors often rely on their natural talent, instead of the Spirit, and insist on looking and sounding respectable; (4) modern individualism has impacted our thinking causing us to lose the biblical perspective of the Spirit; and finally (5) we use the wrong dominant model in the church. Most of our churches have the larger body and smaller groups. The mistake of most churches is to import the larger group into the smaller group rather than allowing the small groups to impact the larger group. This wrongly directed model eventually kills the small group rather than promoting "every member ministry." Leaders, Hjalmarson argues, "must work to create a congregational life of full participation."[74]

One younger leader explained that Christ's leadership is symbolized "by the throne and towel."[75] Leadership in the church needs to imitate the servant leadership of Jesus Christ. Where pastors live out a servant attitude, the congregants have a visible model of spirituality of a life lived for others. A motivated community that emulates their pastor may become a vital community of servants to each other and to the world.[76] Younger evangelicals are becoming weary of the executive model of leadership as an exercise of power that everyone obeys. This is no longer a working ideal for them. They long for how Christ modeled a self-emptying, humble, serving attitude.[77] They recognize that this can only be done with the Spirit's help.

Choosing team ministry and seeking to avoid church bureaucracy propel the younger leaders to leave churches that are run like businesses and launch church plants that are free of these. Avoiding tight control yet encouraging engagement in responsible ministry is a goal to aim for,

---

the Graduate Schools of Theological Studies of Trinity Western University in Langley, BC, Canada.

74. Ibid., 150–51.

75. Ibid., 151. "Dann Pantoja in the 'Paradox of Postmodern Leadership' sees Jesus as the ultimate model of a servant leader. Here is the paradox; Jesus has supreme authority in 'heaven and earth' (Matt 20–28), yet in the kingdom of God Jesus himself rejects power-based leadership. His dual position, Pantoja remarks, is symbolized 'by the throne and towel.'"

76. Webber, *Younger Evangelicals*, 151.

77. Ibid.

yet there is still a need to be aware that as churches grow there will be a need for organization.[78] One young leader's overview of church ministry was to move away from staff-led, committee-run hierarchies and head toward team-based ministry where decision-making is dispersed to lay-led ministry teams. This direction provides a corrective for staffers who want to hoard power and church members who expect hired staffers to do the work rather than jointly being engaged in ministry.[79] Webber considers many innovative ideas that work for these young evangelicals in ministry. He asks the reader to conscientiously consider the potential insights that can be found in these pioneering leaders in the Church.

SPIRITUAL ABUSE DEFINED AND DESCRIBED

The following five books address the subject of spiritual abuse, give a definition for this term, and provide understanding into this recurring condition in the Church: *The Subtle Power of Spiritual Abuse*,[80] *Healing Spiritual Abuse*,[81] *Churches That Abuse*,[82] *Recovering from Churches That Abuse*,[83] and *Wounded Workers*.[84]

The topic of spiritual abuse has instant appeal to countless people since so many have experienced it. People who have suffered spiritual abuse have found consolation in these books. The authors, David Johnson and Jeff VanVonderen, Ken Blue, Ronald Enroth, and Kirk Farnsworth pave the way for wounded people to grasp what exactly happened to them and provide insights for those who research church leadership issues. People have suffered a range of abuse under church leaders, which can be measured from mild to severe. A significant number of Christians had not initially considered that their experience was spiritual abuse, but after making a concerted effort to understand their situation they soon came to the realization that the definitions and examples given in these books quite accurately described their experience.

78. Ibid.

79. Ibid.

80. Johnson and VanVonderen, *The Subtle Power of Spiritual Abuse.*

81. Blue, *Healing Spiritual Abuse.*

82. Enroth, *Churches That Abuse.*

83. Enroth, *Recovering from Churches That Abuse.*

84. Farnsworth, *Wounded Workers.*

The Subtle Power of Spiritual Abuse endeavors to provide a balanced and reasonable look at the abuse victim's experience, how leaders unknowingly drift into abusive behaviors, and how victims can achieve recovery and spiritual restoration. This book was one of the most referenced books among the participants of this study.

The question as to whether spiritual abuse is *subtle* arises. Is it behavior which is unacknowledged by the perpetrator or is all spiritual abuse quite obviously intentional and deliberate? Are some leaders simply uninformed or unaware about spiritual abuse?[85] Improper understanding of biblical leadership, ingrained habits, poor modeling, and a feeling of insecurity within an individual and/or in the leadership task may contribute to unwarranted leadership behaviors. According to a number of authors this behavior is intentional. Hurtful leadership actions may be motivated by a variety of reasons. Basically, leaders may follow a controlling model because of poor biblical understanding or unexamined traditions in their organization. Other leaders are simply manipulative for personal gain. The consequences for congregants, in either case, remain the same.

Blue's book, *Healing Spiritual Abuse*, equips the enquirer to understand what spiritual abuse is. He informs the reader that his book is "The Biblical Answer to the Wounds of Legalism." The reader is helped to examine whether their feeling of fault and failure is actually directly caused by them or may be caused by perceptions generated by leaders. By comparing biblical passages, examining case studies, and considering examples of abusive behavior in leaders, the reader is given the hope of breaking free from bad church experiences. The author basically asks: Are you a victim of spiritual abuse? He provides a standard[86] for the

---

85. Blue comments that: "Spiritual abuse may differ from some other forms of abuse in that it is rarely perpetrated with intent to maim" and that "spiritual abusers are curiously naïve about the effects of their exploitation." They rarely intend to hurt their victims because they are "usually so narcissistic or so focused on some great thing they are doing for God that they don't notice the wounds they are inflicting on their followers." *Healing Spiritual Abuse*, 12. Although I can appreciate this point of view, other authors seem to be persuaded that in most cases this behavior is consistently premeditated. Nevertheless, in some cases, the leader may simply be blind to the effects of their own behavior.

86. To aid in assessing one's church, Blue notes the symptoms of abusive religion according to Jesus in Matt 23. He states: "If your church rates high on these negative indicators, it is significantly spiritually abusive. 1. Abusive leaders base their spiritual authority on their position or office rather than on their service to the group. Their

reader to assess their experience in order to be able to give an informed answer to this somber question.

Abusive leaders today are compared to the inclinations and practices of the Pharisees in Jesus's day. Because of the severity of the exile, the Pharisees set themselves up as the moral watchdogs of Jewish society to keep their religion pure before Yahweh. The Pharisees were rigid and obsessive about physical and moral cleanness and barred those from community who would not conform; controlling who would be accepted and who would be rejected.[87] The power base of the Pharisees was the seat of Moses.[88] "Abuse requires power and the Pharisees had it."[89] There is a strong connection with the religious performance of the Pharisees with church leaders today who set up religious performance, rather than faith in Jesus, as the criterion for acceptance or rejection.[90] By appealing to position, unique claims, or special anointings, leaders can succeed in creating a hierarchy in their church so that they can more easily control those beneath them. They can also use this validation to defend themselves against any who might challenge them.[91] According to the New Testament, truth and its authority are not rooted in personality or office. The Apostle Paul confronted Peter when he was "not acting in line with the truth of the gospel." Paul "opposed him to his face, because he was in the wrong."[92] Paul's actions declared that, "the truth always outranks

style of leadership is authoritarian. 2. Leaders in abusive churches often say one thing but do another. Their words and deeds do not match. 3. They manipulate people by making them feel guilty for not measuring up spiritually. They lay heavy religious loads on people and make no effort to lift those loads . . . 4. Abusive leaders are preoccupied with looking good. They stifle any criticism that puts them in a bad light. 5. They seek honorific titles and special privileges that elevate them above the group. They promote a class system with themselves at the top. 6. Their communication is not straight. Their speech becomes especially vague and confusing when they are defending themselves. 7. They major on minor issues to the neglect of the truly important ones. They are conscientious about religious details but neglect God's larger agendas." *Healing Spiritual Abuse*, 134–35.

87. Ibid., 25.
88. Ibid., 26–27.
89. Ibid., 26.
90. Ibid., 25–26.
91. Ibid., 29.
92. Gal 2:11–21.

position or title in the church. Truth and its authority are not rooted in a personality or office."[93]

Some leaders have developed a twisted image of the Church. Once leaders place themselves at the top of an ecclesiastical hierarchy they can then spread the misbelief of "spiritual covering" that serves as a tool for control. "Spiritual covering pictures a chain of command with authority flowing through the chain from top to bottom. Those lower on the chain are to see those above them as their 'covering' and submit to them as they would to Christ himself."[94] The teaching of spiritual covering which is another controlling tool used by abusive leaders can be dismantled. There is very little biblical basis for the idea of covering and this teaching goes against numerous biblical teachings to the contrary including the egalitarian nature of church fellowship, the fraternal nature of church discipline, and the parity among members of the church.[95] Although Christ gave his disciples spiritual authority and the power to heal the sick and cast out demons, he never delegated his authority *over people* to anyone.[96]

Some church leaders rationalize that their autocratic style of leadership and their hierarchical church structure is done to ensure "church unity." This is flawed thinking since real unity can never be achieved by coercion. The problem lies in the fact that Christian authoritarianism confuses spiritual unity with unanimity. Although uniformity can be achieved with autocratic controls, it is essentially external. In contrast, unity in a Christian community is primarily a spiritual mystery. It can only happen when people are willing to take risks and freely submit to one another. The goal of uniformity is correct behavior, while a right spirit is the fruit of unity.[97] The biblical pattern is that true authority arises out of service and submission is voluntary. The conclusion is that when leadership is defined and walked out this way, there is less chance for spiritual abuse to find a foothold.[98]

If the New Testament teachings on servant leadership by Christ and by Paul can be found without difficulty in various places in Scripture,

93. Blue, *Healing Spiritual Abuse*, 30.

94. Ibid., 30.

95. Ibid. See Matt 18; Matt 23:8–12; 1 Cor 12:14–26.

96. Ibid., 30–31.

97. Ibid., 31.

98. Ibid., 34.

how is it that sensible and intelligent people submit themselves to spiritual abuse? According to human need, it appears that most people wish to be led. People would rather follow the line of least resistance, letting those in positions of power make decisions for them.[99] People's innate longing for God is essential. Leaders who pose as mediators for God can therefore play on people's desire for a leader as well as their yearning for God. An alarming scenario is that the spiritually keen are the most at risk to be victimized.[100] In the final analysis, the cure for both abused and abuser is a sufficient dose of God's mercy and grace.[101]

Some readers will be put in a position of deciding whether they will fight for change or simply leave. Since most abusive systems are very well rationalized and well defended it is unlikely that abusive leaders will respond favorably to rational objections and constructive criticisms.[102] Often the most loving thing that can be done for abusive leaders is to leave them.[103] One must allow time to go through the grieving process, make room for forgiveness, and seek a healthy spiritual community in order to recover from the distress of an abusive leadership situation. *Healing Spiritual Abuse* is an informative book that peels back the hidden layers of spiritual abuse in order to expose its insidious nature and the damaging affects in the Church.

Providing help for those wounded by legalism, authoritarian leadership, and spiritual intimidation, is the goal of Enroth's book, *Churches That Abuse*. Enroth has interviewed people who have been victims of harsh treatment by leaders. His book is "about people who have been abused psychologically and spiritually in churches and other Christian organizations."[104] In this study, the term spiritual abuse is used in a very specific sense. Enroth defines spiritual and pastoral abuse this way: "Spiritual abuse takes place when leaders to whom people look for guidance and spiritual nurture use their positions of authority to manipulate, control, and dominate."[105]

99. Ibid., 36.

100. Ibid.

101. Ibid., 119.

102. Ibid., 135.

103. Ibid.

104. Enroth, *Churches That Abuse*, 30.

105. Enroth, *Recovering from Churches*, 7.

In many cases, churches and church leaders do not begin from a point of spiritual abuse. This happens gradually. As leaders begin to see the power of their influence, they change. Whether these leaders were consciously or unconsciously aware, they took advantage of vulnerable people and convinced them that God had given them, as the spiritual shepherds, the right to exercise authority over the flock.[106] Enroth describes the factors that influence leaders to take on the role of controller and how people are drawn to these leadership personalities and become victims of the system. By using guilt, fear, and intimidation, members are controlled. Unhealthy dependency is an underlying intention since the unfortunate reality is that "In all totalitarian environments, dependency is necessary for subjugation."[107]

In his study of authoritarian groups, public discipline, ridicule, and humiliation became the common experience of participants.[108] The fact that there is little or no feedback available to members from the outside provides an unhindered environment where leaders can demand corporate obedience to them with unquestioning loyalty to the group.[109] The damage created in these groups is that true freedom in Christ is forfeited for human power.[110] Leaders who practice spiritual abuse exceed the bounds of legitimate authority by lording it over the flock. All too often these leaders have the audacity to intrude into the personal lives of members.[111] As many people regrettably find out, abusive leaders are self-centered and adversarial and there is little chance for any type of reconciliation or restoration.[112] The desire to control others and to exercise power over people is part of the human condition since the fall. Abusive leaders often lack compassion and a gentle spirit, as power has blinded their conscience. In this defective environment there is little sign of remorse and repentance.[113] There is, therefore, a strong need to develop discernment skills among Christians. This needs to be a priority in the Church so that there is less likelihood of believers following aberrant

106. Enroth, *Churches That Abuse*, 234.
107. Ibid., 109.
108. Ibid., 163.
109. Ibid., 175.
110. Ibid., 235.
111. Ibid.
112. Ibid.
113. Ibid., 237.

teachers or false doctrines.[114] This book aims to provide help for people who have made their way out of abusive church settings and gives aid to those who desire to help damaged Christians.

Enroth's complementary book, *Recovering from Churches That Abuse*, provides a further look at this Church dilemma and supplies understanding regarding the inner nature of this problem by giving theological reflections, case studies of those interviewed, and commonsense help for those who find themselves in this situation. This book, as the title declares, looks at the recovery process. Enroth describes his perspective as a sociologist who looks for patterns in human behavior and has tried to present an *insider perspective* by using a life-history approach to illustrate patterns of spiritual and emotional abuse.[115] This approach recognizes that every person defines the world differently. Therefore, it is imperative for sociologists to understand what events mean to the people experiencing them. The priority is to recognize that the "subject's definition of the situation takes precedence over the objective situation" and that "the way an individual perceives an event or situation impacts his or her behavior."[116]

While recognizing that some readers might consider spiritual abuse too strong a term to use in connection with unhealthy churches and Christian organizations, Enroth admits that he does not know of a better term to describe this collection of traits than this one.[117] It doesn't much matter what label we apply to it, the fact is that spiritual abuse is an issue that the Christian community needs to recognize in order to take seriously and to confront. Sadly, it is far more widespread in the evangelical mainstream than most Christian leaders are willing to admit.[118] It is becoming quite recognizable by those who examine this issue in the Christian Church that spiritual abuse happens in a wide spectrum of

114. Ibid. Discernment is needed in the local church in order to evaluate people who are being hired for leadership roles.

115. Enroth, *Recovering from Churches*, 109.

116. Ibid., 64.

117. Ibid., 110.

118. Ibid. I would agree with Enroth. In conversations with many people, in varied contexts, I had the opportunity to share about the topic of my research. Both Christians and non-Christians registered spontaneous comments that they or people they knew were definitely victims of spiritual abuse and would likely fit my criteria for participants. These chance encounters suggested a wider spread occurrence of the sociological and ecclesiological factors that have been introduced in this research study.

churches, parachurch organizations, and ministries from many different denominational backgrounds. Many people assume that this can only be a problem in churches that exist on the margins of mainline evangelicalism. Enroth's experience exposes that assumption and challenges Christians to come around in their thinking to the disheartening realization that spiritual abuse takes place in many denominations and in many ministry settings. It would be convenient to believe that leadership abuse happens only in radical churches on the fringes; then there would be no cause for immediate concern or any need to take action.[119]

It can be verified that the struggles of those who recover are often hidden from view. These struggles are brought into the open through these narrative accounts and it is demonstrated that recovery is not always an easy process.[120] Some suggestions that may help smooth the road to recovery are outlined[121] yet the reader is reminded that the road to recovery is different for each person and that there is no simple formula.[122] For that reason there is no attempt to suggest a one-two-three process of recovery.

The following are Enroth's nine suggestions to aid in recovery:

1. For closure to take place there needs to be an acknowledgment of abuse. Denying what has happened will only stall recovery.

2. Find someone who will listen to your story, who supports your desire to gain healing and restoration.

3. Talk freely about your experiences, doubts, feelings, and hopes.

4. Recognize that you will probably go through a grieving process—grief for the lost years, the lost friends and family, the loss of innocence.

5. Expect to feel guilt, fear, and shame. It is crucial to find people who will support and validate your own step of faith and can help you address your hard feelings.

---

119. Ibid., 16.

120. Enroth addresses the wounded with his hope for this book: "In this book I seek to be the voice of the voiceless, and I hope that in listening, you will learn and be warned and find hope for recovery from churches that abuse." *Recovering from Churches*, 5.

121. These suggestions provide confirmation of what I had previously theorized.

122. Enroth, *Recovering from Churches*, 5.

6. Expect to feel foolish and experience self-doubt. You may ask yourself over and over, "Why did I let this happen to me?" Feeling foolish and regretful about poor decisions is a sign of growth; you will soon leave those emotions behind.

7. You will need to trust again, in stages. Above all, learn to trust God again. Renew your walk with him; rebuild a quiet time; don't give up on the Church, despite its imperfections.

8. Relax! Enjoy your new freedoms. Take time for physical recreation, art, music, and just plain fun. Thank God (1 Tim 4:1–5) for all the good things he has given us to enjoy.

9. Remember that forgiveness is crucial to recovery. It has been said that forgiveness is for the benefit of those giving it, not for the benefit of those receiving it.[123]

The need for relationships in a healthy community is one of the primary needs of those affected. There is a common concern among victims that they won't be understood by church friends. Some wait a long while before feeling that they can safely tell their story. Sometimes when they attempt to inform others about their disheartening church situation they are met with skepticism about their spiritual stability, their mental health, or both. These encounters make the victims feel misunderstood, guilty, or even rejected. Those who have suffered spiritual abuse may then wonder whether they should risk revealing their past. It is important for those who want to be helpful to be "sensitive, nonjudgmental, and accepting—even if they find it difficult to understand how something so bizarre could happen to another Christian."[124] Those who desire to minister wisely and with compassion to those who have been abused will find this book a useful resource.[125]

This book concludes by affirming that battered Christians can recover. A question is asked if rehabilitation is possible for churches that abuse. Although difficult, churches could choose to change. Unfortunately

---

123. Ibid., 65.

124. Ibid., 22.

125. Both of Enroth's books, *Churches That Abuse,* and the sequel, *Recovering from Churches That Abuse,* have been made available online at no cost. These resources are instantly available to anyone who is interested and they contain welcome insights into how to be aware of this distressing church condition and how to recover from it. See also D. Ryan and J. Ryan, *Recovery from Spiritual Abuse.*

many churches do not experience positive change. The reason there is little change is because the "modifications are only cosmetic or superficial" and that the "desire to gain legitimacy and acceptance from the larger Christian world"[126] outweighs a genuine desire. It is very hard for leaders who have developed destructive patterns to be willing to admit failure or weakness and to seek healthy change.

Farnsworth's book, *Wounded Workers*, complements the aforementioned books. Although the title of his book may not direct people as quickly to the topic of spiritual abuse, *Wounded Workers* is an invaluable resource that gives readers tools for uncovering organizations that are neurotic, addictive, or are spiritually abusive. There are guidelines for recovery from a counseling psychologist's point of view. This book is geared particularly for people who have found themselves in harmful church or workplace environments. It is instructive for pastors, church workers, church consultants, denominational overseers, parachurch workers and leaders, those involved in Christian organizations, and Christians in general.

This book is intended as a recovery manual for wounded workers.[127] It begins at the point of the reader's woundedness and helps to put words to their wound. It helps the reader to accept the reality of the hurt and gives them guidelines for successful recovery. It is not just the individual that poses a problem in Christian organizations, but that many problems are systemic and involve the entire organization.[128] This view "differs significantly from the traditional view that these are individual matters that must be dealt with exclusively on an individual basis."[129] I would be in agreement. In relegating such situations to be individual problems and assuming that these individuals also may have personality or dysfunctional problems, the seriousness of the systemic ailment becomes marginalized and situations may be brushed off as incidental issues.

Since it is customary for organizations to name workers who appear to be disturbed or disruptive and to deal with them directly; those seen as irrational to be indoctrinated; those seen as irresponsible to be disciplined; those seen as incompetent to need performance evaluations; and those seen as mentally or emotionally impaired to need mental

---

126. Enroth, *Recovering from Churches*, 68.

127. Farnsworth, *Wounded Workers*, 10.

128. Ibid., 12.

129. Ibid., 10.

health interventions, the organization itself is rarely included as a factor that might need to be considered in the situation. The individual takes the brunt of the situation but the organization itself is never called into question and is seldom held accountable in any way.[130] There is a need for Christians not to ignore the wounds inflicted on the workers by dysfunctional leaders and organizations. It may be that dysfunctional leaders and organizations not just be dealt with on an entirely human (psychological, sociological, or economic) level.[131] It is important to recognize the spiritual dimension and be aware that the enemy is determined to disrupt and distort God's work even in the midst of God's people.[132] The reader will be refreshed by this unbiased portrayal of organizational weaknesses, which gives hope to individuals who have or are now facing marginalization for these packaged reasons.

It is vitally important to hold organizations accountable since "Organizations can be dysfunctional, just as individuals can be."[133] This fact allows wounded workers to have a broader perspective of the whole situation. They can begin to better understand how they can cope.[134] Descriptions of dysfunctional organizations run from the ordinary to the extraordinary. Three major types of dysfunctional organizations have been named: the neurotic, the addictive, and the spiritually abusive. Each type is given a separate chapter. Two tests are provided in each chapter; one to test the organization and the other as a self-test for the reader. The reader is asked to consider if they may have personality characteristics or spiritual strongholds that they bring to the situation that makes matters worse.[135] A two-pronged approach gets beneath the surface of organizational dysfunction as well as personal dysfunction and brings instruction and balance to a distraught individual.

A clear outline is provided for the three phases of the recovery process. These include: phase one—recognizing what is, phase two—remembering what should be, and phase three—responding to what can be done about it. The author has endeavored to provide a gentle but forthright approach to help the reader to examine the causes of their

130. Ibid.
131. Ibid.
132. Ibid.
133. Ibid.
134. Ibid., 12–13.
135. Ibid., 14.

pain and then to move on through these progressive stages of recovery. The topics of "servant leadership" and a biblical perspective on "calling" are examined. The reader is exhorted that their number one job is to refuse to be compromised, that they must remain true to their calling, and that they must keep their convictions in the midst of their torment. This is the key to the recovery process. Further, the hand that turns the key is the biblical reality check of the individual's Christian identity and their Christian ideals.[136] This book was thorough and engaging. It is a well designed aid that is a welcome resource for wounded individuals or for interested church leaders so that they can grasp the significance of the personal damage perpetrated by abusive organizations and the necessary elements in recovery from them.

Tom Smail, Andrew Walker, and Nigel Wright's book, *The Love of Power or the Power of Love*, provides another viewpoint on the abusive leadership issue along with related material. The three authors consider problems within the Charismatic and Word Faith movements. This book contains the central theological reflections about the Charismatic renewal in its current stage of development (1994). An excellent treatment of the teaching on the finished work of Christ on the cross is found in the first chapter. This foundational theological underpinning provides spiritual food for the reader to undergird them in their Christian walk. This solid and necessary teaching sets the tone for the rest of the book.

Chapter topics include: the relationship between the renewing Spirit and the crucified Christ that the New Testament expounds and implies; a treatment of John Wimber, whose teaching and practice is used as a base for exploring some of the practical challenges and theological questions that the contemporary renewal has had to face; an approach to demonology based on the New Testament which avoids paranoid obsessions and destructive exaggerations; and definitions of key elements of the Word Faith movement. It also covers charismatic worship; the gift of prophecy in relationship to the so-called Kansas City prophets, and the connection between miraculous Charismatic phenomena and Christian holiness. The last part of the book gives each author's personal story and how they became involved with the charismatic renewal. After reading this book, a reader will be informed and fortified in order to wisely discern how to handle similar situations in the future.

---

136. Ibid., 15.

The important issues of the cross and the Spirit are intentionally looked at in order to consider a theology of renewal. Having good theology is the same reason that people have good maps. When a church is moving ahead and sensing the touch and renewing of the Spirit of God, it can then appreciate how valuable good theology is to the group. Good theology will keep a church spiritually harmonious rather than becoming overweighed in certain areas.[137]

Noting that Pentecostal theology, like all other Christian traditions, has its limitations, the roots of many practical exaggerations and aberrations in Pentecostal and Charismatic theology can be narrowed down to the fact that "the basic structures of Pentecostal theology make it difficult to recognize the close and intimate relationship between the renewing and empowering work of the Spirit and the center of the gospel in the incarnation, death, and resurrection of Jesus Christ."[138] This failure involves not just a theological imbalance between different aspects of the gospel, but is at the root of the problem and that some sections of the renewal movement were (and maybe still are) currently threatened.[139] It is of utmost importance to link the foundational gospel message with a viable and balanced theology of the Holy Spirit. One must be aware of the need to take one's theological bearings from the cross first. From this point of reference, the believer can begin to see where power belongs and that "the only power with which Jesus works is the power of that utterly self-giving love that was itself weak and helpless on Calvary."[140] Jesus did not overcome the violent force of evil by exercising greater force and violence, but by renouncing them altogether. This was the power of Calvary love. This is how God delivers, heals, and saves.[141]

What is needed in the local church in order to minister healing, renewal, and effective evangelism is a growing openness to constantly receive Christ's Calvary love. This love will then be demonstrated in specific ways in the relationships of its members and will extend to those outside its own fellowship because such a church will get near to people by its acceptance of them and will intercede for people in a way that

---

137. Smail et al, *Love of Power*, 15.

138. Ibid., 19.

139. Ibid.

140. Ibid., 27.

141. Ibid., 28.

Christ demonstrated from the cross.[142] "God's healing and renewing power is not something other than or apart from that love; that love itself is the most powerful thing on earth and in heaven."[143]

Smail, Walker, and Wright provide a valuable resource as their book gives indepth answers and theological reflections concerning many persistent questions that a reader may have. The authors have taken on a difficult challenge to remain fair and to be balanced in their assessment of the problems that still face the Pentecostal, Charismatic, Vineyard, and Word Faith belief systems. Their thoughtful analysis and attentive conclusions give understanding regarding certain beliefs, which might otherwise pose a hazard to harmonious biblical understanding of the theologies of both gospel and Spirit in the Church today.

POSITIVE CHRISTIAN LEADERSHIP

Henri Nouwen's book, *In the Name of Jesus*, contains reflections on Christian leadership. There is one complementary theme that intersects with Smail's thoughtful discussion on the cross and the Spirit. Nouwen stresses the fact that to be loved by God and to love God in return is paramount in establishing a foundation for being the competent leader that God seeks to develop. Leaders often struggle with inward and outward fears. In order to be a leader of the future one must simply be vulnerable in just being oneself. The fact that one is loved by God and that one's being and relevance is tied forever to that fact gives freedom to minister in Christ's name. When leaders are intentionally resting in Christ's finished work, they can radiate God's love and gracious concern wherever they are called to minister. Nouwen's book can nourish weary leaders and help to stimulate renewed Christ-like compassion.

Twisted Scriptures, by Mary Alice Chrnalogar, is written primarily to those who find that the church discipleship program that they have gotten involved in is not only unhealthy but also abusive. This book was carefully written to engage those who are starting to question if their discipleship mentor, along with the church philosophy they are affiliated with, is geared to victimize those who come under their oversight. *Twisted Scriptures* shows that devious leaders can use the Scriptures in ways that suit their purposes and consequently will bring people into

---

142. Ibid.
143. Ibid. See Rom 5:5.

spiritual bondage. The Scriptures become unknowingly misrepresented and people simply follow without question or without discerning the dangers resident in such a belief system. Jesus warned of the religious leaders in his day who nullified the Word of God for the sake of tradition. He drew from the words of Isaiah when he restated that God was worshiped in vain because their teachings were but rules taught by men.[144]

Although this book is especially directed towards those who have found themselves in these church settings, it also provides suitable insights into abusive leadership and the factors that influence people to come under these leaders. The reader is invited to consider how easily someone can be manipulated into believing that because they have a discipleship mentor that they should listen to all of their advice without question. The author presents each chapter topic as though she were sitting with the reader and enquiring about their situation. Those who see their circumstance mirrored in this book can get immediate help. The reader is further alerted to a common tactic used to recruit people at the outset. People are showered with attention and caring. Most people find this attractive, but the rules that are under the surface in the discipleship methodology are hidden from view to the unsuspecting beginner.[145]

As the unwary individual gets settled into the system, the undeclared rules begin to emerge. Questioning the discipler or the church leadership, or simply wanting to quit, now come under the topic of sin and rebelling against authority.[146] Showing that unbiblical definitions are kept concealed, that new meanings are given for key words, and that true biblical concepts are conveniently altered exposes the intentions of aberrant discipleship practices. Not until the discipler feels that the trust factor is in place will the rules begin to emerge before the now pliable devotee.[147]

At the end of each chapter there is a checklist of questions that readers can ask themselves in order to evaluate their present discipleship experience. This is a fitting resource for those who feel alone in their struggle but need to find out if they are truly in an unhealthy relationship regime with their discipler and if this program is sponsored by

144. Matt 15:6, 9.

145. Chrnalogar, *Twisted Scriptures*, 2.

146. Ibid.

147. Ibid., 3.

their present church affiliation. The author's commentary along with the evaluation questions helps to empower individuals to break free from enslaving situations and begin to search for a healthier church home.

Chrnalogar echoes the concerns presented by other authors who write on this topic. The title of her book provokes enquiry and establishes the fact that theological deviations have set the stage for Christians to be gently lured and easily manipulated by leaders with a premeditated agenda. The only way that they can confidently carry out this type of discipleship is by willfully twisting the Scriptures to suit their own interpretations. This author is another example of an individual who is breaking the silence and providing relevant teaching for those who are suffering under foolish and hurtful malpractices under the guise of serving Christ and making disciples for his Kingdom. This book alerts conscientious leaders of the inner workings of these flawed discipleship systems and how they can help those harmfully affected.

Stephen Arterburn and Jack Felton coauthored the book *Toxic Faith*.[148] Their book centers on a specific unhealthy faith system, which not only affects individuals but involves entire church communities. An addictive practice of religion is a toxic faith system. The authors define how people get entrapped into an unbalanced view of religion that is toxic. They show that the same elements that are involved and support a dysfunctional family system are also involved in supporting a dysfunctional church family system. The various roles which are played in the system and who plays them are exposed. Individuals are confronted with the realization that when this system is challenged it is dealt with quickly through shaming and rejection.[149]

Previously wounded individuals are susceptible to such a system. Readers can examine their own situation in order to assess whether it may be harmful. It can be acknowledged that one dominant negative emotion prevails—fear. The fear of giving up a power and prestige position to face failure and insignificance is a strong motivator. The religious coconspirator faces the fear of letting the persecutor down. The religious enabler fears ridicule and shame. The victim of religious abuse must

---

148. One participant commented: "The last time I heard Stephen Arterburn speak about this book, he said he had received more comments at conferences, more emails, more letters on *Toxic Faith* than anything else he'd written, and he's written quite a bit!" participant no. 56.

149. Arterburn and Felton, *Toxic Faith*, 161.

follow and blindly believe. Only those who are now outcasts have any measure of freedom. Their desire is to let the truth be known and to be free from this toxic system.[150]

The authors provide a treatment center and have helped many individuals. Though people never come to them as religious addicts, they are depressed, alcoholic, anorexic, overweight, suicidal, and despairing in many other ways. They soon are helped to recognize the roots of their problem—toxic beliefs and a toxic faith. Once this realization has been understood, their recovery is in sight.[151] The aim of this recovery plan is for the religious addict to break through the denial that addiction exists.[152]

The characteristics of a healthy support group should include the following: acceptance, unconditional positive regard, freedom of expression, and a non-autocratic and non-controlling atmosphere. One final guideline is that there is a need to work with the family of the person.[153] Two further descriptions complete the resources available in the book. There is a description of seventeen characteristics of healthy faith[154] and eight core dimensions that indicate the maturity of one's faith.[155]

One key benefit of this book is that it establishes the fact that toxic faith systems do exist. There is hope for those who seek to understand their addiction and then to get the necessary help. For those who seek to help those in toxic systems there is a recognition that individuals cannot do it alone, they need the help of others to get free and to stay free.[156] Although many people will agree that their church situation is not as extreme as the one described by these authors, they can be alert to the many negative factors that influence their own church situation. They can then assess whether their situation is mild or severe or somewhere in the middle. They can use this extreme model as a guide in understanding the dynamics that are involved in order to critique their present

150. Ibid., 206.
151. Ibid., 225.
152. Ibid., 226.
153. Ibid., 241–43.
154. Ibid., 247–62.
155. Ibid., 256.
156. Ibid., 239.

experience of church. They can also be aware of the elements involved in the recovery process that have aided those described in the book.[157]

Although a number of suitable books and articles on the topics of church leaving and spiritual abuse can be obtained, the Internet offers ample pertinent information, theological reflections, and insightful ways to aid people. As stated before, many of the website/blogsite hosts began to post their reflections in an attempt to work through their own distressing experience of church. Insights shared online now become wisdom for those who have had a similar occurrence and for those who minister to those affected.

GRACE, IDENTITY, AND COMMUNITY

The following literature offers theological foundations regarding God's grace, reading God's Word, identity in Christ, healthy church body life, and spiritual wholeness through grief and forgiveness. In order to encourage Christians to relate well to God, to fellow Christians, and to a needy world, they need to understand that their identity in Christ is primary. Their understanding of being identified with Christ and being part of God's spiritual family bolsters their understanding of what it means to be a Christian.

When this foundation is in place, there is opportunity for Christians to move forward in how to help one another as community in which the broken and disconnected can find help and connection, and where people can go from initial salvation in Christ to a place of discipleship and journeying together with others through the enabling power of the Spirit of Christ. When leaders undergird Christians in the basic theological concepts of God's grace, identity in Christ, and biblical community, it paves the way for healthier spiritual communities.

There are a number of books that point to the grace of God as a foundational teaching for new Christians and as a refresher for those further along in faith. The book entitled *The Transforming Power of Grace,* by Thomas Oden, is one that helps leaders and followers to be refreshed in the fundamentals of their conversion. Gordon Fee's book *Paul, the Spirit, and the People of God* enables Christians to see that their

---

157. Other helpful books that consider the topic of spiritual abuse and recovery are: Stephen Arterburn, *Faith that Hurts Faith that Heals*; Ron Burks and Vicki Burks, *Damaged Disciples*; Marc A. Dupont, *Walking Out of Spiritual Abuse.*

salvation is more than an individual event but that there is a spiritual family that they have been born into.

The author of *The Transforming Power of Grace* makes the point that grace is the root of Christian spirituality.[158] The task of a leader is to show how grace seeks out the lost soul, reawakens the spiritually demoralized, and elicits spiritual growth.[159] "The purpose of caregiving is to make the truth of grace plausible and appropriable in the inner life of the individual. The purpose of preaching is to attest the history of grace effectively at work amid the history of sin."[160]

This book is best understood as a resource for personal spiritual formation. The classical Christian teaching of grace undergirds and empowers the daily walk of faith. Since much of our cultural environment goes directly against the stream of the teaching of grace, Christians who remain ignorant of the history of grace are not apt to take deep root spiritually.[161] The teaching of grace, therefore, stands as a penetrating challenge to all pretensions of self-sufficiency.[162]

The broad nature of God's grace can be described in this way: "Grace is an overarching term for all of God's gifts to humanity, all the blessings of salvation, all events through which are manifested God's own self-giving."[163] God's grace can be defined this way:

> Grace is the favor shown by God to sinners. It is the divine good-will offered to those who neither inherently deserve nor can ever hope to earn it. It is the divine disposition to work in our hearts, wills, and actions, so as actively to communicate God's self-giving love for humanity. (Rom 3:24; 6:1; Eph 1:7; 2:5–8)[164]

The reader is helped to acknowledge that grace has a history. This history is of human communities, not merely of individuals. It is an uplifting reality to consider that Christians "do not reason toward grace independently separated from an actual historical community of memory and testimony." The actuality is that believers cannot respond to grace

---

158. Oden, *Transforming Power*, 15.

159. Ibid.

160. Ibid.

161. Ibid., 17.

162. Ibid., 38.

163. Ibid., 33.

164. Ibid.

apart from a community of belief. One does not come to faith out of a vacuum.[165] That the Church exists at all only proves the history of grace through the countless generations.[166]

Comprehending the biblical teaching of God's grace is foundational to spiritual formation and the believer's daily walk with Christ. "Only that which is enabled by divine grace will endure in the church. All plays and maneuvers circumventing grace will atrophy."[167] It can be rightly said that "Many perennial distortions of faith might have been prevented had more sustained attention been given to the biblical teaching of grace."[168]

In order to build a solid biblical foundation and discern the voice of God from all other voices, Christians need to be guided in the importance of reading God's Word for themselves. A primary habit that needs to be cultivated is learning to immerse oneself in the Scriptures. Leaders have a responsibility to model an attitude of reverence for and excitement about Scripture. They have a spiritual obligation to show how to read it systematically and thoughtfully.[169] Christians can benefit by the guidance church leaders give in order to develop regular times of Bible reading and to grow in the habit of *listening* to God.

There are many books written that could help Christians to read the Scriptures with greater understanding. The following selected excerpts from a few different authors focus on the topic of reading the Scriptures intentionally. "Reading Scripture is not the same as listening to God. To do one is not necessarily to do the other."[170] "We have to read before we can listen. But we can read without going on to listen."[171] The goal of reading Scripture is to extend the range of personal and corporate listening to God who reveals himself in and through it. Considering how God has spoken to his people in the past along with how people have responded when he speaks will be spiritually enlightening.[172] Christians need to grasp that "The intent of revelation is not to inform us about

---

165. Ibid., 22.

166. Ibid., 22–23.

167. Ibid., 21.

168. Ibid.

169. Lawrenz, *Dynamics of Spiritual Formation*, 60.

170. Peterson, *Working the Angles*, 61.

171. Ibid., 72.

172. Ibid., 62.

God but to involve us in God."[173] Christians develop skills in discernment as they spend time with their Bible. As believers spend time in God's Word the voice of Jesus will become known. One truth that will be instilled over time is that the inner witness will never contradict the written witness. Being immersed in the Father's teachings will develop the intuitive capacity to recognize the inner witness.[174]

One's theological understandings about God are clarified by paying attention to the teachings and narrative accounts in the Word of God. Misbeliefs about God and assorted folk theologies that have been acquired over time can be exchanged for solid biblical grounding. Spiritual weakness can be replaced by spiritual fortitude. God's love, care, and presence can be experienced in vibrant new ways in a Christian's life. A. W. Tozer made the point that there is a wrong conception of Scripture that is a hindrance. This is the view that "A silent God suddenly began to speak in a book and when the book was finished lapsed back into silence again forever. Now we read the book as the record of what God said when He was for a brief time in a speaking mood."[175] He chides that with notions like that faith can be stunted. He focuses on the detail that God is not and has never been silent. He points out that the second person of the Holy Trinity is called the Word. He challenges believers to reorient their thinking and approach their Bible with the idea that it is a book whose author is now speaking.[176]

Fee's book, *Paul, the Spirit, and the People of God*, establishes the concept of spiritual community. He emphasizes the fact that "God is not just saving individuals and preparing them for heaven; rather, he is creating *a people* among whom he can live and who in their life together will reproduce God's life and character."[177] The question that Paul answers in 1 Corinthians 12:13 is not how people become believers but how the incredible mixture of them, comprised of Jew and Gentile, slave and free, make up the one Body of Christ. Since all alike were immersed in and made to drink their fill of the Spirit, this is how this diverse company has been formed into one spiritual entity in Christ.[178]

173. Peterson, *Reversed Thunder*, 13.

174. Smith, *Voice of Jesus*, 31.

175. Tozer, *Pursuit of God*, 77.

176. Ibid.

177. Fee, *Paul*, 66.

178. Ibid., 66–67.

It is the work of the Spirit in a believer's life that ensures that they grasp the revealed truth of the Gospel.[179] Although people enter this spiritual community one at a time, the goal of salvation in Christ is a people for God's name. Getting saved has to do with faith in Christ that also includes faithfulness to Christ. Paul's theological reasoning includes the idea that "one gets in in order to stay in" and that "salvation for Paul includes the whole process, not simply the beginning point."[180] Paul views the Spirit as the identity marker of the converted. It is, therefore, the experience of the Spirit that is crucial and it is the Spirit alone who identifies God's people in the present eschatological age.[181] Since no one can make the basic Christian confession of Jesus as Lord, except by the Holy Spirit,[182] it follows that if anyone does not have the Spirit, that person does not belong to Christ at all.[183] Therefore, it is the work of the Spirit in a life that brings forth the new birth but also it is the Spirit in that life that is what the Christian life is finally all about.[184]

Personal holiness needs to be considered in the context of community. Christian ethics flows out of community not out of individual personal holiness. The Epistles were written to a church community not just to individuals. It is important for Christians to keep going back to that historical and theological point otherwise many spiritual truths get muddled in the process. For example, the exhortation in Ephesians 5:8 to be "filled with the Spirit" was written to the entire spiritual community there. This passage should be considered, quoted, and explained from that context. The second issue is that ethics has to do with life in the Spirit. The danger is in failing to recognize that the Christian life is simply not a continuation of life under law disguised as being by the Spirit. God's intention was to create an eschatological people who live the life of the future in the present. This life, birthed by the Spirit, will reflect the character of the God who became present first in Christ and then by his Spirit.[185]

179. Ibid., 75.

180. Ibid.

181. Ibid., 88.

182. 1 Cor 12:3.

183. Fee, *Paul*, 88–89. Rom 8:9.

184. Fee, *Paul*, 95.

185. Ibid., 98–99. Fee notes that, "Even though it was God's presence that distinguished Israel as God's own people, their identity as that people was bound up with

Instead of giving Christians in the early churches rules to live by, Paul gives them the Spirit. They were to be finished with rules and move ahead to living the life of those who by the Spirit were being renewed into the likeness of the Creator.[186] Paul's perception of Christian ethics was a theological issue that was tied to the known character of God.

> Thus: (1) the *purpose* (or basis) of Christian ethics is the glory of God (1 Cor 10:31); (2) the *pattern* for such ethics is the Son of God, Christ himself (1 Cor 4:16–17; 11:1; Eph 4:20), into whose likeness we were predestined to be transformed (Rom 8:29); (3) the *principle* is love, precisely because love is at the essence of who God is, (4) and the *power* is the Spirit, the Spirit of God.[187]

When the mind is renewed by the Spirit, Christians understand that love must rule over all—for it is only by a renewed mind that they discover how best to love. Only by dependence on the Spirit can the people of God know what is pleasing to God.[188] Fee helps the reader to grasp what the Spirit fully intends the Church to be.

Although the title *Community 101* may appear unsophisticated, Gilbert Bilezikian's contribution is a resource dedicated to understanding leadership and community in the Kingdom Age. It is tied together with the theme of reclaiming the local church as a community of oneness. The chapters cover these four main topics: only community is forever, oneness, ministry, and leadership.

This book is pertinent to this study as it instructs regarding a new covenant approach to nonhierarchical leadership ministry in a spiritual community founded on the New Testament revelation of the completed work of Christ and his establishing of the Church. The biblical model of community[189] and leadership is far superior to any other model. The model, which unfolded in the Old Testament era, established what worked for that time and why that model does not work today. In establishing the Church as God's spiritual kingdom on earth, necessary

---

their obedience to the Torah, the law. . . . Paul argues, the Spirit, and the Spirit alone, identifies the people of God under the new covenant," 100.

186. Ibid., 106. Col 3:10.

187. Fee, *Paul*, 106.

188. Ibid., 105.

189. Stanley Grenz's book, *Created For Community*, gives a theological foundation for community. In order to establish a sound basis for Christian community, beliefs need to have a solid biblical foundation.

adjustments must be made to effectively navigate in this Spirit-enabled, Spirit-empowered environment.

One such adjustment is the need to recognize the place of women in ministry. There is a need to give voice to an egalitarian view of ministry that includes women and men, based on their gifting in the Church. The great paradigm shift from old to new covenant did not occur at the beginning of Christ's earthly ministry but at its end.[190] The perceptive reader of Acts will quickly note that the first proclamation of Peter, made immediately after the outpouring of the Holy Spirit, concerned a radical change in ministry roles. By the coming of the Spirit a new era was inaugurated. This radical change meant that "ministries that had been previously restricted were now universally accessible to all believers without distinctions of gender, age, or class."[191]

Peter had declared that the empowerment of all Christians to participate in the ministry of the Church as God's prophets and proclaimers of his Gospel had now come.[192] There was no suggestion of reverting back to the parameters of the former dispensation. The standards of ancient Judaism had now been superseded by the ushering in of the new age of the Spirit. With this promised reality now in place, the claim that women should not participate fully in the ministry of the Church because Jesus's apostles were male needs to be challenged. Those who make such a claim simply do not comprehend the scriptural dynamic of the radical change that occurred from the old covenant to the new. They, instead, try to force on the Church the standards of ancient Judaism.[193]

The persuasion of a host of people in today's Church to situate the traditions of ancient Judaism in the era of the Spirit shows itself again and again. "The argument that women should be barred from some church ministries because Christ's apostles were all men represents a regression to preresurrection conditions."[194] The logical outcome of barring women would be that not only women would be excluded from ministry but also any Gentile. This would mean that church ministry should only be assumed by Jewish men. By recognizing Christ's gift of oneness to the

---

190. Bilezikian, *Community 101*, 79. 1 Cor 11:25.

191. Bilezikian, *Community 101*, 79.

192. Ibid.

193. Ibid.

194. Ibid.

new community, all considerations of race, class, and gender become irrelevant to the life of the Church.[195]

Barring women ministers is a prime methodology in many unhealthy church settings. It is strongly felt among some groups, that in order to follow God's plan for the Church in this era, that gender restrictions must be adhered to or their church will not be taking the necessary biblical stand regarding the place of women in ministry. Many authoritarian leaders have a negative mindset towards women taking part in church ministry. The false teaching of gender hierarchy undermines biblical community. It is important to recognize that the issue of gender hierarchy not only affects women in the Church, but it also affects men. Holding a position of gender hierarchy is an underlying and damaging belief that influences leadership and stifles ministry participation opportunities in the local church. This misbelief posed as a valid Christian belief is particularly hurtful for women.

The ideal of community, although exciting, does not happen by itself, because the maintenance of community requires intentionality, perseverance, and sacrifice.[196] Authentic community requires forethought, organization, coordination, and cooperation. Biblically, these features are identified as "ministry." Ministry often is something that is done by special people called "ministers" or "priests" and that the problem with this interpretation of ministry is exactly that. It excludes most of the members of the community from being significantly involved in building it. This weakness necessitates a closer examination of the biblical text in order to determine from Scripture what ministry is, how it is to be done, and by whom.[197] Despite variations in a basic definition, the New Testament view of leadership includes three essential features which seem to remain constant for all churches: Leadership is a servant ministry, based on spiritual gifts, and is always plural.[198] In recognizing the legitimacy of leadership by Christ, it must also be agreed that, "Jesus transformed the concept of leadership by redefining its style and the motivation for doing it."[199] There is no command for any Christian to exercise authority over

195. Ibid., 80.
196. Ibid., 129.
197. Ibid., 65.
198. Ibid., 130.
199. Ibid., 131.

another, but instead there are strict orders for all Christians, including the leaders, to act as servants within their communities.[200]

Comparing hierarchical and democratically constituted bodies, one can grant that "With the right spirit, hierarchical structures can be made the instrument of servanthood just as democratically constituted bodies can fall victim to abuse at the hands of power driven individuals."[201] Therefore, what really matters is the attitude with which leadership is approached. This is the determinative factor in the life of a community rather than the formal definitions of its constitutional status.[202] Understanding the link between the nature of the new community and Christ's ministry is vital.

Therefore, when a community looks at the rationale for administration of the church, the obvious resolution would be that the decisions that shape the church's life and affect its constituency rests squarely with the congregation.[203] The early Church, in the Acts chapter 6 account, modeled the involvement of "the whole group" in their decision making process. Although the Apostles facilitated the process, they encouraged and supported the community's corporate decision. The Church was simply expected to corporately take care of its affairs without authoritarian intervention.[204] "Biblical headship is a servant function, driven by a passion for meeting needs rather than by the desire to exercise authority over others."[205] Bilezikian's clear presentation gives refreshing biblical direction and hope for leaders and church communities to model authentic missional communities.

Another helpful resource that addresses the issue of the place of women in church ministry is *Women in the Church* by Stanley Grenz. *Women in the Church* deals with the theological issues that make a case for women to be involved in ministry according to spiritual giftings rather than gender. The place of women in the Church, regarding their suitability based on God's calling and their spiritual giftings, is a Church leadership issue.[206] Grenz takes the apparently problematic texts

---

200. Ibid.

201. Ibid., 136.

202. Ibid.

203. Ibid., 140.

204. Ibid., 141.

205. Ibid., 166.

206. Many authors address the issue of women in ministry. Here are two helpful books: *Daughters of the Church* by Ruth A. Tucker and Walter Liefeld and *Why Not*

of Scripture and demonstrates that biblical analysis soundly supports an egalitarian view. When this view is considered, an imbalance in the idea of the submission of women to men in the Church is demonstrated. The further implication is that the egalitarian view demonstrates that it is a better model for marriage and the family. Grenz's rationale for an egalitarian view and for writing his book was "to show that the vision of male-female mutuality is grounded in the Bible, is the logical outcome of evangelical theological commitments, and best serves the practical needs of God's people."[207]

The egalitarian view is not built on the myth of androgyny, which is the claim that men and women are essentially the same. Since both genders view the world differently, the differences between the sexes demand the inclusion of both in leadership.[208] The Van Leeuwen study group made a significant observation: "If male-dominated, overly hierarchical modes of church management remain in place . . . then the ordination of women turns out to be a questionable victory."[209] Grenz strongly resists such a regrettable outcome. "Indeed, we have done the entire people of God a disservice if we merely give women access to the power structures of the church while maintaining unbiblical hierarchical organizational patterns."[210] In light of Gibbs's discussion on the need to change lingering assumptions about church leadership, the biblical basis for both women and men in church ministry must be considered with other church issues that are facing the Church in the twenty-first century.

In contrast to books on leadership abuses in the Church, *Churches That Heal*, by Doug Murren, comes as a welcome herald of what a local church could do to reorient their thinking to being a healing community in a broken world.[211] The introduction to the book registers the fact that

---

Women? by Loren Cunningham and David Joel Hamilton. The women's ministry issue is also addressed on the website: Christians For Biblical Equality.

207. Grenz, *Women in the Church*, 18.

208. Ibid., 230.

209. Ibid.

210. Ibid.

211. Other books that look at developing healthy churches are: *A Caring Church*, Charles A. Ver Straten; *The Practices of a Healthy Church*, Donald J. MacNair with Esther Meek; *What People Expect From Church*, Robert L. Randall; *Healthy Christians Make a Healthy Church*, John H. Oak; *The Connecting Church* and *Making Room For Life*, Randy Frazee.

not all churches have an environment that is conducive to healing. He is also very aware that there are many toxic churches today. Toxic churches are communities where guilt, manipulation, fear, and shame reign. The inevitable results are that it poisons the spiritual atmosphere and makes healing all but impossible.[212] Often the best healers are the ones who have experienced pain.[213]

Churches that heal, major on relationships. Since many churches do not make relationships a priority, they fall short in their capacity to heal. Communities need to consider that forgiveness is the central factor in emotional healing. In a healing church, people are not defined by the mistakes of their past but they are encouraged to grow beyond them because biblical love is unconditional.[214] Murren's book provides a sensible guide and a vision that churches can steward their corporate experience of pain and minister God's grace to the hurting.[215]

Two books that further echo the theme of stewarding the corporate experience of pain to minister God's grace to the hurting are Larry Crabb's book, *Connecting*, and Peter Scazzero's book, *The Emotionally Healthy Church*. Crabb gives the essential overview for the human need to connect while Scazzero informs people how they could visualize what this might look like in their spiritual communities.

After Crabb had been involved as a professional psychologist for over twenty-five years, both in practice and in teaching, he recounts a major shift in his approach to counseling ministry. His book *Connecting* unfolds his story. He boldly goes against a popular view and states that what our culture calls psychological disorder is really a soul crying out for what only community can provide. It is not a matter of a damaged psyche or a disorder requiring treatment but something that a community can offer those who are disconnected. Simply exhorting people to do what is right and then holding them accountable is not the answer to their internal need. When groups tend to emphasize accountability then it may be a sure sign that they don't know how to relate. "Rather than fixing psyches or scolding sinners, we must provide nourishment for the disconnected soul that only a community of connected people can

212. Murren, *Churches That Heal*, 5.

213. Ibid., 6.

214. Ibid., 95.

215. Ibid., 251.

offer."[216] It is clear that "The crisis of care in modern culture, especially in the Western church, will not be resolved by training more therapists. We do not need a counseling center on every corner." A workable solution would be to focus on caring community. The need is to develop communities where the heart of God is at home and the community shepherds one another as they journey together.[217]

Crabb is countering faulty thinking that "the church's job is done when it instructs people in biblical principles and then exhorts them to do right." He adamantly feels that: "It's about time to find a better way to help each other when we struggle than the way of our therapeutic culture, which looks beneath every troublesome emotion or behavior pattern to find a psychological disorder that needs repair."[218] His renewed vision is based on the extreme spiritual benefit of the new covenant. God has placed something wonderful and resilient within Christians that no abuse, rejection, or failure can ever destroy. The need is not to relate to one another as moralist to sinner or therapist to patient, but as saint to saint, father to child, friend to friend. The need is to help each other believe that, by the grace of God, there is something good beneath the mess. Even when all that can be seen in lives is the mess, people need to be encouraged to believe that God's people can nourish the good and encourage its release.[219]

God's Spirit does search the heart, rebuke, and exhort, but Crabb also sees an integral aspect of God's working in someone's life through connecting. The center of what God does to help someone change is to reveal what he is really like and then to pour his life into them. A critical element in the revealing process is to place a believer in a community of people who are enough like God to give them that taste firsthand. Connecting, then, plays a vital, indispensable, powerful role in effectively addressing the core issues of people's souls, the issues that lie beneath all the personal, emotional, and psychological problems.[220]

216. Crabb, *Connecting*, xvi.

217. Ibid., xvi–xvii.

218. Ibid., xvii.

219. Ibid., xviii.

220. Ibid., 9. John Ortberg also reasons: "Sometimes in church circles when people feel lonely, we will tell them not to expect too much from human relationships, that there is inside every human being a God-shaped void that no other person can fill. That is true. But apparently, according to the writer of Genesis, God creates inside this man a kind of 'human-shaped void' that God himself will not fill," Ortberg, *Everybody's Normal*, 32.

It is important to observe how God helps people become more like Christ and to learn from this method. First, God provides his people with a taste of Christ delighting in them—the essence of connection—accepting who they are and envisioning who they could be. Second, God diligently searches within each of them for the good that he has put there—an affirming exposure. He remains calm when badness is visible and he keeps confidence that goodness lies beneath. Third, God engagingly exposes what is bad and painful—a disruptive exposure. He takes opportunities to reveal grace in the midst of the difficult content of our hearts.[221]

Crabb confesses that in his previous counseling methodology that he spent too much time with the flesh. He realizes in hindsight that he did not emphasize enough that beneath all the bad is goodness. His renewed focus is to more fully reveal God's grace and create a fuller appreciation for what that grace does. True change depends on experiencing the character of God. Although he agrees that, "Someone has defined spiritual direction as recognizing what God is up to in someone's life and joining the process," he recognizes that this is not what is typically done. In a search for solutions, a core ingredient might be easily overlooked. Rather, the prime need is to search for the good that God may be releasing through this trial.[222] The issue isn't how bad people are but rather how good God is. It is God's kindness that leads men to repentance. "Connecting helps to not only enliven the good but also to destroy the bad, and it does so by surprising us with forgiving love."[223]

The usual pattern for most people in dealing with a hurting friend is to retreat, to reprove, or to refer. These are done by establishing a safe distance between the emotionally troubled, scolding people into holier living, or simply referring them to a trained counselor.[224] Maybe the struggles that are assumed to be symptoms of a psychological disorder are in fact evidence of a disconnected soul. Connecting with a source of life, not professional treatment would be a natural solution. Ordinary people have the power to change other people's lives because the power is found in connection. Defined, this connection is when the truest part of one soul meets the emptiest recesses in another and finds something

---

221. Crabb, *Connecting*, 10–11.

222. Ibid., 12–16.

223. Ibid., 18–19. See Rom 2:4.

224. Crabb, *Connecting*, 25–26.

there; when life passes from one to the other—an experience of shared life. Exhorting without loving connection just has no power.[225]

Two "helping" models are examined: the exhortation/accountability model and the treatment/repair model. In the first model, efforts to help consist of admonishment to do what is right, resulting in painful consequences for violation, and occasionally, rewards for cooperation. The power that is depended upon to influence someone's life becomes pressure in all its ugly forms, including guilt, shame, threat, fear, and manipulation. The second model is to figure out what is wrong and find a way to fix it.

God designed Christian communities to connect—it is the nature of his family. In order to be a healing community, that community must be fully persuaded that Christians have an innate appetite for holiness. Furthermore, the community needs to focus on releasing what is good, that is, that which is resident in the believer—the very nature of Christ. The conclusion is that it is a connected community, rather than good advice or deeper insight that is at the center of things. The rationale for this is because connected community is the defining center of God. It would appear that when this truth is grasped then there is a greater chance to journey toward connection.[226] The new covenant is a neglected and pivotal doctrine in shaping the local church's approach to personal growth and to connecting relationships.[227] The basic truth of it provides this delightful insight: "God help me to believe the truth about myself, no matter how beautiful it may be."[228]

The Church can be a healing community characterized by the fact that as the people within it bond together in small healing communities they can celebrate the life that they share. They are instructed in that life so that they can go out to connect even more deeply and invite others to enjoy that same intimacy.[229] The latent potential of community life is more than just going to church but that there is a resource simply waiting that could be powerful to heal brokenness and to overcome the damage done by abusive backgrounds. It is a force that can encourage

---

225. Ibid., 29–32. See Gibbs, *Leadership Next*, 106. "Leadership is about connecting, not controlling."

226. Crabb, *Connecting*, 40.

227. Ibid., 79.

228. Ibid., 159.

229. Ibid., xiv.

the depressed to move forward and stimulate the lonely to reach out. This resource is realizing that the center of Christian community is relating to a few.[230]

The question then becomes: Where is the place for professional counselors? Two kinds of problems need to be distinguished: those that require the services of a technically trained professional (psychoses, Attention Deficit Disorder, and the like) and those that represent struggles of the soul. An appreciation of biblical anthropology, Trinitarian theology, and new covenant blessings provide the framework for all helping efforts.[231] Informed diagnosis and treatment is helpful, yet there are a wide range of concerns that do not easily fit into the four main categories, such as personality disorders, nonextreme mood problems and existential despair, relational difficulties, and a host of everyday problems such as insecurity, indecisiveness, superficiality (denial), resentment, worry, and sexual struggles (including perversions and addictions). These are concerns of the soul. Their roots lie in disconnection, that is, in a response driven by the flesh in order to handle life's disappointments. It is energizing to grasp that though the root is the flesh, the cure is ultimately the spirit. This is demonstrated by a new heart that trusts God and perseveres in faith.[232]

These problems do not require the services of a trained expert. Sometimes all that people require is involvement from a wise elder or kindness from a peer or older friend. Crabb believes that connection is the solution to disconnection. He encourages the reader to consider the fact that as long as the resources of community remain undeveloped, professional counselors will closely resemble what real friends, wise shepherds, and seasoned spiritual directors do, since qualification to effectively counsel has more to do with wisdom and character than with training and degrees. The need, then, is for wisdom and character to be developed in Christian communities.[233]

The focus should be on being spiritual communities that become dispensers of grace accompanied by wisdom. When churches require cooperation more than connection, a vibrant dynamic of community is missed. A healing community, therefore, would be a people who place

230. Ibid., xiii.
231. Ibid., 205.
232. Ibid., 204–5.
233. Ibid., 205–6.

connecting at the center of their purpose and passion—not evangelism, teaching, preaching, missions, music, social action, or numerical
growth—but connecting with God (worship), others (loving service),
and self (personal wholeness). Loving God and loving others are foundational to the Christian life and reside at the core of God's intention for
his people.[234]

When connecting lies at the center of community, priority will be
given to issues such as: What constitutes friendship? What does it mean
to shepherd others; to be an elder? Doing so should answer the question:
What is *spiritual direction* and who can do it?[235] Church leaders as well
as a number of congregants will have the skill to know when to refer
people to professional experts for help. On a regular basis it will then be
the community that will care for the souls of its people through friends,
shepherds, and spiritual directors.[236] The reader is helped to rethink
these issues in order to place *connecting* in its appropriate place because
of the work of Christ in the life of individual Christians and because of
the beauty and power of the Spirit resident in the local church.

Scazzero, author of *The Emotionally Healthy Church*, like Crabb,
found himself in a personal crisis. He had to examine his philosophy of
ministry in the crucible of family crisis. This catalyst helped Scazzero to
recognize that he, as a leader, needed to change. As he considered various problematic leadership situations in the Church, he grieved.[237] From
growing problems within his own leadership team he was faced with the
realization that even though they could talk about the Bible, they didn't
know how to live what they had learned. The lack was identified as a
failure in the discipleship model that did not include growing from emotional infancy or adolescence into emotional adulthood. He knew that
"as go the leaders, so goes the church" and that they could not grow an
emotionally healthy church if they, as leaders, were not addressing issues
beneath the surface of their lives.[238] Many Christian leaders he meets are
emotionally numb. Through a concerted effort to work through his own

234. Ibid., 206.

235. Ibid.

236. Ibid., 207.

237. Scazzero, *The Emotionally Healthy Church*, 44. Scazzero's conclusion was that
the problematic examples that he had observed stemmed from a faulty paradigm of
Christian discipleship.

238. Ibid., 45.

emotional pain, he introduced his church leadership to the paradigm that emotional health and spiritual maturity are inseparable. It was a step of faith in a new frontier.

Part Two of his book explores a scriptural basis for this new model of discipleship. "Contemporary discipleship models often lift up the spiritual over the physical, emotional, social, and intellectual components of who we are."[239] Good biblical theology does not allow such a division. The thesis for his book is that emotional and spiritual health cannot be separated. "It is not possible for a Christian to be spiritually mature while remaining emotionally immature."[240] The fact that a leader may be a dynamically gifted speaker for God in public yet remain an unloving spouse and parent at home needs to be questioned. A subtle bias has filtered into our churches that to be emotional is less than spiritual; that spiritual maturity can be achieved apart from an integration of the emotional aspects of who we are.[241] The answer is complex but the image of God in Christians includes many dimensions such as the physical, social, emotional, intellectual, and spiritual.[242] Since emotions are the language of the soul it is important not to ignore one's emotions. Scazzero echoes Allender and Longman who contend that, "Ignoring our emotions is turning our back on reality; listening to our emotions ushers us into reality. And reality is where we meet God."[243]

The author encourages the reader to consider taking the emotional inventory provided in the fourth chapter. The next six chapters outline six essential principles. These include: look beneath the surface; break the power of the past; live in brokenness and vulnerability; receive the gift of limits; embrace grieving and loss; and make incarnation your model for loving well. Each chapter is introduced with a similar pattern. Here is an example of principle one:

> In emotionally healthy churches, people take a deep, hard look inside their hearts, asking, "What is going on that Jesus is trying to change?" They understand that a person's life is like an iceberg, with the vast majority of who we are lying deep beneath

239. Ibid., 49.

240. Ibid., 50.

241. Ibid., 51.

242. Ibid., 51–52.

243. Ibid., 53; Dan Allender and Tremper Longman III, *Cry of the Soul* (Dallas: Word, 1994).

the surface. They invite God to bring to their awareness and to transform those beneath-the-surface layers that hinder them from becoming more like Jesus Christ.[244]

One of the reasons that the author puts this item first is because for the first fifteen years of his Christian life he rarely took time to look deeply into his heart. Although he was purposeful in the disciplines of the Christian life such as prayer, Scripture reading, listening to God's voice, confessing sins, journaling, and even fasting, he deluded himself into believing that he had been looking inside when he had not. As a pastor, he learned that unless people experience sufficient anguish and discomfort, most will not do the hard work of taking an honest look inside. It is through one's personal pain that the hunger for change is developed.[245] In leadership training, young people were willing to experience significant changes in their lives when exposed to a discipleship model that integrated emotional and spiritual maturity. Older people appeared to require crisis or extreme distress to engage in serious reflection and change.[246]

In contrast to Jesus, who was deeply aware of who he was and what he was doing, most Christians, though self-conscious, are simply not self-aware. Scripture portrays Jesus "as one who had intense, raw, emotional experiences and was able to express his emotions in unashamed, unembarrassed freedom to others."[247] In today's language, Jesus would be considered "emotionally intelligent."[248] The crisis in ministry is that individuals cannot enter into someone else's world when they have not entered into their own world. Since the ultimate purpose is to allow the Gospel to transform, the end result ought to be that Christians are better lovers of God and other people.[249]

In order for individuals to explore some of the disturbing and dark aspects of who they are, it is crucial that they are grounded in God's grace and that they confidently stand before God as his beloved. It is the revelation of God's free grace that gives his people the courage to face the painful truth about themselves. As God's children step out onto the

244. Scazzero, *Emotionally Healthy Church*, 69.

245. Ibid., 74.

246. Ibid.

247. Ibid., 75.

248. Ibid. This term was popularized by Daniel Goleman.

249. Ibid., 78.

tightrope of discovering the unpleasant things about themselves, they realize that they have a safety net below—the Gospel of Jesus Christ."[250]

A spiritual community committed to seeking the emotional and spiritual health of its people will be a messy place, but people need to understand how their past affects their present ability to love Christ and others. Since people can only change through direct intervention of God, it is important to cultivate a safe and healing atmosphere—a place for deep emotional and spiritual healing to be the norm. Many authors agree with the concept that "The New Testament world is unable to imagine living out healthy family life apart from the context of a healthy church life."[251] Although becoming a Christian gives someone a new identity and forgiveness for the past, it does not erase the past. God's desire is to heal brokenness and patch up wounds. Therefore, the consensus is that the local church can be the spiritual family where hurting children are "reparented."[252]

The fifth principle is entitled "Embrace Grieving and Loss." This chapter is relevant for those who have suffered grief and loss through their church experience. Knowing that the soul grows larger through suffering, it is important to allow grief to develop maturity. Churches that help people to embrace grief know that this is the only pathway to becoming a compassionate person like Christ. Since everyone experiences sorrows, people need to be invited to grieve and grow through them.[253]

The issue of forgiveness is not a quick process. It is not possible to truly forgive another person from the heart until people allow themselves to feel the pain of what was lost. There is a caution against thinking that forgiveness is simply an act of the will. This clearly demonstrates a lack in understanding the grieving process.[254] "The process of forgiveness always involves grieving before letting go—whether you are the person giving forgiveness or asking for it."[255] There is hope for those who grieve by acknowledging that although biblical grieving can feel as if it is only going to make things worse, in time this process will lead to life.[256]

250. Ibid., 83.
251. Ibid., 99.
252. Ibid.
253. Ibid., 152–55.
254. Ibid., 157.
255. Ibid.
256. Ibid., 170.

As a community has learned to absorb and grow through pain, they will bear the fruit of God-like compassion toward others. The ability to embrace losses and grief together will equip a community to love others as Jesus did. This leads to making incarnation the model for loving well. Incarnation needs to be a priority. The need of the Church is not to "fix" people, or whatever else may have current appeal, but simply to love well. The final challenge for the reader is to apply the six principles of emotionally healthy churches to themselves (as leaders) and then to the rest of their church community.[257] The reason is that this is the pathway to experiencing more of heaven on earth. The last two chapters of his book describe how to initiate such a journey. There is a discussion guide that is a helpful tool in restructuring Christian discipleship.[258] Both Scazzero and Crabb have touched on common themes that influence the Church. Their personal pain along with thoughtful discussion provides a refreshing look into how to minister wisely and more intentionally to those who hurt and grieve.

It is critical for those who minister by listening to people's needs to realize that many people have already experienced much insensitivity in their lives. It is vital to seek to maintain an attitude of kindness, mercy, and concern, undergirded by great faith in the character of God. Many times it is precisely that the needy person has not had a valid picture of the character of God that they now are struggling. It is an opportunity to reshape distorted images of God to a biblically corrected image. Many authors agree that people who suffer from a distorted concept of God have difficulty experiencing his grace. They need compassionate helpers to assist them to realize the spiritual benefits involved in their salvation and to be folded into a caring community.

When people have experienced the distress and grief of spiritual abuse as well as having experienced the effects of distorted biblical doctrines, it is essential that they have the opportunity to tell their stories in a safe environment. Those who intentionally listen to their account of experienced loss, disappointment, and grief, are sincerely appreciated by those in need. It is not necessarily a time to instruct them, but rather a time to comfort and particularly to bring the comfort of the Lord. This is also applicable when a Christian goes through a time of great change or difficult adjustment in life and could use the help of a fellow believer

257. Ibid., 172–93.
258. Ibid., 197–211.

to help process these events. The upset of being spiritually abused or disfellowshiped are such times. Sensitive helpers who listen appropriately, identify with the loss, and give emotional and spiritual support can be beneficial during these times.[259] Thoughtful, heartfelt listening has been identified again as the primary healing tool needed for caring church leaders and Christians who seek to help people.

PENTECOSTAL AND CHARISMATIC ISSUES

A number of books that focus on Pentecostal, Charismatic, Vineyard, and Word Faith beliefs consider which beliefs are biblically founded and which are not. This comparison helps the reader to consider their situation and if what they are hearing in their churches is authentic and viable in light of a biblical review or if their beliefs fall under those topics which are essentially fruitless and unprofitable to embrace. Along with spiritual abuse and leadership issues, the book *The Love of Power or the Power of Love*, devotes some thought to questionable interpretations of Scripture. The issues of biblical integrity and intellectual credibility are addressed. The three authors provide a biblical rationale why certain beliefs and practices are unprofitable and should not be continued.

Other books that show weaknesses in some Pentecostal and Charismatic beliefs are Lee Grady's *What Happened to the Fire?* and Rob McAlpine's *Post Charismatic?*,[260] published in April, 2008. Grady looks at his religious affiliation and challenges those who are in the Pentecostal and Charismatic branch of Christianity to investigate with him areas that are in need of examination and remedy. This book explores the following topics: shallow theology and weak biblical interpretation; pride in spiritual gifts; hyper-mysticism and lack of discernment; spiritual abuse and heavy handed leadership; exaggerated claims of healing, miracles, and manifestations.

Grady's book, written in the early 1990s, was written around the same time as a number of books that dealt with specific problematic areas in the Church and is still relevant today. Distressing beliefs and practices were confronted in the hope that these would be recognized

259. Two websites aimed at helping people in the recovery process are D. Ryan's *The National Association for Christian Recovery* and VanVonderen's *Spiritual Abuse Recovery Resources*.

260. McAlpine, *Post Charismatic?* I was able to read McAlpine's study, then available online (accessed March 2006; site now discontinued).

and cleaned up. The Pentecostal and Charismatic branch of the Church has seen visitations of the Holy Spirit in seasons past. By purging the misbeliefs and accepted folk theologies it was hoped that authentic renewal would revive and refresh the entire Church.

How unprofitable beliefs and practices can undermine the genuine and the spiritually beneficial arouses the reader's attention to discern if these elements can be found in their church setting. The dangers that result when unfruitful practices remain unchecked are considered. The reader is helped to recognize areas of church life that need to be detoxified. These include spiritual abuse and heavy-handed leadership. Abusive leadership along with unsound practices diminishes the impact of the Gospel. If these suggestions are followed, a more robust way of doing church could result. This positive course of action will benefit the spiritual and emotional health of the local church.

In summary, this literature review has established that various authors identify the reality of spiritual abuse. This chapter also provides some helpful insights into how people can cope with it. The need to help rebuild a solid theological foundation in wounded people becomes the task of caring helpers in healthy spiritual communities. This includes an understanding of the grieving process, forgiveness of leaders, and how to begin to rebuild a solid theological foundation in people's lives. This foundation includes the grace of God, the spiritual identity of a Christian, and understanding the purposes of the local church.

The theoretical context for this study revolves around the fact that many individuals in the Church have suffered unnecessary injury in their home church. Organizational dysfunction can be recognized as a common problem in numerous church settings. The literature reviewed provides insights for those representing healthful spiritual communities in how they might effectively minister to individuals experiencing this trauma and how they might provide strategic help for church fellowships who are seeking change. Understanding the nature of spiritual abuse can be the beginning of a solution for this multifaceted Church ministry problem.

3

What Does the Bible Say?

MANY PROBLEMS IN CONGREGATIONS arise because of unbiblical theological beliefs and leadership malpractices that result from these beliefs. It is necessary for Christians to reexamine specific biblical and theological principles and discern healthy church leadership practices that flow from these principles and to consider what may contribute to abusive situations. This chapter will consider the biblical and theological foundations that proceed from the research question.[1] It will explore the mar factors affecting Christians, the inaccuracy of legalism, the hierarchical/authoritarian model of leadership, the origins of the hierarchical/authoritarian model of leadership, a critique of this model, leadership from a New Testament perspective, and the journey towards restoration.

THE MAR FACTORS

The term "mar" is appropriate for the spiritual and emotional impairment in people who have experienced spiritual abuse. Defined, "to mar" is to cause something to be "injured, damaged, or impaired."[2] If something has been injured or damaged in a person's spiritual life through his or her Christian experience, that which has been marred needs to be healed and restored. The mar factors are damaging teachings or events in a person's life and their remedy requires a more secure theological foundation. Abused people have some specific distorted areas of Christian belief and understanding—areas that need to be discerned and set straight so that their spiritual life might be renewed. Areas of distortion in under-

---

1. How have Christians recovered after experiencing perceived spiritual abuse in a local congregation?

2. *Webster's*, s.v. "Mar."

standing the Christian faith[3] include the following: misunderstanding salvation by grace and sanctification by the Holy Spirit; inability to interpret God's Word with a measure of skill; inability to discern whether teachings are biblical truth or not; inability to recognize genuine biblical leadership; a lack of Christian community; and failure to understand how God's people should be treated by church leadership.

The following description expands on these distortions in belief and the personal impairment they create. A renewed biblical understanding in these areas will help people to be restored and to establish harmony in their spiritual walk.

1. Mar Factor: Legalism. A theological understanding of the grace of God has been marred. This has distorted the potential for a healthy spiritual life.[4] The person needs to understand that the gift of salvation is by God's grace and that one's spiritual identity is to be found solely *in Christ*.[5]

Failure to grasp salvation from a grace perspective also influences how people understand the work of sanctification by the Spirit, along with an understanding of how the gifts of the Spirit and ministry gifts ought to function. Many people in works-based congregations do not grasp the Spirit's intentions in the ongoing work of sanctification in their lives. Although believers accept the fact that salvation is by faith, they struggle with the concept of "keeping their salvation" and their sanctification is, therefore, by works. When Christians struggle with feelings of shame, of never measuring up, and of feeling like they have to constantly try to earn God's approval, they often do not grasp why their Christian

---

3. D. Ryan and J. Ryan, *Recovery from Distorted Images*. One primary distortion in the Christian faith begins with distorted images of God according to Dale and Juanita Ryan.

4. Enroth, *Recovering from Churches*, 21. Enroth references David Miller, *Breaking Free: Rescuing Families from the Clutches of Legalism*, (Grand Rapids: Baker, 1992), 34–35, which states that legalism in a church renders dysfunctional everything a person touches, including family: "There is a corruption in the heart of the legalistic family that will eventually break through the surface and adversely affect the children. . . . The damage comes not from what is done to the children but rather through the more subtle messages they learn about themselves and others. . . . Legalism inevitably turns children into church mice and Christian leaders into authoritarian monsters."

5. Eph 2; Gal 5:1: "It is for freedom that Christ has set us free. Stand firm, then, and do not let yourselves be burdened again by a yoke of slavery."

life is so spiritually draining.[6] Misunderstanding the sufficiency of Christ's finished work puts rigorous and sometimes unrealistic demands on individual believers. One consequence is that they demand from others that which only Christ can fulfill.

A deficient understanding of sanctification supports a legalistic belief system. Uncertain understanding in this crucial area hinders spiritual growth and opens the door to misbeliefs. A corrected view of the role and ministry of the Holy Spirit and a renewed appreciation for the work of sanctification in the believer's life needs to be discerned. This includes an improved understanding of how the gifts of the Spirit ought to work; what church ministry practices are beneficial and what practices are not; and developing a greater sensitivity to the Spirit's leading individually and discerning the will of God corporately.[7]

2. MAR FACTOR: A FAULTY HERMENEUTIC. The inability to wisely interpret Scripture makes a person vulnerable to erroneous teachings and the malpractices of controlling leaders. If people do not know the principles that guide sensible biblical interpretation, they will not recognize potential, discern spiritual abuse, or discern biblical truth from error.[8] Healthy, robust discipleship comes from the ability to interpret the Scriptures for oneself, in the company of a healing community, rather than having to rely on poor church leadership that unfortunately, too often, has modeled manipulation of the Scriptures for their own purposes.

3. MAR FACTOR: FULLY UNDERSTANDING HEALTHY CHURCH LEADERSHIP. People's experience of healthy leadership has been marred because of their experiences with abusive leadership.[9] Developing a biblically-

6. VanVonderen, *Tired of Trying.*

7. Gal 5:16–18. See Morris and Olsen, *Discerning God's Will Together.*

8. In Enroth's book, *Recovering from Churches That Abuse,* he mentions Stephen Martin, a staff member at Wellspring [Retreat Center], who considers instruction in sound study methods and the interpretation of the Bible important. In abusive groups, twisted hermeneutics are often used to instill fear and guilt and thus become a form of spiritual intimidation. "Since leaders of abusive churches typically twist the Scriptures, education in hermeneutics would help the ex-member gain the right perspective on Scripture passages. In talking with former members at Wellspring, I have found a number of them who have difficulty with or even an aversion to reading the Bible because it has been misused by the group to abuse them. Learning the proper application and interpretation of Scripture goes a long way toward healing the wounds of abuse," 30. This has been verified by the experience of some of the participants of this study.

9. Cudmore, "Victim Suffering." Cudmore confirms this by stating: "The abusive treatment to victims denies them participation as willing and capable members and

sound understanding of Christian leadership based on Christ's teaching and the New Testament example will create a renewed appreciation for godly leadership expressed in healthy communities.

Deficient leadership prevents the development of a vital concept of Christian community. A church experience that is inflexible and lacks in demonstrating God's love damages not only the experience of authentic community but also prevents the expression of a valid ecclesial model. These harmful affects take their toll on individuals and families who innately long for genuine community. Building a biblically-based theology for authentic Christian community enables a believer to assess whether a potential church community is healthy or not.

4. MAR FACTOR: PERSONAL SPIRITUAL AND EMOTIONAL INJURY. A person's spiritual life has been severely marred by personal injury inflicted by church leadership. How believers have been treated by leadership will affect them spiritually and emotionally. People can grow spiritually by understanding and experiencing the benefits of forgiveness and compassion; the benefits of growing through their disillusionment and pain; recognizing the benefits of suffering, which ought not to be wasted in a believer's life; reinstating legitimate biblical beliefs, and experiencing the benefits of correcting misguided beliefs and practices.

Pivotal distressing experiences have the potential to propel people forward to understand what has happened to them. They find that they are now on a quest to get theological answers for themselves that help them process the pain of this experience. People search for wisdom in what God might be trying to teach them through this unexpected circumstance. As individuals experience acceptance and care through trusted confidants and among loving communities, healing begins. Misbeliefs and folk theologies are replaced with biblical truth and fractured relationships are replaced by genuine community.

This research has identified key negative beliefs that contribute to personal abuse situations. These negative results are not new. Within Scriptures these abuses have already been identified as hurtful. The early Church had the same problems and their leaders provided responses to

---

confuses them as to what genuine Christian leadership entails. . . . The impact of certain leadership traits is one key to the process of healing the suffering of individuals and of revitalizing valuable organizations that represent the Christian faith," 8.

these abuses. They taught what was wrong and how to deal with these issues in order to express Christianity in appropriate ways.

THE INACCURACY OF LEGALISM

One primary misbelief that Christians must wrestle with is the theological inaccuracy of legalism[10] as it does not represent the grace-filled message of the Gospel of the Kingdom but brings a distortion to people's understanding of God's character and their experience of his salvation. Legalism does not bring freedom but brings tension and dissatisfaction in their Christian life. The teaching, or rather, the misbelief of legalism, demonstrates how the various mar factors are intertwined. First, how one interprets the Word of God, how one essentially understands their salvation, and how one discerns truth from error are simultaneously negatively affected. Furthermore, a stifled understanding of the sanctification process, a lack of experiencing authentic community, and a lack of experiencing caring leadership also take their toll in the life of a Christian. These Christians prove to be spiritually vulnerable and are often found to be in places where control and manipulation are exercised as well.

Christians who have experienced various forms of legalistic teachings have not fully comprehended God's grace towards them. They have not grasped that they are fully loved by God and that salvation and sanctification are on the basis of the cross of Christ and not merited by one's personal righteousness.[11] This survey comment expresses what others have felt:

> I had a warped sense of who God is . . . I have learned that some churches do not have a clue about the incredible significance of grace in the life of the believer, ministry of the minister, and in the Church as a whole. . . . When I (and I am sure many other people as well) came into contact with this authoritarian church, it was at the time of my salvation. I knew absolutely nothing about the Bible, church, doctrine, etc. All I knew was that God was real and that this church was involved with my coming to know that He is

10. Legalism is defined as a doctrinal position that is essentially opposed to the biblical teaching of God's grace. Legalism requires observance of specialized biblical interpretations and traditions in the group. The failure to keep these rules is labeled as sin. Those who do not keep certain rules or repent from perceived offending behaviors are often shunned or excommunicated from the group.

11. Eph 2:1–10; Rom 11:6.

real. . . . commencing from that moment, and progressing over a period of several months, I was taught that the pastor was God's representative for me and that in order to hear from God, or even stay saved, I *must* be submissive/obedient to him, I *must* tithe, I *must* not miss any church activity/outreach/prayer meeting/rally, etc., I *must* cut off ungodly influences in my life (non-Christian friends and family), I *must* not watch TV or go to the movies, I *must* have nothing to do with other "lukewarm" churches, and on and on the "I *must's*" went . . .

The church I was involved with preaches a corrupt form of the Gospel, a works-Gospel basically. In other words, you get saved by grace through faith, but you soon learn that you can lose your salvation at any moment unless you work hard to maintain it.[12]

The Galatian churches struggled with legalism and their experience shows that this is not uncommon. This common theological inaccuracy needs to be replaced by a deeper perception and acceptance of God's unconditional love and immeasurable grace through Christ's substitutionary sacrifice on their behalf.[13]

The book of Galatians gives insights into how quickly erroneous beliefs and practices could be peddled as part of the Christian Gospel message.[14] According to the Christian Judaisers of Paul's day, since Abraham had been circumcised to seal the covenant with Yahweh, it was logical to expect that believing Gentiles, in order to be made complete in their faith, should also be circumcised.[15] What seemed to be a sound and reasonable practice, and entirely necessary for both Jew and Gentile to believe and to participate in together, was revealed instead as inherently flawed theology and practice according to the Apostle Paul. He pointed out that any change in the original Gospel delivered to the churches in Galatia, whether the change was preached by Paul himself or an angel from heaven, was to be outrightly and eternally condemned.

Galatians was written with a sense of urgency.[16] Paul was intent on making sure that these Gentile believers were not ensnared by expired and unnecessary Old Testament Torah practices. The Apostle was ap-

12. Participant no. 89.

13. Heb 9:26, 28; 10:1–14.

14. Fee explores the book of Galatians in one chapter of his book *God's Empowering Presence*, 367–471.

15. Douglas, *New Bible Dictionary*, 402.

16. Ibid., 401.

palled at the widespread acceptance of such a Gospel. In fact he argued that such a "Gospel" was not a Gospel at all but was filled with theological inaccuracy.[17] Paul was uncompromising in his campaign to rectify this deviant Gospel position and bring back a lucid understanding of the true Gospel. His purpose, therefore, was resolute and unwavering. This type of thinking and this religious activity was not only outright error, but was fundamentally offensive to the pure Gospel message.[18] Adding circumcision and other Jewish practices to the truth of the Gospel—even those that seemed reasonable and culturally acceptable—was, in fact, error and flagrant hypocrisy.

The apparent lack of spiritual discernment on the part of the churches in Galatia, even though they were founded by the Apostle Paul himself, demonstrates that believers can be sidetracked by error yet remain oblivious to it. Believers can be lulled into feeling that what is being presented is biblical and orthodox, and thus be beguiled. The Galatians were unaware of the problem and needed someone to arouse their spiritual senses in order to recognize how certain error had been blended with the truth. These churches were not alert to the inroads of this corrosive and contaminating influence among them.

Paul's correction of the Galatians demonstrates that biblical error can happen anywhere or anytime. It is therefore important that Christian communities are alert and vigilant against this very real possibility that the truth of the Good News of salvation can become reengineered by legalism. Incorrect teaching with a Judaistic bent came easily among the Galatians because of the culturally Jewish presence. The legalistic principles were easy to believe, simple to follow, culturally acceptable, and socially comfortable. They were simply accepted and added into their basic understanding of the Gospel message. Paul writes Galatians to put a quick end to the adding on of extras to the Gospel.[19]

Such admonishment is one task of the leader. New Testament passages combine the idea of Christ-like leadership with the task of warning God's people about false teachings. Paul set an example when he was

17. Gal 1:6–9.

18. This undermining issue needed to be dealt with promptly in order to prevent further inroads of this Judaistic bent which would ultimately undermine the veracity of the Gospel in the churches of Galatia. The Gospel of Jesus Christ was to be delivered uncluttered and uncontaminated with legalistic or heretical tendencies in order to have its desired and salvific effect.

19. The Council at Jerusalem in Acts 15 had to deal with this issue early on.

faced with a delicate yet imperative situation regarding the truth of the Gospel. Although Peter, a fellow apostle, was giving in to hypocrisy, Paul did not shrink from taking on the responsibility to confront him. He recounts to the Galatians the necessity of publicly confronting Peter in Antioch:

> When Peter came to Antioch, I opposed him to his face, because he was clearly in the wrong. Before certain men came from James, he used to eat with the Gentiles. But when they arrived, he began to draw back and separate himself from the Gentiles because he was afraid of those who belonged to the circumcision group. The other Jews joined him in his hypocrisy, so that by their hypocrisy even Barnabas was led astray. When I saw that they were not acting in line with the truth of the gospel, I said to Peter in front of them all, "You are a Jew, yet you live like a Gentile and not like a Jew. How is it, then, that you force Gentiles to follow Jewish customs?
>
> "We who are Jews by birth and not 'Gentile sinners' know that a man is not justified by observing the law, but by faith in Jesus Christ. So we, too, have put our faith in Christ Jesus that we may be justified by faith in Christ and not by observing the law, because by observing the law no one will be justified.
>
> "If, while we seek to be justified in Christ, it becomes evident that we ourselves are sinners, does that mean that Christ promotes sin? Absolutely not! If I rebuild what I destroyed, I prove that I am a lawbreaker. For through the law I died to the law so that I might live for God. I have been crucified with Christ and I no longer live, but Christ lives in me. The life I live in the body, I live by faith in the Son of God, who loved me and gave himself for me. I do not set aside the grace of God, for if righteousness could be gained through the law, Christ died for nothing!"[20]

The New Testament provides direction for all Christians to exercise discernment. There is a need for the local church to learn the principles of discerning God's will together.[21] It is important for leaders to instruct congregants in sound doctrine and in the practice of discerning truth from error. Awareness of counterfeit doctrine bolsters a Christian community to practice biblical discernment together[22] in order to ensure that a community remains watchful and therefore vibrant. This practice

20. Gal 2:11–21; see Rom 3 and 4..

21. 1 John 4:1; 2 Pet 2:1–3.

22. See Morris and Olsen, *Discerning God's Will Together*.

will also fortify those who could minister to people influenced by deviant teachings.

Competent, godly leaders guide healthy communities authentically by imitating the leadership practices modeled by Christ.[23] They warn God's people about false teachers and erroneous teachings.[24] Godly leaders and all congregants need to exercise spiritual discernment in order to recognize error and the inroads of aberrant teachings and practices.[25] If a congregant believes that a leader is promoting error, they can look to biblical guidelines outlined by the Apostle Paul.[26] The best way to recognize the counterfeit or the unprofitable is simply to place the genuine along side it.

Paul taught much about the work of the Spirit in the book of Galatians. Paul's emphasis was that freedom in Christ is the scriptural antidote to legalism. He clearly exhorted the Galatians that it was for freedom that Christ had set them free. Because of this reality they were to "stand firm" and not to allow themselves to "be burdened again by a yoke of slavery."[27] Paul's summary admonitions pointed to the fact that they were corporately to "live by the Spirit" and to "keep in step with the Spirit." In this way they would ultimately prove that being "led by the Spirit" was an indicator of the truth that they were no longer under old covenant stipulations of the law but under the realities of the new covenant. The promise given in the Old Testament and reiterated by Christ was now their reality.[28]

Paul unfolded facts about those in the Galatian churches who were trying to force circumcision on everyone. They were solely interested in making a good impression outwardly and boasted about Galatian "flesh." This cunning tactic would release the perpetrators from being persecuted for the cross of Christ. They were intentionally avoiding this inevitable happening. Another obvious detail that Paul pointed out was that these

23. Mark 9:33–35; 10:42–45; Luke 22:24–26; John 13:12–17; 1 Pet 5:1–3; Eph 4:11–15; Phil 2.

24. Acts 20:28–31; Rom 16:17; 2 Pet 2:1–3; 1 Tim 1:3–4; 2 Tim 3:16; 4:1–2.

25. Eph 4:11–15; Heb 5:14; 6:1; 1 John 2:13–14; 1 Cor 2:15–16; Phil 4:7; Col 2:8–10.

26. 1 Tim 2:19–20. Paul provided instruction that accusations were not to be brought against an elder unless there were two or three witnesses. If sin was involved, elders were to be rebuked publicly so that others would take warning. (Regrettably, in some places, this practice has been adapted to deal with congregants.)

27. Gal 5:1.

28. Gal 5:16, 18, 25; Jer 31:31–33; John 14:15–18; Luke 24:49; Acts 1:4, 5, 8; 2:32–39.

zealots were simply unable to obey the law themselves. Paul solidifies his own life focus by stating his theological intentions in these words: "May I never boast except in the cross of our Lord Jesus Christ, through which the world has been crucified to me, and I to the world."[29] He concludes this letter by affirming that "Neither circumcision nor uncircumcision means anything; what counts is a new creation."[30] This final declaration confirmed the need for the Galatian churches to press forward in faith with their full trust based on the finished work of Christ. They should not waste any more time by trying to live under the mistaken impression that the old and new covenants had somehow merged into one new belief system that included circumcision.

THE HIERARCHICAL/AUTHORITARIAN MODEL OF LEADERSHIP

This section will give an overview of the hierarchical/authoritarian model of leadership and consider some of the affects on congregants. The hierarchical model of leadership has been around for an extensive period of time and has been applied in diverse Christian leadership contexts. It would, therefore, be a mistake to assume that all hierarchical leadership in Christian institutions is authoritarian and controlling. It is often not so much a church's structure for leadership, but how individual leaders or a group of leaders perceive their leadership position and their relationship to their flock.[31] It would be legitimate to presume that "hierarchical structures can be made the instrument of servanthood just as democratically constituted bodies can fall victim to abuse at the hands of power driven individuals."[32] Therefore, what really matters is

---

29. Gal 6:14.

30. Gal 6:15.

31. In Heb 13, reference is made in verse 17 to: "Obey your leaders and submit to their authority." This verse is in the context of the final admonitions of the author of Hebrews. A few verses before this comment seem to portray the kind of leader that was ideal to obey: "Remember your leaders, who spoke the word of God to you. Consider the outcome of their way of life and imitate their faith" (Heb 13:7). Obeying one's leaders then and now involves discerning the leader's character and behavior in order to imitate them. Obeying leaders with integrity would, therefore, not be burdensome but would be biblically encouraged, since they were to be fully accountable. "They keep watch over you as men who must give an account. Obey them so that their work will be a joy, not a burden, for that would be of no advantage to you" (Heb 13:17).

32. Bilezikian, *Community 101*, 136.

the attitude with which leadership is exercised. The determinative factor is the spiritual life of a community and its respective leaders rather than the formal definitions of what the constitution states.[33] Nevertheless, a number of problems are associated with the hierarchical/authoritarian model of leadership.

Simply defined, a "hierarchy" is a system of church government by priests or other clergy in graded ranks. A "hierarch" is the presider over sacred rites, basically the leader or chief of a religious group.[34] Although a hierarchy may work well in the military, it is generally not suitable for the Christian Church. Hierarchical and authoritarian leadership can often slip into abusive patterns. What appears to be a reasonable system of church governance can get molded to suit the designs of certain types of leaders. Unfortunately, these leaders distort church authority in ways that eventually misrepresent biblical principles for church governance. Leadership then becomes a command and control style, which slowly erodes the effectiveness of that church body and leaves those under that regime dependent and immature in their Christian lives.[35]

In order for devious leaders to ensure their position and control in a group, maltreatment of those under them becomes the natural and predictable result. The participants in this study were subject to such maltreatment under an authoritarian and controlling leadership style, and a few pastors who completed a survey indicated that they had helped people who had been mistreated by this type of leadership behavior. Authors who addressed this subject[36] along with numerous Internet articles also verify this fact. When leaders maintain and enforce control by using oppressive measures, become dictatorial, controlling, or are unwilling to allow others to participate, authoritarian leadership becomes abusive. Abusive spiritual authorities overstep their bounds[37] and use their position of leadership to mistreat those under their care.

33. Ibid.

34. *Webster's*, s.v. "Hierarch."

35. Enroth confirms spiritual dependency: "Spiritually abusive groups routinely use guilt, fear, and intimidation as effective means for controlling their members. In my opinion, the leaders consciously foster an unhealthy form of dependency, spiritually and interpersonally, by focusing on themes of submission, loyalty, and obedience to those in authority. In all totalitarian environments, dependency is necessary for subjugation," *Churches That Abuse*, 109.

36. See chapter 2.

37. Johnson and VanVonderen, *Subtle Power*, 21.

A single individual or a select group of leaders may see their place in leadership as elitist. These leaders consider that they are "the called of God" and that they are somehow ranked above the flock. A common misbelief has been meshed with an elitist view. Many church leaders see themselves at the top of an ecclesiastical hierarchical structure. The popular belief of spiritual covering has been generated. "Spiritual covering pictures a chain of command with authority flowing through the chain from top to bottom. Those lower on the chain are to see those above them as their 'covering' and submit to them as they would to Christ himself."[38]

For such leaders, their word becomes law, unquestioning obedience to authority is required, and those who question or challenge can be scrutinized, disciplined, or even excommunicated. Some leaders face minimum accountability. These pastors, along with the directors of the church, develop into an administration system that cannot be easily challenged. In order to be an affirmed congregant in this type of system, member participation involves that they: submit, obey, attend, and pay. These governors of church affairs dictate how people in the congregation should be treated when their authority is questioned.

Many participants in this study verified that authoritarian leadership was evident in the church in which they were actively involved. Control, spiritual abuse, and lack of accountability ranked high. This participant reflected on control by leaders and what they had learned:

> In my former church, Christ was head of the pastor and the pastor was head of all in the church and had godlike authority over them since he was God's sole representative (the headship doctrine, otherwise known as the strong discipleship/shepherding doctrine). The damage this does to marriages is terrible.
>
> I have learned that it was for freedom that Christ died. And just like in the days of the Pharisees, some churches are completely ignorant of what this means, but instead load heavy burdens on believers while striving to control them utterly. We [later] looked for one [a church] which did not seek to control its members but rather sought to serve them and empower them while teaching them how to serve and empower others.[39]

This negative tendency can be found in a hierarchical system: "In a hierarchical system, the strong man or person in charge hands

---

38. Blue, *Healing Spiritual Abuse*, 30.

39. Participant no. 89.

down decisions that may not be questioned or criticized. Even if issues are allowed to be discussed, the strong individual leader arrogates the right to make final decisions for the group."[40] All too often, people in the church are confronted with certain policies that must be followed. Loyalty, mutual friendship, or church service no longer matter, making confrontation devastating. There is little room for restoration[41] and disillusionment and grief overtakes those affected. Those who offend in this type of hierarchy are either asked to leave or things are made so uncomfortable for them that they must take their distressed families out of this unhealthy church system.

THE ORIGINS OF THE BELIEF AND PRACTICE OF AUTHORITARIAN LEADERSHIP

In the context of the contemporary Christian Church, an Old Testament leadership style can easily be developed by the fusion of a Mosaic model with that of the Aaronic/ Levitical priesthood. Yahweh's calling of the priesthood, together with the narrative accounts of Moses's calling and leadership, creates this popular interpretation of leadership and provides some of the foundational principles for a reworked Old Testament model of leadership in today's Church.

A look at the Pentateuchal narrative helps to refresh this concept. Moses carefully documented the miraculous deliverance of the Jewish nation. Egypt had been decimated and the Pharaoh and his army had been destroyed. Moses was given the supreme task of being Yahweh's chief spokesperson.[42] Acting as mediator of the covenant, Moses took the words and the judgments spoken by God on Mount Sinai down to the people.[43] Moses was God's chosen leader over the Israelite nation. Moses's brother, Aaron, would help in this monumental task of leading the children of Israel on God's behalf. Although the Israelites repeat-

40. Bilezikian, *Community 101*, 162.

41. VanVonderen, *Tired of Trying*, 71. VanVonderen recommends that people attempt to take a trusted person and try to confront the abusive leader, as it is important to do so. If the leader does not listen, then inform the people to whom the abuser is accountable. If leaders or those responsible do not or will not listen to a problem but people are treated as though they are the problem, he advises that it is time for them to get out of there. Since there are plenty of good churches, people should be willing to make a change.

42. Num 12:5–8.

43. Sailhamer, *The Pentateuch*, 296.

edly failed to have faith in their God, Moses was known as a man of faith and a close follower of his God. The writer of Hebrews recognized this.[44] According to the Old Testament narrative, Israel repeatedly failed to have faith in Yahweh, they often broke the commandments, and they rejected God's leadership by rebelling against Moses (and sometimes Aaron) through whom that leadership was manifested.[45] This dependent and unorganized multitude of families, with a common history and heritage, needed instructions in how to worship and obey their God. Moses would direct and oversee this fledgling nation on Yahweh's behalf.[46]

Israel was to be a kingdom of priests and a holy nation before Yahweh.[47] It would essentially be a nation that would be distinctive[48] among the surrounding nations. The people's manner of worship,[49] their laws,[50] and their lifestyle would be the antithesis of those of the other nations. Their worship of Yahweh would pose a sharp contrast to the requirements of the deities of the adjacent nations.[51] Israel's divine purpose was to give the other nations a significant model to consider—with Yahweh being the supreme deity over all other deities. Moses carefully documented the regulations that Yahweh had instituted which would help the Israelites to live together as a people and to function as a na-

44. Heb 11:23–29.

45. Douglas, *New Bible Dictionary*, 798.

46. Although Moses was the called and skilled first leader of Israel, early on the concept of delegating responsibility to other leaders was instituted. The magnitude of the task of overseeing and ministering to the needs of Yahweh's people in this newly constituted nation was becoming evident. Moses was quickly becoming overwhelmed with his new task. Jethro, Moses's father-in-law, observed how the task of the administration of justice by his son-in-law was quickly bringing strain on him and also the people. Jethro's simple but effective solution was to suggest that Moses find men of character among the people who would share in the ministry oversight of this nation. Since that time, what many have called "The Jethro Principle," referring to the delegation and sharing of tasks to avoid ministry burnout, has been based on this Old Testament narrative passage in Exod 18.

47. Exod 19:5–6.

48. Deut 4:32–39.

49. Deut 12:29–31.

50. "The laws are intended to distinguish the Israelites from the inhabitants of the land that they were about to possess: 'Do not defile yourselves in any of these ways, because this is how the nations that I am going to drive out before you became defiled'" (Lev 18:24). Sailhamer, *The Pentateuch*, 347.

51. Deut 4:1–40.

tion under Yahweh's care and protection.[52] The sons of Levi would be the token representatives for the whole nation—as a kingdom of priests ministering before their God.[53] The priesthood had already been established in the family of Aaron. The priests who served at the tabernacle could only be from the families of Aaron's remaining sons, Eleazar and Ithamar.[54] They were to wear special garments to set them apart in this ministry.[55]

Both Aaron's sons and the sons of Levi were chosen for prescribed priestly tasks. The different responsibilities determined which group did the ministry tasks.[56] Three previous incidents in Israel's history led to God's selection of the tribe of Levi to be his servants in the work of the tabernacle.[57] Simeon and Levi had been rejected from participation with the tribes of Israel because with their violence they killed men in anger.[58] The members of the family of Levi had rallied behind Moses and the Lord after the golden calf incident. At that time the Lord chose the tribe of Levi for himself.[59] Lastly, God had a claim to every firstborn Israelite who had been "passed over" in the Exodus.[60]

The tribal families who were to officiate as priests in this prescribed system of national worship were chosen by Yahweh alone. Moses did not make an appeal for volunteers for this task. There was no involvement in the choice of priests by the nation, either by democratic vote or by casting the lot.[61] Only men from the tribe of Levi between the ages of thirty and fifty without physical blemish were eligible. There was no place in a patriarchal society for women to participate in the priesthood, or for men

52. Deut 4:37–38; 10:12–22.

53. Scripture references regarding the Levites can be found in Num 1:47–54; 3:6–16.

54. Sailhamer, *The Pentateuch*, 372. Aaron's firstborn, Nadab and his brother, Abihu were replaced by Eleazar and Ithamar after the incident of judgment found in Leviticus 10. See also Exod 29:9 and Num 3:30.

55. Sailhamer, *The Pentateuch*, 305.

56. Ibid., 374.

57. Ibid., 373.

58. Gen 49:5–6.

59. Exod 32:26, 29.

60. Sailhamer, *The Pentateuch*, 373. Sailhamer goes on to note that: "the sin of the golden calf marked a decisive change in Israel's relationship with God in the Sinai covenant."

61. Scriptures regarding the lot can be found in 1 Chr 26:13; 24:5–31; Neh 10:34.

younger or older than the age stipulated, even from the chosen families. Priests who were intoxicated or those found ritually unclean were also restricted from taking part.[62] The only human involvement was to monitor and confirm that the stipulations that Moses had received directly from Yahweh were followed.

The instructions for the consecration of the priests for work in the tabernacle are given in Exodus 29:1–37.[63] One tribe out of the twelve tribes was chosen by Yahweh to take on this prescribed assignment in place of the firstborn of all Israel. The details and the intricacies of the priestly duties[64] were clearly rehearsed to Moses by Yahweh. The responsibility of the priests was to obey and exhibit great care in the execution of their many priestly tasks. This prescribed worship and sacred administrative structure functioned mainly during the old covenant era.[65]

Two of the Old Testament servant roles were priests and prophets. The king was yet another role of significance. The priests were inducted into ministry by right of tribal birth. The prophets received a personal call from Yahweh to represent him among the people. Moses outlined the qualifications for the future king who would shepherd the nation. He would be Yahweh's choice. The concept of divine election is referenced in Deuteronomy.[66] The Lord chose Israel as his people; he chose a place to establish his name, and he chose priests from the tribe of Levi.[67]

The true prophet of Yahweh in the classical tradition of Old Testament prophecy was first found in Moses.[68] A prophet received a

---

62. For restrictions and guidelines for serving as a priest, see Sailhamer, *The Pentateuch*, 354–57.

63. Sailhamer, *The Pentateuch*, 329. Yahweh relinquished his right to all firstborn Israelite males and put in their place the tribe of Levi (Num 3:11–13). Yahweh gave the gift of the service of the priesthood to the Levites. As representatives of the tribes' firstborn (Num 3:40ff.) the Levites were part of the far-reaching principle of representation. This demonstrated the concept of a people dependent upon and totally surrendered to God. The responsibility of the people was to recognize and honor the role of the priesthood who stood and ministered to Yahweh on their behalf. They would support the priests through the tithe system.

64. Heb 8:5; 10:1. Also, the ordination of Aaron and his sons (Lev 8), priests begin their ministry (Lev 9–10), and rules for priests to live a holy life (Lev 21).

65. There were times when this structure did not function, for example, during the exile.

66. Block, "The Burden of Leadership," 263. See Deut 17:5.

67. Deut 4:37; 7:6–7; 10:15; 14:2; 12:5, 14; 18:5; 21:5.

68. Douglas, *New Bible Dictionary*, 975.

specific and personal call by Yahweh. This call was an introduction into God's presence. The prophet's task was to stand before men as a man who had been made to stand before God.[69] The prophet had an awareness of history and they owed to Moses their ethical and social concern.[70]

> History became revelation because there was added to the historical situation a man prepared beforehand to say what it meant. Moses was not left to struggle for the meaning of events as or after they happened; he was forewarned of events and of their significance by the verbal communications of God. So it was with all the prophets. Alone of the nations of antiquity, Israel had a true awareness of history. They owed it to the prophets, and under the Lord of history, the prophets owed it to Moses.[71]

The prophetic aspect was to include justice. The priest was to preserve knowledge and to provide instruction since he served as a messenger of the Lord.[72] The priest was called to care for the wounded and tend the flock, while the prophet cried out for the wounded and brought justice to the oppressed.[73] Two of the primary concerns of prophetic ministry were identification with the oppressed and provision for the poor.[74]

Although these servant leader qualities were the ideal for Israel's spiritual leaders, this model was not fully followed. It was replaced by a deficient model and later it degenerated into a corrupted model. As the nation progressed, the true prophets of God had to challenge the wayward leaders of the theocracy. Although the model of servant leadership is clearly observed in the Old Testament text, at different times in Israel's history the leaders had become habitually careless in their duties and calling to serve Israel. The leaders had often become more interested in serving themselves than the people. The time before the exile was a significant season that characterized severe erosion of the servant

69. Ibid. 1 Kgs 17:1; 18:15.

70. Douglas, *New Bible Dictionary*, 975. "Even before his call Moses concerned himself with the social welfare of his people" (Exod 2:11–19). Afterwards, "as the prophetic lawgiver, he outlined the most humane and philanthropic code of the ancient world, concerned for the helpless (Deut 24:19–22 etc.) and the enemy of the oppressor (e.g., Lev 19:9ff.)."

71. Ibid.

72. Mal 2:7.

73. Farnsworth, *Wounded Workers*, 139.

74. Ibid., 140.

quality ideal in Israel. Ezekiel was given these words to prophesy against the "shepherds" of Israel. These shepherds included all of the nation's leaders—the prophets, the priests, the Levites, and the civil authorities—all were diseased with the same malady.

> The word of the LORD came to .me: "Son of man, prophesy against the shepherds of Israel; prophesy and say to them: 'This is what the Sovereign LORD says: Woe to the shepherds of Israel who only take care of themselves! Should not shepherds take care of the flock? You eat the curds, clothe yourselves with the wool and slaughter the choice animals, but you do not take care of the flock. You have not strengthened the weak or healed the sick or bound up the injured. You have not brought back the strays or searched for the lost. You have ruled them harshly and brutally. So they were scattered because there was no shepherd, and when they were scattered they became food for all the wild animals. My sheep wandered over all the mountains and on every high hill. They were scattered over the whole earth, and no one searched or looked for them.'"[75]

Since the nation of Israel was a theocracy, the national leaders who governed were under the same set of laws as the religious leaders. Even though the nation's leaders had often failed miserably and eventually the nation was forced into exile, servant leadership was the embedded model for Old Testament leaders. The ideal of a servant leader who would come was also part of the message that Isaiah had declared and was part of their future hope.[76] This individual was Yahweh's chosen servant who would come as his anointed one, the Messiah.

With the coming of the New Testament era it may have appeared that Christ taught and exemplified a new model of leadership. What seemed to be evident was Christ's intention to reinstate a servant leadership model that simply had been lost. This reinstated model would have the noticeable feature of the servant's complete dependence on the Holy Spirit. Although Christ's leadership style was embedded in the Old Testament, it appeared to be something radically different. The common people recognized how different Jesus's ministry was from their religious leaders.[77] They were extremely jealous of the attention of the people and

75. Ezek 34:1–6.
76. Isa 42:1–4.
77. Mark 1:27; Luke 4:32.

resisted the methodology of this threat to the religious system that they carefully guarded. Their interest in this unorthodox and unpredictable rogue threat from Galilee was to simply eliminate him at their earliest convenience.[78] Jesus was not only the Son of God, but he was also the Son of man who confirmed that his motivation and empowerment was solely by the Holy Spirit. He fulfilled and embodied the promised ideal of Isaiah 42. Therefore, what understanding can be gleaned for the Church in the new covenant era to shape a viable biblical model of servanthood?

Before going deeper into that topic, there is a preliminary question that must be asked: In light of the priestly and prophetic qualities for ministry in the Old Testament model, are pastors, in the age of grace, to be equated with either Moses, Aaron, and/or the Levitical priesthood? Who, exactly, represents the Levitical priests in today's Church? Are they represented by pastoral leaders in the Church? This question might quickly be answered this way: "No, of course not. The priests who ministered to the Lord, on behalf of the nation, point to the spiritual calling of every believer today. There are no legitimate priests or prophets after the Old Testament order." Although this is apparently believed and ardently declared, there is a need to examine this thought further.

The priesthood of Aaron prefigured that of Christ.[79] The writer of Hebrews assures readers that since Jesus has become a high priest forever; they can have hope.[80] Peter reminded his readers that the royal priesthood instituted by Moses was a foreshadowing of the future priesthood of all believers—which is now a spiritual reality.[81] It is significant to note that the New Testament sees the Church's priesthood as corporate and that no individual minister or leader is to be called "priest" to designate the ordained ministry or the ordained minister.[82] That is, every true believer born into God's family can be considered a legitimate priest before God. On this same premise, every believer can be regarded as

78. Matt 12:9–14; Mark 3:1–6; Luke 6:6–11. Since the original servanthood model for priests and prophets had been corrupted, there was need to renew the original model of servanthood and also to demonstrate and fulfill the Isa 42 ideal.

79. Sailhamer, *The Pentateuch*, 305. Heb 5:5; 7:26; 9:11.

80. Heb 6:19–20.

81. 1 Pet 2:1–12. Verse 9 declares, "But you are a chosen people, a royal priesthood, a holy nation, a people belonging to God, that you may declare the praises of him who called you out of darkness into his wonderful light."

82. Douglas, *New Bible Dictionary*, 972.

a redeemed son,[83] to be a prophet for God, and to be a royal heir of God—because of the exaltation of the Risen Christ.[84] There is no longer a need for a human mediator[85] between redeemed children of God and their Father in Heaven. Both the priesthood of Christ and the priesthood of the baptized have in their respective ways the function of sacrifice and intercession.[86] The priesthood and prophethood of all believers has been established through the finished work of Christ on the cross,[87] his victorious resurrection, and the outpouring of the Holy Spirit.[88] All believers since the day of Pentecost share in this mutual spiritual calling and royal duty before the Triune God.

A look at the historical record of the early Church shows some overlapping of these terms regarding their use in certain functions of a minister.

> In the early Church the term "priesthood" and "priest" came to be used to designate the ordained ministry and minister as presiding at the Eucharist. They underline the fact that the ordained ministry is related to the priestly reality of Jesus Christ and the whole community. When the terms are used in connection with the ordained ministry their meaning differs in appropriate ways from the sacrificial priesthood of the Old Testament, from the unique redemptive priesthood of Christ and from the corporate priesthood of the people of God.[89]

Although there seems to be an apparent differentiation of these terms, this historical usage also contributes to confusing the function of the

---

83. Gal 4:6–8.

84. Acts 2:32–33; Eph 1:4–10.

85. Moses became the mediator of the covenant at Mount Sinai between Yahweh and Israel. "After hearing God speak, the people requested that God speak only to Moses and that Moses then speak to them" (Exod 20:18–19). See Sailhamer, *The Pentateuch*, 282. Because of the fear of the people, Yahweh accommodated the concerns of the people and Moses served as a mediator. This can also be found in Deut 5.

86. Schrotenboer, *Evangelical Response*, 56.

87. A Christian is one who is dead to sin, has been made spiritually alive in Christ, and one who rests in the finished work of Christ. Believers need to be grounded in the fundamentals of their life "in Christ" and in how to live for God by the power of the Holy Spirit. See Rom 6:1–23; 12:1–21.

88. Acts 2; Joel 2.

89. Schrotenboer, *Evangelical Response*, 56.

Old Testament priest and priesthood with the New Testament understanding of these functions.

Moses longed for all of God's people to be prophets. Speaking to Joshua, Moses declared, "Are you jealous for my sake? I wish that all the LORD's people were prophets and that the LORD would put his Spirit on them!"[90] Moses desired a much different type of community than the one formed under the law at Sinai. He preferred a community led not by a person like himself but a community guided by God's Spirit.[91] The view expressed here by Moses is identical to the accounts of the later Israelite prophets in their description of the new covenant.[92] It can be observed how the old covenant leadership model played out. Even within the Pentateuch Moses's role and the leadership seemed to change. The shortcomings of the leadership style were becoming obvious and the failure of the people was increasingly apparent. A different type of rule, similar to the kind of leadership seen in the Spirit-controlled office of the prophet, begins to appear.[93]

In light of the above, it is important not to forget that Miriam challenged her brother's leadership in Numbers chapter 12. His leadership was contrasted with the kind of leadership provided by priests and prophets. The question of Moses's leadership, found in Numbers 16, seems to still be an issue for the writer of the Pentateuch. Although the account of Miriam and Aaron's opposition to the leadership of their brother is brief, it leaves many details unexplained. The context of the previous chapter, about the kind of leadership exemplified in Moses, is put into question by the initiation of a new type of leadership, the leadership of elders who are led by the Spirit.[94] The issue is raised whether Moses's leadership was no better in God's eyes than that of other prophets like Miriam. Apparently, the purpose of this chapter was to vindicate Moses's divinely given leadership. A comment about the character of Moses has been interjected into this passage which is noteworthy: "Now Moses was a very humble man, more humble than anyone else on the face of the earth."[95] The final word on this matter was Yahweh's. Although Yahweh

---

90. Num 11:29.

91. See Jer 31:31–34; Joel 2:28; Ezek 36:22–27. Sailhamer, *The Pentateuch*, 386.

92. Sailhamer, *The Pentateuch*, 386.

93. Ibid.

94. Ibid.

95. Num 12:3. Parentheses in original.

did speak to prophets like Miriam, it was not in the same way as he spoke to Moses. Moses the mediator was not simply like the rest of the prophets—he was God's servant. God did not speak to Moses in visions and dreams, but face to face.[96]

The final words of Moses at the end of Deuteronomy looked forward to the eschatological and messianic prophet of God.

> Since then, no prophet has risen in Israel like Moses, whom the LORD knew face to face, who did all those miraculous signs and wonders the LORD sent him to do in Egypt—to Pharaoh and to all his officials and to his whole land. For no one has ever shown the mighty power or performed the awesome deeds that Moses did in the sight of all Israel.[97]

The coming of the Messiah referenced by Peter in Acts 3 looked back to the passage in Deut 18:18: "For Moses said, 'The Lord your God will raise up for you a prophet like me from among your own people; you must listen to everything he tells you.'"[98]

Some pastors may feel that because they are called and ordained into the ministry that their calling is like the calling of a Levitical priest or as a leader like Moses to the people. Desiring a divine call and being set apart for service is a worthy aspiration, but the fact is that *all* of God's people have now been called into service for him, not just the leaders. Since Moses was the mediator between God and the people as well as the priests ministering before God on behalf of the people, it may be quite easy for some leaders to consider themselves in the place of the Old Testament calling of a leader that was mediatorial.

The issue of going to God for a vision for the local church also has the unspoken mental picture of the leader following in the footsteps of Moses who went alone to God on the mountain and received the Ten Commandments. The idea that the people simply wait passively for their "Moses" to return with the plan of God for them is often the mutual expectation. Some have called this "the Moses syndrome." Leaders who retain this model have missed out on the biblical concept of the local church and the role of godly leadership. They have not regarded the corporate factor of this assembly and the potential of the corporate wisdom

96. Sailhamer, *The Pentateuch*, 387.

97. Deut 34:10–12.

98. Acts 3:22.

of God to be found in the midst of his people—this new spiritual entity. The understanding of the egalitarian nature of the Church has been replaced by a grandiose idea of leadership, which is far from the model that Jesus gave the Church. This model, instead, turns out to be a pretentious and unrealistic view of leadership that has the seeds of disappointment and discouragement built within it.

New Testament passages demonstrate that with the coming of Christ the predicted change from old covenant to new community took place. The relation of the ministry of select priests in the Old Testament is that this office now belongs to everyone who knows Christ as Lord. Peter's First Epistle teaches that the Christians he was writing to were to consider themselves as "a chosen people, a royal priesthood, a holy nation, a people belonging to God"[99] In John's letter to the churches, he wrote that Christ had made his followers to be "a kingdom and priests" in order "to serve his God and Father."[100] The outpouring of the Holy Spirit was a great release of divine power that had a profound effect on the three institutions of the old covenant: the priesthood, the prophetic function, and the kingly office.[101] God's people are the spiritual house where God's Spirit lives and they are also the priests who serve within it. The task of offering acceptable sacrifices to God is no longer restricted to a privileged few men among them but is open to all of God's people.

Though the concept of the priesthood of believers has been recognized as a New Testament reality, the concept of the "prophethood" of all believers has escaped the theological understanding of many. However, the Scriptures build a convincing case in support of the prophethood of all believers. The responsibility of God's people to proclaim the Good News of Jesus is the primary prophetic act that the Spirit gifts his people to accomplish. The Gospel is God's message for salvation and judgment today. The theological notion of the universality of the prophethood of believers is a New Testament reality. The post-Pentecost outpourings of the Holy Spirit actualize and illustrate the universality of the prophethood of believers about which Peter spoke in his Pentecost address.[102] The transfer of the Spirit from the risen and exalted Lord to his dis-

---

99. 1 Pet 2:9. In Rom 15:15–16, Paul tells the Romans that his ministry includes the priestly duty of proclaiming the Gospel to the Gentiles.

100. Rev 1:6.

101. Bilezikian, *Community 101*, 69.

102. Stronstad, *Charismatic Theology*, 63. See Acts 2; Joel 2.

ciples is similar to the transfer of the Spirit from Moses to the elders.[103] Moses's desire that all God's people might be prophets was fulfilled at Pentecost. This transfer of the Spirit to the disciples was the fulfillment of the promise of the Father. With the gift of the Spirit poured out on the disciples, the age of the prophethood of all believers had dawned.[104]

In the old covenant community, a few individuals were called to proclaim a message from Yahweh to the people. Since Peter's announcement on the day of Pentecost, the new availability of the Spirit is for all believers—everyone now has access to the ministry of prophecy.[105] It would also appear that "God's ultimate plan was for the Word to be so richly available within each congregation that each believer could contribute to this ministry."[106] All were expected to become knowledgeable enough to be competent to instruct one another.[107] Therefore, believing in Jesus Christ as the Son of God defines one's spiritual calling as a new covenant priest and prophet, roles which were foreshadowed in the old covenant text. All those who have the abiding Spirit of the Father and of the Son[108] can stand as rightful heirs and participants in God's Kingdom and therefore are suitable ministers of his grace to a broken and needy world.

A CRITIQUE OF THE HIERARCHICAL/ AUTHORITARIAN MODEL

Even though the common belief in the priesthood of all believers is meticulously proclaimed as a New Testament concept, in actuality there has often been a drift back into the old covenant model. The unspoken expectation for the priestly office with a prescribed authoritarian model, rather than a servant model, seems to remain fixed in people's thinking. This embedded thinking is found in both church and parachurch organizations. The blurring of the lines between a servant model of leadership and a hierarchical/authoritarian model of the relationship between the leader and the followers continues to cloud leadership beliefs and

103. Stronstad, *Charismatic Theology*, 77.

104. Ibid. See Num 11. See also Sailhamer, *The Pentateuch*, 384–87.

105. Stronstad, *Charismatic Theology*, 71.

106. Ibid., 72.

107. Ibid. The competence of the Christians in the Rom 15:14 passage can be contrasted with the lack among those referred to in the Heb 5:12 passage.

108. John 14:16, 26; 15:4–10; 16:7, 13–16, 27.

practices. An apparently Old Testament authoritarian model, which has been blended with New Testament leadership principles, has unconsciously been intertwined. The unwarranted merging of the leadership tasks from this type of Old Testament model with a New Testament one ends up sustaining a hierarchical and authoritarian model. This leadership is accepted without question and has become the norm in many Christian organizations.

Why has a hierarchical model of Christian leadership worked to some degree in congregational churches? A hierarchical model is relatively efficient—a top down model has worked in various contexts as a method of church governance. This model of leadership has historical precedence and provides authority to execute the tasks of church administration and ministry. It is straightforward for Christian leaders to follow. This model is often the expected leadership style in many denominations and organizations. Unfortunately, some leaders take advantage of the situation and believers become wounded through the negative behaviors that this type of leadership tends to allow. Congregants are often inclined to tolerate forceful tactics by spiritual leaders and the corporate church culture seems to accept, rather than challenge, deviant leadership actions.

There is concern for churches that value an authoritarian model of leadership. Leaders are often permitted to control most, if not all, ministry areas of the church. Their efforts might be applauded except for the fact that in such settings leaders prevent congregants from serving God in the church, their giftings are unsolicited, and their potential remains undeveloped.[109] These Christians fail to experience sensing God's leading and directing them as they do acts of love and service for him. They fail to achieve growth into maturity in Christ. They miss out on feeling affirmed as a valuable and spiritually mature participant in the church's ministry task. They lack the reward of joy in service to Christ and will ultimately miss out on promised eternal rewards. In effect, leaders often break the eighth commandment and are found to be stealing from their neighbor. Using this definition of stealing: "to deprive another person of what he or she has a right to,"[110] can be expanded to say that "to steal is to

---

109. Cudmore confirms this by stating that "The abusive treatment to victims denies them participation as willing and capable members and confuses them as to what genuine Christian leadership entails," "Victim Suffering," 8.

110. Packer, *I Want to be*, 296.

deprive another person of what God, in His love, has sought to provide for them."[111] Basically, "love to our neighbor requires us to hold sacred not only his person (sixth commandment) and his marriage (seventh commandment), but also his property and his due."[112] Sadly, too many leaders fail at this point and there is great loss to all and to the Kingdom of God as a whole.

A mixed model of leadership confuses New Testament principles of leadership. This fashionable hybrid is a result of resorting to an Old Testament authoritarian model of sacred administration, rather than an Old Testament servant model. Many Christian groups act upon a misunderstanding of the function and responsibility of Christian leadership. The paradigm of church ministry leadership, which was taught and modeled by Christ, has become a curious blend of old and new concepts. Hierarchical structures have become the accepted means of administering church affairs. The hierarchical/authoritarian model has continued to be retained without question and it is still the one deemed appropriate for Christian ministry.

Because of the magnitude of the Old Testament record there may be a natural tendency to be impressed with the perceived authoritarian manner of leadership in Israel. The incontestability of the historic record of the century's-old protocols of church administration allows this persuasion to remain. This hybrid model, that is, the fusion of a Mosaic model with that of the Aaronic/Levitical priesthood with a number of New Testament flourishes, has been easily established in the minds of the majority of Christians. It is rarely challenged and is assumed to be a fully biblical model for Church leadership today. This philosophy of Christian leadership has evolved into a practice that is accepted and useful and cannot be quickly dispelled.

In his book *Servant Leadership*, Robert Greenleaf took on the challenge to critique the hierarchical model of leadership.[113] He showed that there are two major conflicting organizational traditions. The one has been widely adopted and this may be the major cause of most of the trouble. People seem to be "wedded" to it and its assumptions go untested by the majority. The hierarchical principle that places one per-

---

111. Scott Anderson, sermon May 18, 2008, Parkside Church, Cloverdale, BC, Canada.

112. Packer, *I Want to be*, 296.

113. Greenleaf, *Servant Leadership*, 74–79.

son in charge as the lone chief atop a pyramidal structure is the widely accepted tradition that comes from Moses. This is the model by which nearly all institutions such as businesses, governments, armies, churches, and universities have been organized. People have been doing it this way so long that it is rare for anyone to question the assumptions that underlie the model. The main consideration is that one person is held responsible. It is only logical then, that in order to have stronger leadership, it is important to strengthen the control of the one person at the top. Unfortunately, the outcome in most cases exacerbates rather than alleviates the problem.[114] The basis for the second tradition comes from Roman times, which placed the principal leader as *primus inter pares*— which is, first among equals. There remains a first, a leader, but that leader is not the chief. Although the differences may appear to be subtle, there is an important difference. The job of the *primus* is to constantly test and prove that leadership among a group of able peers.[115]

Greenleaf pondered the question: "Why, the world over, do most trustee bodies choose to delegate administrative responsibility to a chief ... rather than to a leadership team with a *primus*?"[116] The weight of tradition is one reason, but trustees also simply appear uninterested in the obligation of assigning administrative responsibility to a team of equals. There needs to be a radical shift in thinking from the hierarchical principle, that is, only having one chief, to having a team of equals with a *primus*. A call for change in trustee attitude and the role necessary to assure its success needs to precede it.[117] This course would not be easy or without risk, but the limitations of the hierarchical principle outweigh these factors.

The following are nine flaws with the concept of the single chief:

1. A lone chief atop a pyramid is abnormal and corrupting.[118] No one is perfect and each of us needs the help and correcting influence of close colleagues. When one person is placed at the top of the pyramid, that person no longer has colleagues, only subordinates. The pyramidal structure tends to weaken informal

114. Ibid., 74.
115. Ibid.
116. Ibid., 75.
117. Ibid.
118. Ibid., 76.

links for communication; it stifles honest reaction and feedback and puts limits on chief-to-subordinate relationships that can seriously penalize the whole organization.[119]

2. An image of omniscience often evolves from these warped and filtered communications.[120] In time this will eventually defeat any leader since it causes a distortion of judgment. It has been found that judgment is best sharpened through interaction with others who are free to challenge and criticize.[121]

3. People at the top of pyramids tend to suffer from very real loneliness. There is an uncertainty regarding the motives of those around the chief and chiefs also seem to be out of direct contact with the grapevine. Their direct source of information is more what other people choose to tell them. They miss the relevant knowledge that seems informally available to others.[122]

4. When decisiveness is required the input of one person in charge is needed. Yet on closer examination, it appears that top persons everywhere demonstrate the burden of indecisiveness. Although decisiveness is usually conspicuous and heroic, indecisiveness is often subtle, hard to detect, and sometimes tragic. The cost to the institution, therefore, is greater from indecisive moments than from those that are decisive.[123]

5. The complaint about too few leaders rests on the institutional structure that there can only be one leader at a time. The reality is that no matter how large an institution, having only one person at the top substantially limits the full scope of leadership of that one person.[124] This innate design structure progressively limits the opportunity for other leaders to emerge.[125]

119. Ibid.
120. Ibid.
121. Ibid.
122. Ibid., 76–77.
123. Ibid., 77.
124. Ibid.
125. Ibid.

6. The perception that the chief at the top of the pyramid of any large institution is grossly overburdened.[126] The flaw is that the job not only destroys many but also damages the institution itself. The demands of the office destroy these persons' creativity long before they leave the office.[127]

7. There is a major interruption when that person leaves. The intensive time required to search for a suitable replacement jeopardizes the efficiency of the institution. The apparent search for the perfect replacement also demeans others' assets and liabilities in comparison. This produces inevitable disillusionment among others since 'the chosen one' turns out to have feet of clay like everyone else.[128]

8. Leadership by persuasion is hindered because the single chief holds too much power. The skill of persuasion from the top gets interpreted as a command instead. From the standpoint of the followers, no one else can effectively speak for the chief because they want to know what he, alone, thinks. When more responsibility converges on the single chiefs than they can handle, they must appear to be handling it alone. This unfortunately sets up the leader as a performer and their creative powers tend to be diminished. The sad outcome is that the concentration of power tends to stunt the growth of the person in the institution. So instead of this person being the model of growth in stature, growing awareness, developed skills in communication, and increased human sensitivity, the opposite seems to be representative. Reduction rather than growth becomes the downward influence and this factor imposes its limitation on everybody.[129]

9. The prevalence of the lone chief places a burden on the whole society because it gives control priority over leadership.[130] The picture that leadership portrays to the younger generation is that it is a struggle to get to the top. It nourishes the fallacy that one

---

126. Ibid.
127. Ibid.
128. Ibid., 77–78.
129. Ibid., 78.
130. Ibid.

must be boss to be effective. The ultimate negative consequence is that such leadership conduct affects everyone.[131]

Other models may serve better than the single chief model of leadership. The solution to this flawed model rests upon a reworked role for trustees and their chair. The trustees, with the support of the chair's own staff, closely monitor the performance of an administrative and leadership team, which is a group of equals with one of the first among equals. This paradigm adjustment would get closer to a worthy aim, that of a responsible serving institution.[132] This direct assessment provides insights into the weaknesses in the traditional model and is well on the way to offer a reasonable solution.

The question of "who is a servant leader" provides a basic contrast between the servant first and the leader first model.[133] The person who is servant first makes sure that other people's highest priority needs are being served. The following questions could be asked: Are people growing as persons? Are they becoming healthier, wiser, freer, and more autonomous? Are they more likely to become servants themselves? Will the least privileged in society receive benefit or be further deprived?[134] It seems obvious that more servants should emerge as leaders and that people should follow only servant leaders, but this is not a popular position.[135] The most reasonable response of followers is that they will esteem only those leaders who have proven that they are trusted as servants.[136]

An egalitarian model of leadership is the best model to replace the hierarchical organizational tradition of Moses. It is, therefore, a crucial need in the Church, based on the New Testament, to shift from a hierarchical/authoritarian model of leadership to an egalitarian model with a servant-leadership base. It might be a surprise to find that from among those who don't look as though they would be "leadership material" may instead be a multitude of true servants just waiting to be marshaled.

131. Ibid.
132. Ibid., 78–79.
133. Ibid., 27.
134. Ibid.
135. Ibid., 24.
136. Ibid.

LEADERSHIP FROM A NEW TESTAMENT PERSPECTIVE

The New Testament model of leadership was taught and demonstrated by Christ himself. Jesus established an egalitarian servanthood model of leadership for those in the new Kingdom. This model was based on the equality of its participants. The basic spiritual principles of leadership are seen within the divine relationship of the Trinity. Although there is role differentiation, all the members of the Trinity share authority. They worked together to develop the plan of redemption by exhibiting interdependence, unity, and diversity. Such a model of leadership has servanthood rather than mastery over others at its center.[137] "The Persons of the Trinity act together, in unique but inseparable ways, and never do anything apart from one another. Leaders must seek a similar kind of participation in organizations."[138] The goal is consensus, not merely agreement. A common position can be reached as people possessing varying levels of authority are engaged in the conversation.

The dynamics observed in the Trinity provide practical implications for how leadership should function. Leadership should never be authoritarian, coercive, or dictatorial. The priorities of Christ-like love and service, not a command and control methodology, characterize relations within the life of the Godhead. The best plan for leadership following this model would be to navigate between hierarchical (top down) and egalitarian (leaderless team) styles of leadership. Although in the Trinity the Father is the source of its life, nevertheless, all three members of the Trinity act in a unified, loving, and conciliar way. It is the task of leaders to strive to fuse these apparent opposites.[139] Basing one's view of leadership on a trinitarian understanding of the Godhead elevates and prioritizes an egalitarian servanthood model of leadership.

Leadership primarily deals with the structure of decision-making and secondarily with communication. These elements are both needed for effective leadership and mutual accountability.[140] After considering the Trinity there are lessons that leaders can glean. There should be a multiplicity of leaders with shared authority. The value of unity and diversity among leaders can be foundational. Each person's unique and

---

137. Banks and Ledbetter, *Reviewing Leadership*, 84.

138. Ibid., 86.

139. Ibid.

140. Ibid.

complementary role should be celebrated. Relationships should be the priority, not the task of an organization. Mutual respect and dependence can grow through relationships. As people listen and discern the merit of one another's contributions, leadership begins to naturally occur through more than one person. Leadership can then rotate according to whoever is pointing the best way forward at a particular time.[141]

The concept of servant leadership is not entirely a New Testament concept. The idea of a servant leader was an embedded Old Testament ideal for Israel's leaders which included priests, prophets, judges, and kings. Later in Israel's history the prophet Isaiah describes this servant ideal.

> Here is my servant, whom I uphold,
> my chosen one in whom I delight;
> I will put my Spirit on him
> and he will bring justice to the nations.
> He will not shout or cry out,
> or raise his voice in the streets.
> A bruised reed he will not break,
> and a smoldering wick he will not snuff out.
> In faithfulness he will bring forth justice;
> he will not falter or be discouraged
> till he establishes justice on earth.
> In his law the islands will put their hope.[142]

Matthew quotes from this passage and affirms that Jesus fulfilled what the prophet had talked about.[143] The concept of servanthood from a New Testament perspective can be defined in a number of ways. It involves *being gentle*, that is, being humble, kind, and considerate, not contentious or disrespectful. It involves *bearing with*, that is, patiently enduring with affectionate regard those who are weak or disheartened. It involves *building up*, that is, strengthening those who are timid or discouraged. It involves *bringing justice*, that is, helping those who have been injured or dishonored. Lastly, servanthood involves *blessing others*, that is, sacrificing self-interest for the good of others, for those who are without hope and direction.[144]

---

141. Ibid., 85. The authors have referenced Stacy Rinehart's book *Upside Down: The Paradox of Servant Leadership* (Colorado Springs: NavPress, 1998).

142. Isa 42:1–4.

143. Matt 12:18–20.

144. Farnsworth, *Wounded Workers*, 126–27. The opposite of these descriptions

Benevolence is bearing with others when they don't seem to measure up and endeavoring to be redemptive in discipline. In fact, redemptive discipline is pleasing to God. God cannot be pleased with what often happens in Christian organizations. A better plan would be that, "The Lord's servants are to be ready first and foremost to teach rather than terminate, and to gently correct rather than condemn the ones who disagree with their message and who perhaps even oppose them."[145] Leaders are to tend the sheep, not to rule them with force and leaders are to care for the weak, the sick, and the wounded.[146] These are solid biblical guidelines for aspiring leaders and reminders for those who may have gotten weary.

Church discipline needs to be returned to biblical balance.[147] Too often corrective church discipline has been done poorly and ineffectively. Loving confrontation with Christ-like love, in order for healing, reconciliation, and restoration to take place should be the aim. *"Church discipline* is the training *of* the church *by* the church."[148] In the larger theme of discipline as a whole, it must be recognized that corrective church discipline is but a part.[149] Too many leaders try to use either the church or the Bible or both to control God's people. Church leaders need to realize that they "are themselves under the authority of scripture, but its authority is never to be coercive; it does not make leaders into rulers."[150]

In further considering a Christ-centered approach to leadership it can be observed that Jesus was on assignment from God. He inverted the world's power scale and showed the strength of servant power. He showed the force of example, portrayed his mission to suffer, and unfolded the apparent paradox undergirding the power of the cross.[151] Jesus demonstrated that having a clear sense of who one is, which comes through developing intimacy with God, is where leadership begins. Therefore, knowing oneself is the key to one's effectiveness as a leader. "Because leadership takes place within the Trinity, it is in essence 'a divine attri-

seems to portray leaders who instead injure their followers.

145. Ibid., 131.

146. Ibid.

147. White and Blue, *Healing The Wounded.*

148. Ibid., 18.

149. Ibid., 20.

150. Ibid., 40.

151. Banks and Ledbetter, *Reviewing Leadership,* 79.

bute' that is at the very heart of our being. It is a God-given dynamic in our nature and therefore a basic dimension of being a person."[152] It would be beneficial to explore the members of the Trinity in a renewed attempt to glean a better understanding of shared power, how to relate to others, and leading. "The nature of God, expressed in the Trinity, offers a superb representation of unity within diversity, community, freedom, and a collegial approach that is nonhierarchical."[153] Being created in the image of God innately points to a way of leading that honors the nature of God as expressed in the Trinity. When leadership takes on the nature of God, people begin to experience the sacramental nature of leading.

Since the nature and character of God were revealed more fully by the coming of the Son, mankind has been offered a more complete view of God. The New Testament Scriptures proclaim that the Father exercised his power over evil and triumphed by raising Jesus from the dead.[154] Jesus demonstrated in his incarnation how a leader should serve. He gave an example of how to relate to one another and to God (by submitting to his will). The disciples of Jesus initially had a distorted concept of leadership. From the Gospel accounts we read that James and John tried to coax Jesus to give them a distinct position of privilege and honor.[155] This account gives the context for Christ's teaching on appropriate leadership in the Kingdom contrasted with the Gentile leadership style. Christ gave his disciples a concise teaching on how leadership should operate in the Kingdom of God. In the incarnation, Jesus demonstrated how God's people ought to relate to one another and to God. This new leadership paradigm was based on serving.

> You know that those who are regarded as rulers of the Gentiles lord it over them, and their high officials exercise authority over them. Not so with you. Instead, whoever wants to become great among you must be your servant, and whoever wants to be first must be slave of all. For even the Son of man did not come to be served, but to serve, and to give his life as a ransom for many.[156]

---

152. Ibid., 85. Banks and Ledbetter quote from Williams and McKibben: "Our leadership positions may vary and our positions of leadership may be different, but that doesn't alter the fact that we are all called to be leaders." The goal of leadership is "enabling persons to become all that they were created to be," *Oriented Leadership*, 24.

153. Banks and Ledbetter, *Reviewing Leadership*, 87.

154. Acts 2:22–28.

155. Matt 20:20–28; Mark 10:35–45.

156. Mark 10:42–45.

When the disciples argued about who would be the greatest[157] in the Kingdom they tried to keep it from him, but Jesus put them on the spot and asked what they had been arguing about. An argument had started among them about who would be the greatest. Jesus took the opportunity to give them instruction. Mark recorded what Jesus said: "If anyone wants to be first, he must be the very last and the servant of all." Jesus then took a little child into his arms and said, "Whoever welcomes one of these little children in my name welcomes me; and whoever welcomes me does not welcome me but the one who sent me."[158] Matthew stated that Jesus called a little child and had him stand among them, and said:

> I tell you the truth, unless you change and become like little children, you will never enter the kingdom of heaven. Therefore, whoever welcomes a little child like this in my name welcomes me. But if anyone causes one of these little ones who believe in me to sin, it would be better for him to have a large millstone hung around his neck and to be drowned in the depths of the sea.[159]

Jesus was helping them to consider the priorities that mattered in his Father's Kingdom rather than their preconceived ideas of leadership, which esteemed position, power, and prestige.

Jesus had to frequently rebuke the religious leaders of his day. The conflict between Christ's view of how the Pharisees and Sadducees demonstrated leadership and how they should have led stirred up levels of strife between them. In their efforts to uphold holiness among the Jewish nation at that time, their harsh methods outweighed their admirable intentions. Christ criticized their appalling and insensitive methodologies and used them as a reference for what not to do. The areas where they had strayed from a divine view are enumerated throughout the Gospels.

During the Last Supper,[160] Jesus exemplified leadership by serving others. Even though his impending arrest and death weighed heavily on his heart, he took the time to reinforce one singular truth that his life had demonstrated—serving was how the work of the Kingdom of God was to be accomplished. The disciples' concept of leadership was based

157. Matt 18:1–6; Mark 9:33–37; Luke 9:46–48.
158. Mark 9:35–37.
159. Matt 18:3–6.
160. Luke 22:14–27.

on honor and prestige. Christ's teaching must have appeared paradoxical to them and they did not fully comprehend what he meant. There was noticeable discomfort and initial rejection of their teacher's paradigm of leadership in favor of their more familiar model. It was only after Christ's post-resurrection appearances among the disciples and the coming of the promised Holy Spirit that all of the teachings of Christ converged and the disciples began to understand what he had earlier taught and demonstrated.[161] Based on the example of Christ and the exhortations of the New Testament text, leadership in the Kingdom of God is a style of leadership different from that which is promoted in the secular world. The Lord reinstated a shepherding servant model as a singular guide for those leading his people. A delightful reality unfolds when relationships are structured on mutual servanthood and not power, the world can then get a taste of heavenly reality where love is manifested and God's peace rests.[162]

Peter explained to those gathered on the day of Pentecost that this Jesus who had been crucified and buried, was the very one God had raised to life. This Jesus had been "exalted to the right hand of God" and God had made him "both Lord and Christ."[163] John also describes his position as the Sovereign Lord in the book of The Revelation: "Jesus Christ, who is the faithful witness, the firstborn from the dead, and the ruler of the kings of the earth."[164] As the Risen Lord, the Father gave him full authority. The predicted change from the old covenant to the new covenant had taken place. The old covenant was now history and the new one had been instituted.

The Apostle Paul led the way in articulating an understanding of leadership as well as practicing leadership in various early church contexts. Paul was concerned that the churches conduct themselves in an orderly manner and that the members be guided and properly cared for. Yet, other than when a church's actions were inadequate, he says very little about how the gatherings should be regulated. Paul never suggested that it was the role of one or a few people in a spiritual community to regulate its gatherings. It is everyone's responsibility as they discern together what they sense the Spirit seems to be saying. Organization in

161. Luke 24:38–49; Acts 1:1–8; 2.

162. Webber, *Younger Evangelicals*, 147.

163. Acts 2:31–36.

164. Rev 1:5.

the early churches stemmed from a highly participatory and charismatic process and was not determined in advance by a few. It is curious that the word *authority* rarely appears in Paul's writings. Paul's authority was only exercised for constructive purposes.[165]

Paul uses the language of family when talking about the local church—which is based on the biblical view of God as Father and believers as children. "This conveys an affectionate but responsible parental rather than patriarchal bond."[166] Paul also referred to himself as a mother who suffered labor pains and as a nurse who cared for them.[167] Responsibility was intertwined with an affectionate relationship between Paul and his converts. Nevertheless, Paul did not encourage a childlike dependency on him. He treated believers as adult children and urged them to "grow up" in Christ and to become mature adults in the faith.[168] Paul's basic authority stemmed from the Gospel that he had been commissioned to preach, not by rights from his apostolic commission. Therefore, only as long as his words reflected the Gospel and as long as he was in accord with the Spirit should the churches give him a hearing. His authority was "instrumental, not inherent, and, though powerful because of God's call, it was still subject" to the discernment of the Christian converts in these believing communities.[169]

Paul's associates, like Timothy and Titus, had only functional or derived authority based on the reputation of the work they did and the task of embodying the message Paul had for the churches. Their role was as itinerants and not as residents. Their role was more ambassadorial and exemplary rather than having an official role in the congregations.[170] Their authority was spiritual rather than formal and was exhibited through the quality of their love and faithfulness to Paul's teaching. They, too, were to relate to these believers in a familial way rather than from a position of command. They provided instruction regarding worship and church governance but avoided control in the regulating of the specifics of how church worship and government ought to be conducted. The key roles in the churches were individuals and couples in the church body

---

165. Banks and Ledbetter, *Reviewing Leadership*, 37. 1 Cor. 12:7–11; 14:28, 30, 31.

166. Banks and Ledbetter, *Reviewing Leadership*, 37.

167. Gal 4:19; 1 Thess 2:7.

168. Banks and Ledbetter, *Reviewing Leadership*, 37. 1 Cor 14:20; Eph 4:14.

169. Banks and Ledbetter, *Reviewing Leadership*, 40–41.

170. Ibid., 41.

who were recognized by the community.[171] Since Paul understood his ministry to be "rooted in the gospel and embodied in Christ" he operated in a "highly consultative and collegial way."[172] He spoke of his team as "coworkers" and as "brothers" and highly regarded their personal ministries—they were not merely extensions of him and his work.[173] Though there was willing subordination to Paul, it was voluntary and personal rather than coercive and formal.[174]

The Apostle Paul's role demonstrated certain leadership qualities that could frequently be observed by others. These qualities included:

> . . . considerateness, courage, decisiveness, encouragement, faith, vision, modest self appraisal, humility, the capacity to listen, magnanimity, patience, self-discipline, integrity, wisdom, criticism constructively, differences flexibility, finances scrupulously, time discerningly, and suffering redemptively.[175]

Paul paid attention to communication—with God and with others. His leadership was based on his unique sense of calling by God, a dynamic awareness of being identified with Christ, and an extraordinary versatility in the Spirit as he confronted diverse peoples and situations.[176]

Paul confirmed that, in the Christian community, being motivated by the Spirit assures benefit to all. There was room for an exercise of gifts, a variety of services, and different kinds of working.[177] The activities that resulted from these gifts demonstrated the diversity of the Spirit's working among them.[178] Paul was a firm believer that everyone had a part in the service and that everyone had an equal part in discerning what the Spirit of Christ might be saying to the community. It was the obligation of the entire church community to discern the validity of the various contributions in a meeting.[179]

Paul's use of the language of priesthood appears only metaphorically in his writings and is never used of a literal person or group. The

171. Ibid.

172. Ibid., 42.

173. Ibid. Phil 2:25; Acts 18:18; 1 Cor 1:1.

174. Banks and Ledbetter, *Reviewing Leadership*, 42. 1 Cor 4:17; 2 Cor 8:17.

175. Banks and Ledbetter, *Reviewing Leadership*, 42.

176. Ibid.

177. 1 Cor 12:4–7.

178. Rom 12:4–8; 1 Cor 12:8–11; Eph 4:11–13.

179. Banks and Ledbetter, *Reviewing Leadership*, 37–38. 1 Cor 12:10; 14:30.

kinds of ceremonial activities Yahweh required of mainly one tribe of Israel are now required of all Christians.[180] From the New Testament record, it would appear that what was important was the function that people performed rather than the positions they occupied.[181] Rather than a formal recognition of a church position, there appeared to be a "nonformal, community recognition of a group, not an individual," that was "based on the quality of the ministry people were already engaged in rather than on external qualifications."[182] One cultural insight is that people would be appointed overseers and helpers in the community only if they had first proven themselves in their households.[183] The New Testament "approach to authority recognizes the charismatic gifts or social prominence of certain people but requires that other qualities such as commitment and servanthood also be present."[184] Paul named women among the group and indicated that they played a significant role in the Christian community life as well as among the itinerant group of apostles and prophets and they possibly served as evangelists.[185]

The authority of the ordained minister is rooted in Jesus Christ who received it from the Father[186] and who confers it by the Holy Spirit through the act of ordination. Since Jesus came as one who served,[187] being set apart is being consecrated to service. The act of ordination takes place within a community.[188] The authority of the ordained ministry is not to be understood as the possession of the ordained person but as a gift for the continuing edification of the particular fellowship for which they have been ordained. Ordination is essentially a setting apart with prayer for the gift of the Holy Spirit. Authority can then be seen as one's responsibility before God but it is exercised with the cooperation of the

180. Banks and Ledbetter, *Reviewing Leadership*, 38.

181. Ibid.

182. Ibid., 39.

183. "But houses were workplaces as well as domestic spaces and involved the tasks of supervising slaves in addition to raising families. Proven experience and a good reputation in managing workers were therefore also qualifications for leadership in the church," ibid.

184. Ibid.

185. Ibid. Rom 16:6–7; 1 Cor 11:5; Phil 4:3.

186. Matt 28:18.

187. Mark 10:45; Luke 22:27.

188. Schrotenboer, *Evangelical Response*, 45.

whole community.[189] Christ's authority was and is an authority governed by love for "the sheep who have no shepherd."[190] His authority was manifested by his life of service and ultimately by the total giving of his life in death. Therefore, authority in the Church can only be authentic as it seeks to conform to this model. Christ's authority was unique as the people recognized it and declared: "he spoke as one who has authority (*exousia*), not as the scribes."[191]

From this model a number of appropriate character qualities should be manifested in the lives of those who are set apart for ministry. Ordained ministers must not be autocrats or impersonal functionaries; they are bound to the faithful in interdependence and reciprocity. Only when leaders strive for the inclusion and involvement of the community can their spiritual authority be protected from the distortions of isolation and domination. Spiritual directors can exercise the authority of Christ in the way Christ himself revealed God's authority to the world, by committing their life to the community.[192]

Paul pointed believers to the Risen Christ. Although Jesus Christ was raised to the highest position of power and authority, there was to be no stratified hierarchy of redeemed individuals below him. When it comes to defining church governance from a New Testament perspective, it is difficult to develop a structure of church government that adheres to the authority of the Bible because there is the lack of didactic material and there is no prescriptive exposition of what the government of the local church should be like.[193] The combined elements of governance found in the New Testament text demonstrate that there is no unitary pattern. There were marked democratic elements, notable monarchical elements, (the apostles appointed and ordained officers and instructed the churches), and passages demonstrating that the elders had a strong role.[194]

In the final analysis, even if it were clear that one exclusive pattern of organization in the New Testament emerged, there is serious doubt

189. Ibid.

190. Matt 9:36.

191. Matt 7:29.

192. Schrotenboer, *Evangelical Response*, 45.

193. Erickson, *Christian Theology*, 1083–84.

194. Ibid.

that that pattern would necessarily be normative for us today.[195] A naive persuasion can be constructed regarding one's view of church. Those declaring "We want to be a 'real' New Testament church" may have missed an integral element in their perception of the early church. A suitable response might be: "To which New Testament church are you referring?" Having an understanding of the governance followed in New Testament churches takes more investigation than most people are willing to undertake. To assume that early Christian churches had a singular governing structure in every place misses the dynamic portrayed throughout the New Testament text.

In order to attempt to construct a governmental system, it is necessary to turn to the principles that are found in the New Testament. Two pertinent questions could be asked: "In what direction was church government moving within the New Testament period? and What are the reasons for church government?"[196] Here are some simple guidelines for contemporizing the biblical message to construct a model of local church government suitable for today:

1. One principle that is evident in the New Testament and particularly in 1 Corinthians is the value of order.[197]

2. It is also desirable to have certain persons responsible for specific ministries.[198]

3. Another principle is the priesthood of all believers.[199]

4. The idea that each person is important to the whole body is implicit throughout the New Testament and explicit in Romans 12 and 1 Corinthians 12.[200]

195. Ibid., 1085.

196. Ibid.

197. Ibid. "The situation at Corinth, where total individuality tended to take over, was not very desirable. At its worst it was downright destructive. It was necessary, then, to have some control over the highly individualized ways in which spirituality was being expressed" (1 Cor 14:40).

198. "We are reminded here of the situation in Acts 6, where we are told that seven men were appointed to be in charge of the ministry to widows," Erickson, *Christian Theology*, 1085.

199. "Each person is capable of relating to God directly," ibid., 1085–86.

200. "The multiplicity of gifts suggests that the input into decision making should be broadly based. The Book of Acts stresses group consensus (Acts 4:32; 15:22). There is a special sense of fellowship whenever all the members of a community feel that they

Based on these components a proposal for suitable church government is composed of two basic parts:

1. The congregational form of church government nearly fulfills the principles which have been laid down because it takes seriously the principle of the priesthood and spiritual competency of all believers and it also takes seriously the promise that the indwelling Spirit will guide all believers.

2. Simultaneously, the need for orderliness suggests that a degree of representative government is necessary. Therefore, in some situations, leaders need to be chosen in order to take suitable action on behalf of the group.[201]

Although the issue of church governance may in principle recognize the priesthood of all believers, the practice in numerous churches does not fully reflect this belief. Somehow the influence of some leaders is bent towards a more command and control style which negates an egalitarian model—which could easily be facilitated by them. Often the main concern among such leaders is that *doing* is more important than *being*. Success is measured by how much one has visibly accomplished rather than by inward spiritual growth and personal wholeness.

It is important for God's people, especially the leaders, to have a clear sense of who they are. This can only come through developing intimacy with God. This is where leadership with integrity can truly begin. Therefore, knowing oneself is the key to one's effectiveness as a leader.[202] Being created in the image of God reflects something of the life of the Trinity. Leadership takes place within the Trinity; therefore it is in essence a divine attribute and is at the very heart of our being.[203] Not only is it a God-given dynamic in our nature, but it is a basic dimension of being a person.[204] Although leadership positions may differ, that does not alter the fact that believers in Christ are called to be leaders. Basically,

---

have played a significant part in determining what is to be done," ibid., 1086.

201. "Those chosen should always be conscious of their answerability to those whom they represent and where possible, major issues should be brought to the membership as a whole to decide," ibid.

202. Banks and Ledbetter, *Reviewing Leadership*, 85.

203. Ibid.

204. "This is a democratic understanding of leadership," ibid.

the ultimate goal of leadership is to enable people to become all that they were created to be.[205]

As stated earlier, focusing on the divine example of what leadership involves ought to demonstrate practical implications for how leaders ought to function in the Church today. It should never be authoritarian, coercive, or dictatorial but demonstrate love and service, which characterize relations within the life of the Godhead.[206] The idea of relationship is at the heart of the Trinity and has implications for leadership. Based on this theological understanding, leaders should aim to demonstrate interdependence, exhibit unity in diversity, recognize people's unique contributions, and express shared authority. People will then "begin to experience the sacramental nature of leading when leadership takes on the nature of God."[207] The multifaceted relationships within the Trinity provide insights for new models of shared power, relating to others, and leading. "The nature of God expressed in the Trinity, offers a superb representation of unity within diversity, community, freedom, and a collegial approach that is nonhierarchical."[208]

Leadership grows out of personal wholeness as well as wholeness through a balanced life. "Such wholeness is not so much a quality or a mark of leadership as a precondition and a catalyst for it."[209] Wholeness comes through total abandonment to the gift of God's grace, the merits of the finished work of Christ on the cross, and the promise of the infilling and enabling power of the Holy Spirit. With these essential spiritual priorities in place, there is less likelihood for believers to slip into the "shadow side" of leadership. "These include always needing to be in charge and have everything under control, inflicting pathology and

205. Ibid. See Williams and McKibben, *Oriented Leadership*, 24, 29.

206. "Vision is at the root of discerning and implementing this understanding. A proper vision entails having a clear mental picture of how things should be, regardless of what they are now. It involves loving God and the creation and desiring to live a life of thanksgiving for all that God is and has done. As a result, people with this vision accept the responsibility of stewardship, which involves the human management of God's gift of the world. Such a vision gives aim to daily life, guides commitment, stimulates motivation, informs speech and behavior, clarifies expectations, and develops unity. The Father is the source of the vision, Jesus models its implementation, and the Spirit generates enthusiasm and empowerment for it," Banks and Ledbetter, *Reviewing Leadership*, 85–86.

207. Ibid., 87.

208. Ibid.

209. Ibid.

inadequacies on others, falling into the messiah trap with its attendant danger of workaholism, being a mere persona rather than a genuine person, and failing to overcome the inability to share weakness or face failure."[210]

The Church is an egalitarian spiritual entity with Christ as its Head and Supreme Ruler. There are to be no graded ranks of those who hold greater or lesser authority, but all are to be considered as equal ministers under the Lordship of Christ. "The unity, love, and harmony among the three members of the Trinity exemplify and catalyze the process and structures involved in a vision coming into being."[211] As the persons of the Trinity act together, in unique but inseparable ways, and never do anything apart from one another,[212] a healthy model for leadership among God's people unfolds. Since the aim of organizational leadership is consensus, not merely agreement, but a common position reached as people possessing varying levels of authority engage in conversation, then leaders must look to what they can learn from the Trinity in order to strive for participation in organizations.[213] It is essential to recognize that "a leader is a first among equals rather than a person on the dominant side of an unequal relationship. Such leadership involves authority, but authority that flows from love, and function revolving around service rather than positions and power."[214]

The Apostle Paul rehearsed foundational truths about the spiritual and egalitarian nature of the Church in his letters to the early churches. He reminded the Corinthian church that:

> The body is a unit, though it is made up of many parts; and though all its parts are many, they form one body. So it is with Christ. For we were all baptized by one Spirit into one body— whether Jews or Greeks, slave or free—and we were all given the one Spirit to drink. Now the body is not made up of one part but of many. . . . Now you are the body of Christ, and each one of you is a part of it.[215]

---

210. Ibid., 112.
211. Ibid., 86.
212. Ibid.
213. Ibid.
214. Ibid.
215. 1 Cor 12:12–14, 27.

To the Galatians, Paul clarified that since they were all sons of God through faith in Christ Jesus and that they had clothed themselves with Christ, their new spiritual identity would define them from any natural designations such as ethnic roots (whether Jew or Greek), social status (whether slave or free), or gender (whether male or female). Paul told them plainly that if they belonged to Christ then they were Abraham's seed and as a result were heirs according to the promise. Their identity was now determined on that basis. Now, because of the Spirit, they were true sons of God and legitimate heirs.[216]

> Because you are sons, God sent the Spirit of his Son into our hearts, the Spirit who calls out, "Abba, Father." So you are no longer a slave, but a son; and since you are a son, God has made you also an heir.[217]

To the Ephesians, Paul used the analogy of the human body to illustrate the fact that they were unified by the Spirit who was within them. He reminded them that since Christ had descended and then ascended higher than all the heavens he could now give specific gifts of people to the Ephesian gathering of the saints. People so gifted would prepare God's people for works of service so that the church family would be built up and mature and that unity in the faith and knowledge of God's Son would be evident. This would unmistakably mark them as a community of Christ. Their corporate spiritual maturity would prevent them from being infantile and defenseless against "every wind of teaching and the cunning and craftiness of men in their deceitful scheming."[218]

They would instead be people who would make it their aim to speak the truth in love and consistently grow up into Christ, the Head of the Church. As members of a redeemed community, they were admonished to speak truthfully to one another and to put off falsehood. They were to get rid of all bitterness, rage, anger, and other negative behaviors and they were instead to demonstrate kindness, compassion, and forgiveness as the habit of their new life in Christ. This could be done by the empowering of the Holy Spirit within them.[219]

---

216. Gal 3:26–29.
217. Gal 4:6–7.
218. Eph 4:14.
219. Eph 4:1–14, 25–32.

In 1 John the reader is reminded that the nature and character of the Father ought to be demonstrated among all those who claim a relationship with him.[220] Paul reminded the Galatian believers that they had freedom in Christ and that the fruit of the Spirit would naturally flow from a life of fellowship with the Triune God by the enabling of the Holy Spirit.[221] Through maturing spiritually, by walking with God, those who aspire to be leaders can be expected to demonstrate godly character qualities.

The Apostle Peter exhorted church leaders in his day to be willing shepherds over God's flock; shepherds who would be eager to serve, who would live as good examples, who would avoid the temptations of greed, and lastly, who would shun the inherent tendency to lord it over God's people. Christ's example was to be esteemed while a leadership style that was authoritarian was to be rejected.

> To the elders among you, I appeal as a fellow elder, a witness of Christ's sufferings and one who also will share in the glory to be revealed: Be shepherds of God's flock that is under your care, serving as overseers—not because you must, but because you are willing, as God wants you to be; not greedy for money, but eager to serve; not lording it over those entrusted to you, but being examples to the flock.[222]

In his final words to the assembled elders from Ephesus, the Apostle Paul reminded them of his passion to proclaim the whole will of God among them. He exhorted these spiritual shepherds to keep watch over themselves and the flock and to shepherd the Church of God because of the infinite value placed upon it—it was bought with the precious blood of Christ. Paul expressed grief that truth distorters would arise from among the flock and draw away disciples after them. It was, therefore, hugely important that these spiritual shepherds be on their guard. Paul exhorted them to earnestly follow his resolute example of warning against any such eventuality.

> Keep watch over yourselves and all the flock, of which the Holy Spirit has made you overseers. Be shepherds of the church of God, which he bought with his own blood. I know that after I leave, savage wolves will come in among you and will not spare

220. 1 John 3:1–3; 4:7–21.
221. Gal 5:16–26.
222. 1 Pet 5:1–3.

the flock. Even from your own number men will arise and distort the truth in order to draw away disciples after them. So be
on your guard! Remember that for three years I never stopped
warning each of you night and day with tears.[223]

Paul's final words reinforce the actuality that from the beginning of the
New Testament era there was a need for leaders to remain vigilant. As a
redeemed community they needed to be prepared to recognize distortions of the truth, which Christ had predicted would inevitably arise.[224]

The Apostle Paul exercised loving authority as an apostle and
undershepherd of Christ through his Epistles, by his personal visits,
and by sending chosen and capable laborers to minister on his behalf.
Relevant theological instructions along with pertinent admonitions for
the churches strengthened the believers and established the witness
of the Christian community in those pagan societies. When the need
arose, he used his apostolic authority to guide the affairs of these growing church communities in the many cities of Asia Minor. Generally,
Paul demonstrated his skill as a leader by establishing a strong relational
model.[225] He affirmed and modeled the paradigm of leadership taught
and demonstrated by the Lord Jesus himself.

The New Testament contains a strong rationale for the necessity of
authority structures in secular society—because the fallen world does not
have the mind of Christ. It cannot function in an orderly fashion without
someone taking charge and enforcing rules.[226] Our secular world cannot provide suitable patterns of leadership for Christ-like shepherding.[227]
When it comes to the Church, the suggestion and practice of this type
of authority within the Church cannot be found in the New Testament.
If anything, the Scriptures explicitly forbid Christians to run their communities in the manner of the rulers of the Gentiles or of their high

---

223. Acts 20:28–31.

224. Matt 7:15–23; 24:10–12; 24:23–25; Mark 13:21–23; Luke 6:25–27.

225. Although the Apostle Paul had authority given to him by Christ, his leadership
style also demonstrated a brother sharing his life with the churches of Asia Minor. He
did not lord it over or use demanding tones but persuaded as a father with his children.
Passages from 2 Cor 1:12–14, 23–24, 2:4, and 3:1–18 outline how someone could be a
competent minister of the new covenant.

226. Bilezikian, *Community 101*, 162. See Matt 22:16–21; Rom 13:1–7; 1 Tim 2:1–2;
Titus 3:1; 1 Pet 2:13–17.

227. Nouwen, *Name of Jesus*, 62.

officials who exercise authority over them.[228] The contrast between the organization of governance in the secular world and that in Christian communities is that the former is ruler-to-subject relations, while the latter is a subject-to-subject model of an interactive life based on New Testament principles.[229] In the Church, there is a need for an egalitarian model that operates on the basis of group or representative consensus, not of unilateral, autocratic, top down decision-making.[230]

The Romans 13 passage has been used to support the notion of unquestioning submission to church leaders. The supposition is that if God ordains authority, any challenge to that authority constitutes rebellion to God. In the context it can be noted that the purpose of authority is to do good not just to invoke fear. Unlike this noble purpose, leadership belief and practice has instead weakened the intention of this passage. This passage has simply been misconstrued in favor of authority figures. Paul's message never intended for people to be in psychologically disturbing environments. The outcome is that supporting an unloving leadership suggests submission to abuse, not to leadership.[231]

There are grave repercussions in a leadership model that "arrogates to itself the ministry belonging to others, leadership that claims a monopoly on spiritual gifting, and leadership that substitutes itself for the priesthood of all believers. This type of leadership is not scripturally warranted and does not come from God."[232] There are two reasons why this paradigm of leadership has been so readily accepted. This belief is either the result of a faulty interpretation of the concept of biblical leadership or is evidence of uncritical regression into Old Testament patterns of ministry.[233] Careful reexamination of the theory and practice of ministry is needed in the light of an embedded servant shepherd Old Testament model joined with supportive New Testament teachings along with a willingness to recognize and discard unbiblical traditions that hinder and entangle people.[234]

---

228. Matt 20:25.

229. Nouwen, *Name of Jesus*, 62.

230. Ibid.

231. Cudmore, "Victim Suffering," 13–14.

232. Bilezikian, *Community 101*, 71.

233. Ibid.

234. Ibid.

The desire for power among church leaders influences congregants to exit from their local churches. In pondering the possible reasons for attrition in the churches in Europe over the past few decades Nouwen presented this assessment: "When I ask myself the main reason for so many people having left the church during past decades in France, Germany, Holland, and also in Canada and America, the word 'power' easily comes to mind."[235] It can be easily recognized how ironic this insight is:

> One of the greatest ironies of the history of Christianity is that its leaders constantly gave in to the temptation of power—political power, military power, economic power, or moral and spiritual power—even though they continued to speak in the name of Jesus, who did not cling to his divine power but emptied himself and became as we are.[236]

Although a significant number of churches affirm a congregational form of church governance, in practice a hierarchical leaning has gained subtle preference in many fellowships. While leadership that is expressed hierarchically is often accepted as a valid biblical model, it comes with a price tag. Although it may seem to resemble an appropriate Old Testament model and generally feels comfortable to many people, in reality many church groups are neither following a valid Old Testament model, which included an embedded servant leadership model, nor are they following an effective servant leadership model as demonstrated in the New Testament. It is, therefore, not an appropriate leadership model for the Church today. The ultimate inefficiency of this model is demonstrated by the distress it creates in the Church because it fails to portray the biblical model of leadership that Christ both instituted and intended. Many have been harmed by overbearing leadership behavior. When the secular/power model is found in the Church it is not a good thing. Though this model is alluring and tempting, it is decidedly flawed. It would be natural to conclude that having power—provided it is used in the service of God and fellow human beings—is a good thing. The problem lies in the fact that every time a major crisis happens in the history of the Church it can be observed "that a major cause of rupture

---

235. Nouwen, *Name of Jesus*, 75–76.
236. Ibid., 77.

is the power exercised by those who claim to be followers of the poor and powerless Jesus."[237]

In a leader's attempt to cope with change, there is often a tendency to slip into an authoritarian form of leadership. Since there is rapid change within the culture as well as within the Church—leadership, at such times, becomes critical. Leadership is always an issue in the life of any institution, but it is crucial during unpredictable times. It is incumbent on leaders to be prepared to discard established patterns of operating that are no longer applicable. This goes along with the need to learn new skills and draw from fresh insights in order to be ready for inevitable challenges.[238] Much of the leadership material available apparently does not help leaders to overcome modernity's hierarchical and authoritarian bent. Leaders need to learn how to step back, refuse forms of control, give space for the Holy Spirit to work, and create contexts for the priesthood of all believers to be expressed.[239]

All too often the authoritarian model of leadership provides a pathway to misuse power and is prone to abuse. Power is an irresistible lure; this can be observed throughout human history. "The long painful history of the church is the history of people ever and again tempted to choose power over love, control over the cross, being a leader over being led."[240] When this happens, a dangerous and hurtful consequence occurs—the misuse and abuse of power. There is an abundance of leaders who have not developed healthy, intimate relationships but have chosen power and control instead. When Christians have arrived at the leadership task without the ability to give and receive love, and a feeling that intimacy is a threat, the temptation of power is greatest.[241]

Although the abuse of power can be found in any style of leadership, venerating a hierarchical leadership style with an authoritarian bent can lead to harmful and distressing actions that wound God's people. Loving can be contrasted with controlling and it shows the basic human temptation to choose power over love. Does power offer an easy substitute for the hard task of love? Ever since the snake said, "The day you eat of this tree your eyes will be open and you will be like gods, knowing good from

237. Ibid., 76.
238. Gibbs and Bolger, *Emerging Churches*, 193.
239. Ibid., 208.
240. Nouwen, *Name of Jesus*, 77.
241. Ibid., 79.

evil," there has been a temptation to replace love with power.[242] The need is to resist this alluring temptation.[243]

Since Yahweh has been viewed as an authoritarian God and the chosen leaders of Israel mainly used an authoritarian style of leadership, the natural progression regarding leadership in the Church would be to continue with this evident pattern. The problem lies in the fact that the Church is not in the old covenant era and in the fact that Christ Jesus has already come and revealed in fuller measure the nature of the God of Heaven. The character of God and a fitting view of Church leadership need to be revisited in order to unravel the unconsciously intertwined Old Testament and New Testament concepts. This intertwining is detrimental to an understanding of God's intentions and his ultimate purposes for the Church. The implications of the new covenant for power structures in Christian communities demonstrate that there are no patriarchs in the Kingdom because that place is reserved for God alone. Jesus is the head of any community under God. The very nature of the Kingdom of God insists that all views of power be reexamined as all previous power structures are made relative.[244]

The Father-heart of God is demonstrated in the Old Testament—the Pentateuch alone records abundant examples of God's loving attributes. This fact dispels the view that the God of the Old Testament was solely a God of anger, wrath, and judgment. A brief look in the introduction to the book of Deuteronomy highlights Yahweh's Father-heart and divine care for his people.[245] At the inception of the nation, this encounter of Moses with the Almighty gives the reader an understanding of the divine nature of the Sovereign Lord. Unlike the gods of the surrounding nations, Yahweh's attributes were neither vengeful nor capricious. Although he is Lord of all, he is not aloof, but benevolent and caring in his relationship with his creation. As Paul affirms later, the invisible qualities of the Creator God have always been recognized: "For since the creation of the world God's invisible qualities—his eternal power and divine nature—have been clearly seen being understood from what has been made . . ."[246]

242. Ibid., 77.
243. Ibid., 79.
244. Ibid.
245. Deut 4–7; 10:12–22.
246. Rom 1:20.

The heart of a true shepherd of God's people is based on the shepherd nature of God. God's chosen leaders are to know him intimately and follow his model of care in tending his flock on his behalf. Through the incarnation, Jesus further demonstrated the nature of the Creator God. Christ left a legacy of gracious servanthood for his people to emulate. Having leaders with Christ-like character qualities would be the ideal, but gentle and caring church leadership is far from the actual experience of many Christians. The ideals of New Testament beliefs and practices provide a foundation for a healthy model of Christian leadership. The present statistics of people leaving the institutional church, leaving Christian organizations, and leaving the house church movement, needs attention. Christians from a great variety of denominational backgrounds have left the local church or Christian mission or service organizations. Dictatorial excesses found in Christian leadership situations are a major reason for leaving. This research has also tapped into the disturbing factor of the aftermath of this type of leadership philosophy and behavior. This study lends a voice to the distress among God's people caused by this recurring situation.

The common concept of leadership, which can be found among many modern churches, is quite naturally based on power, control, and unquestioned submission to authority. This is in direct contrast to the concept of the Kingdom of God depicted in the New Testament Scriptures. In order for the Church to resemble the Kingdom of God, it is imperative that current notions of church power be drastically altered.[247] "An effective and comprehensive biblical theology of leadership must draw on the person and work of Christ, the nature and activity of the Trinity, and the way biblical figures were led by God to develop into effective coworkers with him."[248] The model of the Apostle Paul should also be considered. When it comes to leadership in the twenty-first century, it is important to engage in the skills of discernment in order "to sort out what is true and false, fitting and inappropriate, abstract and practice, timely and outdated."[249]

---

247. Gibbs and Bolger, *Emerging Churches*, 192.

248. Banks and Ledbetter, *Reviewing Leadership*, 93.

249. Ibid.

THE JOURNEY TOWARDS RESTORATION

In the Church today, there is a conflict between the ideal and the present reality. Many people have had distressing and demeaning encounters with authoritarian and controlling Christian leadership that creates severe personal anxiety and emotional pain. As a consequence, many leave their local fellowship. They go from enthusiastic and joyful voluntary participation in their local church to a state of deep emotional distress and disaffiliation. Sadly they are detached from their regular place of worship, service, and fellowship. Such devastation requires a path forward to stimulate spiritual restoration and renewed hope.

Spiritual recovery is multifaceted but understanding this process can be aided by eliciting common factors from completed questionnaires. A theology of restoration can be discerned as people have journeyed towards recovery. Individuals have had to pass through and reckon with specific issues in order to progress from a state of despair to one of spiritual and emotional harmony. Individuals who have suffered spiritual and emotional wounding have journeyed from that point of loss and weakness to a realm of spiritual health and strength; and thus have gone from a negative to a positive state. Necessary spiritual and emotional transitions[250] include the following:

1. Going from a state of grief to a state of comfort.

2. Going from a place of suffering to place of healing.

3. Going from a condition of disorder to a condition of order.

4. Going from a state of dismay and turmoil to a state of rest and hope.

It is only by the power of the Holy Spirit in the life of a Christian that comfort and hope can be renewed. As people reckon with the need for changes in their beliefs, their faith becomes stronger as their relationship with God grows. There appears to be no simple theological answer to pain; the only reasonable answer is a relationship with God in the midst of pain. A change in one's theology will result in a faith that changes from an ethical system to a relationship with God; from a faith based on the law to one being based on love.[251] In order to make this transition people

---

250. See Enroth's list of nine suggestions to aid recovery, chapter 2.

251. Cloud, *Changes That Heal*, 302.

have to replace works-based beliefs with a wholehearted acceptance of the grace-full message of the Gospel. Giving up on rules and developing a genuine relationship with the Father celebrates one's adopted status. When people can finally let go of the conventions that have kept things in check for so long they can realize that they are "poor in spirit" and are in need of a loving Father. This realization confirms what being adopted is all about.[252]

Regarding offenses perpetrated by church leaders, there is a need for those who have been emotionally and spiritually injured to progress through several phases. First, they must forgive those leaders. Next, they must begin to have compassion for those still leading, as well as for those still in the organization. Eventually they will seek out or accept opportunities to give voice to the experienced harm. In time, although guarded and discerning, those who have been harmed can often be restored to a peacefully supportive attitude towards worthy leaders.

Forgiveness is a spiritual discipline that believers need to understand and practice in order for restoration to be complete. Forgiveness is a spiritual responsibility that believers in Christ need to practice for their own spiritual well being. The model given for forgiveness is to "Forgive as the Lord forgave you."[253] Forgiveness can be granted as a result of a deeper understanding of the magnitude of God's grace in one's life. The act of forgiveness does not mean that spiritual pain is ignored or excused but that it is recognized and then let go.[254] Personal grief is a process in which the pain and confusion lessen over time as losses are continuously processed.

It is not possible to truly forgive another person from the heart until people allow themselves to feel the pain of what was lost. There is a caution against the idea that forgiveness is simply an act of the will. This demonstrates a lack in understanding the grieving process.[255] One must recognize that the process of forgiveness always involves grieving before letting go—whether you are the person giving forgiveness or asking for

252. Ibid., 302–3.

253. Eph 4:32; Col 3:13.

254. Matt 6:12, 14–15; Mark 11:25; Luke 11:4; Col 3:12–15.

255. Scazzero, *Emotionally Healthy Church*, 157.

it.[256] Although biblical grieving can feel as if it is only going to make things worse, in time, this process will lead to life.[257]

The following examples show three Old Testament characters who demonstrated a forgiving heart after experiencing a deep personal injury from someone close to them. After Jacob's willful offense against his brother Esau, he was forced to leave his home because of the intense anger of his brother. After many years, Jacob returned home with his family, his servants, and his herds—not knowing how he would be received or treated by his offended brother. He was greatly relieved by the reception and expression of forgiveness towards him by his twin brother: "But Esau ran to meet Jacob and embraced him; he threw his arms around his neck and kissed him. And they wept."[258] The past was forgiven and a chance to rebuild a broken relationship was now a possibility.

Joseph's unique situation demonstrates a timeless account of betrayal and the ultimate forgiveness of his offending brothers. The enduring story of Joseph provides insight, comfort, and the strength to forgive[259] to many as they consider his gracious words to his brothers after his agonizing personal losses because of them:

> Then Joseph said to his brothers, "Come close to me." When they had done so, he said, "I am your brother Joseph, the one you sold into Egypt! And now, do not be distressed and do not be angry with yourselves for selling me here, because it was to save lives that God sent me ahead of you. For two years now there has been famine in the land, and for the next five years there will not be plowing and reaping. But God sent me ahead of you to preserve for you a remnant on earth and to save your lives by a great deliverance. So then, it was not you who sent me here, but God. He made me father to Pharaoh, lord of his entire household and ruler of all Egypt."[260]

David, the son of Jesse, was enlisted by King Saul to be his personal servant. After the killing of Goliath, the people's joyful response to David

256. Ibid.

257. Ibid., 170.

258. Gen 33:4. This portrayal of forgiveness is reminiscent of the New Testament parable told by Jesus in Luke 15 of the father who demonstrated wholehearted acceptance and welcome of his wayward son after the son's season of rebellion and shameful living.

259. Gen 37–45.

260. Gen 45:4–8.

fostered envy in Saul's heart. Although it is human nature to associate and identify with those who win or succeed, this reflected back on Saul's prestige in the kingdom and he was negatively affected by the people's response after this national event. The jealously that raged in Saul's heart and the disturbing mental condition of the first king of Israel made the palace a place of intrigue rather than safety. David had to run for his life. He was faced with a dilemma that included how he would regard his father-in-law who was the head of state. David chose a righteous path, which included honor towards the king, God's chosen leader, and forgiveness for his repeated harmful actions.[261]

Christ exemplified forgiveness towards those who had participated in bringing about his unjust trial and crucifixion though he had done no wrong: "Jesus said, 'Father, forgive them, for they do not know what they are doing.'"[262] Forgiveness is available from God to his children and can be given by them to those who have offended and distressed them. This spiritual grace is accomplished by the empowerment of the Holy Spirit. Stephen, the Jerusalem church deacon, empowered by the Spirit, followed the example of his Lord. In the intensity of his hour of persecution by his countrymen, who were led by the religious leaders of Israel, he cried out: "Lord, do not hold this sin against them."[263] And with that cry, he died from the stoning—becoming the first martyr of the Christian Church.

Compassion prepares the way for forgiveness. A two-step process is suggested: first, a person remembers that Christ has forgiven them; then, the believer can choose to forgive others. "Healing starts when the bleeding stops."[264] "Compassion points to the possibility of forgiving the leader who does not measure up to what a leader should be ... Compassion says to let go ..."[265] Turning one's eyes upon Jesus and forgiving is the beginning of recovery.[266]

There is no doubt that it is difficult to forgive those who abuse.[267] One must remember that forgiveness is crucial to recovery. Forgiving

261. 1 Sam 24:10–12.

262. Luke 23:34.

263. Acts 7:60.

264. Farnsworth, *Wounded Workers*, 162.

265. Ibid.

266. Ibid.

267. In *Recovering from Churches*, 66, Enroth credits Peter Sommer, "High Pressure Christian Groups: The Broken Promise," unpublished paper, 1992, 2.

is a journey, sometimes a long one, and people may need some time before they get to the station of complete healing. The intriguing thing is that people are being healed en route. It has been said that forgiveness is for the benefit of those giving it, not for the benefit of those receiving it.[268] When genuine forgiveness is offered, a prisoner is set free. It is then discovered that the prisoner set free is the person who experienced the offense. Believers need to practice forgiveness in order for spiritual well-being to be restored. Forgiveness is based on the Lord's act of forgiveness of his children. Forgiveness is one of the core principles of the Christian faith that provides release and healing while walking through life in a broken world. Forgiveness can be encouraged and supported by a loving Christian community.

The shattered sense of community experienced by people creates a need to develop new and healthy relationships within vibrant believing communities. There is a need to examine the traditional role of the Church along with the new covenant text in order to restore a solid ecclesiological foundation. Christians need to work through their negative feelings of vulnerability, susceptibility, and defenselessness. By being biblically fortified, individuals can, over time, replace these weak sensitivities with biblical knowledge and spiritual vigor. By being listened to and affirmed by a sensitive confidant and eventually by being accepted and loved in a healthy community, individuals no longer remain in the place of being the victim of spiritual abuse.[269] For many, the road to recovery comes through others who have gone that way ahead of them.[270]

It can be recognized that recovery from spiritual abuse is similar to other kinds of victim recovery since deep healing usually occurs within and through relationships with others. People who have been deeply hurt tend to be angry loners and are committed to self-protection. For such people it is necessary to learn to trust and allow oneself to become vulnerable to others and to God. This underscores the need for relational

268. Ibid., 65.

269. Enroth, *Recovering from Churches*, 22. Enroth adds: "Christians who want to be helpful to those who have come out of abusive experiences must be sensitive, nonjudgmental, and accepting—even if they find it difficult to understand how something so bizarre could happen to another Christian."

270. Ibid. One of the individuals in Enroth's book stated their need this way: "What would help me in recovery is to talk to someone who is farther along in recovery than I am."

input.[271] People recovering from spiritual abuse have a deep fear of rejection, of not being accepted. Experiencing acceptance, whether in a small group or in a caring church, is often the beginning of their healing. "Grace is the beginning of our healing because it offers the one thing we need most: to be accepted without regard to whether we are acceptable. Grace stands for gift; it is the gift of being accepted before we become acceptable."[272]

Being involved in a caring community is one of the major contributing factors to healing and restoration for the majority of Christians. Many recovered Christians take steps to express acceptance towards others. Recognizing that healing is a process helps people to cope as well as to move towards spiritual and emotional restoration. People can minister to others from the vantage point of their own pain and recovery after they have been able to clarify their own experience. When believers in Christ continue to experience healing and emotional wellness, they will naturally find themselves helping others by using the wisdom that they have gained. There is opportunity for wounded healers[273] to come alongside and clarify the confusion of thoughts and feelings of others in distress, to help prepare the way for forgiveness, to discern dysfunctional realities, and to look for signs of hope.[274]

An Old Testament passage, which is instructive regarding the processing of personal heartache, is Psalm 142. The psalmist cries from the depth of his grief in his aloneness. By the end of the psalm he recognizes that after the Lord has set him free from his prison, he is able to praise God. Through this experience, he realizes that he has gone from being alone to discovering that the righteous community is there for him. The people there are able to mutually support one another. Going from grief and loneliness to praise towards God and then fellowship with community can become a common experience for many. These people can easily resonate with the experience of the psalmist.

---

271. This is another comment from one of the subjects in Enroth's book, *Recovering from Churches*, 67.

272. Ibid. See also Lewis B. Smedes, *Shame and Grace* (San Francisco: HarperCollins, 1993), 107–8.

273. Nouwen named one of his books *The Wounded Healer*. "In our own woundedness, we can become a source of life for others," cover.

274. Farnsworth, *Wounded Workers*, 164.

As many believers have been wounded through unhealthy leadership in their congregations, there is opportunity for them to find spiritual healing among those who have an understanding of their plight. The Apostle Paul conveys the theme of mutual comfort in the Second Epistle to the Corinthians, particularly 2 Corinthians 1:3–5:

> Praise be to the God and Father of our Lord Jesus Christ, the Father of compassion and the God of all comfort, who comforts us in all our troubles, so that we can comfort those in any trouble with the comfort we ourselves have received from God.[275]

The theme of mutual comfort through bearing one another's burdens can also be seen in Galatians 6:2: "Carry each other's burdens, and in this way you will fulfill the law of Christ." The resource and responsibility of the Church to minister comfort to those who have been wounded—with the same comfort that they experienced through their personal trials—can now be made available to those who have suffered spiritual abuse. It is important to be reminded of this spiritual truth: "The community of God's people owe their life together as a body to their common, lavish experience of the Spirit."[276] Therefore, the community of loving Christians who has experienced God's grace and his comfort in their various trials can be an available resource for others in their time of crisis. Churches that heal steward their corporate experience of suffering by taking what they have learned from their pain and extending it as an outstretched arm from God to the community around them.[277]

People, over time, replace their weak and undeveloped ability to discern with a heightened ability to discriminate and resist that which is theologically and emotionally unsound.[278] Many church leaders have not been intentional in the task of discipling Christians to discern truth from error and to distinguish valid biblical practice from that which is questionable. This has further resulted in Christians not understanding solid principles for biblical interpretation or developing appropriate skills for the hermeneutical task.[279] This lack of skill makes a person vulnerable to persuasive leaders with captivating teachings. Therefore, people

---

275. 2 Cor 1:3–4.

276. Fee, *Paul*, 66.

277. Murren, *Churches That Heal*, 251.

278. See chapter 2.

279. See Virkler, *Hermeneutics*, and Osborne, *Hermeneutical Spiral*.

need to hone these skills and feel confident to interpret the Scriptures for themselves. Fortified disciples are then able to compare their insights with those of other followers of Christ—this is an added protection and guard against weak and unorthodox beliefs and practices. This spiritual discipline is an indication of the common priesthood of believers.

Christians have a habit of leaving the interpretation of the Scriptures up to their leaders. Their trust in leadership is admirable, but blind trust combined with a lack of skills in discerning truth from error for oneself causes many to follow charismatic authoritarian and controlling leaders without question. Later they discover that they have been wrong to trust in this type of leadership practice. In the processing of their experience the need to repent before the Lord of this tendency is also acknowledged. Individuals must then reckon with the distressing reality of why they were effortlessly beguiled and so easily led. Many believers now see the value of emulating the Berean Christians. These followers of Christ were exemplified by Luke in the account in Acts since they made a diligent effort to verify that the Apostle Paul's message was, in fact, true by daily examining the text of Scripture.

> Now the Bereans were of more noble character than the Thessalonians, for they received the message with great eagerness and examined the Scriptures every day to see if what Paul said was true.[280]

Through the grieving and restoring process, spiritual weakness has gradually been replaced by spiritual strength, wisdom, and joy. "The grace-killing religious legalists and spiritual abusers in Galatia had tied up heavy religious loads and laid them on the shoulders of Paul's converts, destroying their joy."[281] Paul pointedly asks them, "What has happened to all your joy?"[282] Lack of joy in the Christian life is all too evident in many places. Jesus's promise of abundant life[283] is often not the experience of those where "grace and peace"[284] is neither preached nor practiced. Yet formerly wounded individuals can regain joy, grace,

---

280. Acts 17:11.

281. Blue, *Healing Spiritual Abuse*, 152.

282. Gal 4:15.

283. "I have come that they may have life, and have it to the full" (John 10:10b).

284. One of the Apostle Paul's recurring phrases in the salutation of his Epistles was "grace and peace" to the community of believers receiving his letters. The Apostle Peter also said: "Grace and peace be yours in abundance" (1 Pet 1:2; 2 Pet 1:2).

and peace. They will no longer crave comfort for their loss but will now be able to give it.

Theological reflection is a significant spiritual discipline that enables followers of Christ to grow and mature in their Christian faith. Healthy theological reflection helps Christians to discover that the road to restoration is really the road to experiencing greater grace in one's life. After events such as those just discussed, God's immeasurable grace now becomes a priority in the spiritual understanding of many. After experiencing disappointment, shattered dreams, and emotional stress, it is often quite astounding for people to recognize that their spiritual life has grown in a way that they could not have ever imagined if they had not had this upsetting, yet pivotal life experience.

Through the spiritual and emotional healing process the interpretation of the circumstances that brought about this distress can open doors to spiritual quickening in areas that were virtually hidden or undeveloped before this time. There is a keener ability to grasp spiritual truths and individuals begin to see where their previous biblical beliefs had not been fully formed. Their interest is in rectifying this debilitating condition. This awareness moves them forward in the healing process.

There is also an empathetic awareness among those of like experience. Although people have come from different places geographically, denominationally, or ethnically, they find that in the telling of their stories, they share renewed comprehension of spiritual truths—evidence of the renewal which has gradually happened in each of them over time. This convergence of relevant spiritual truths—which previously had been weak or undeveloped—can become the foundational material for newly reformed theological and ecclesiological understandings. There is a dawning recognition that their reworked ecclesiology has dispelled the fog of their former grievous situation and that they have been ushered into deeper realms of biblical and spiritual perceptions. At this point, many people are delighted to discover a growing number of opportunities to share and minister to others. Networking with others, the stirring up of buried skills, and the reaching out to others in need open new areas of service in the Kingdom of God.

One participant in this study, who also identified himself as a pastor who teaches and ministers to hurting people, shared this thought in one of his emails:

I speak and teach on this subject; it is very dear to my heart in the healing of God's children. Many, once healed, have a great deal more to offer the Kingdom of Heaven than they realize, as God uses their scars (experience), sacrificed to Him through their dedication, as He used His own scars for healing all mankind.[285]

Considering the complexity of this problem leads to the conclusion that there is a call for caring leaders who will engage and equip their congregations to effectively minister to those who arrive distressed at their fellowship doors. Christians need to understand this recurring situation and be available to those who have experienced wounding under the hands of authoritarian and controlling Christian leaders. Christian leaders need to meet the challenge of living faith-controlled lives. "If spirituality is more than unthinking legalism filled with shoulds and oughts and no joy, then someone must demonstrate the possibility of a joyful faith actually lived out."[286] If the priesthood of all believers is to become a reality, that ministry must start somewhere. Church leaders can make this ideal a reality by teaching and modeling it.[287] Leaders in local churches can provide leadership and facilitate the wide range of ministries exercised through the membership of the body.

Faulty beliefs, authoritarian leadership, and fractured community stand in the way of healthy spiritual formation and believers who have suffered from these distortions in their Christian faith need compassionate Christian helpers to untangle the many strands which have interconnected to choke emotional and spiritual harmony. Because of an unconscious and unprofitable habit of blending incomplete Old Testament and New Testament leadership concepts, many Christian groups need to retrace theological steps back to a valid biblical model of leadership in order to have renewed spiritual health and vigor. Those who have processed their personal grief need to be encouraged to go forward on their journey with Christ among a healthy Christian community. The following chapter will help to demonstrate what the participants in this study have gone through emotionally, what they have learned spiritually and intellectually, and how they have grown through this unsettling experience in many profitable ways.

285. Participant no. 20, email message to researcher, 2007.

286. Rice, *Pastor as Spiritual Guide*, 185.

287. Ibid.

4

What Does This Research Say?

WHAT DO THE PARTICIPANTS in this study have to say to the Church? What can be learned from their trial by fire? This chapter explains the design, the procedures, and the results of this ministry research project. The research question for this dissertation was: How have Christians recovered after experiencing perceived spiritual abuse in a local congregation?

Participants for this study were Christians who:

1. Experienced emotional and spiritual distress under authoritarian and controlling church leaders and who have ceased to be associated with those congregations.

2. Recognized and processed their spiritual grief and pain and experienced spiritual recovery.

3. Are willing and able to share how they processed and recovered from their negative experiences.

DESCRIPTION OF THE RESEARCH PROJECT

This research focused on Christians who exhibited Christian maturity and had regular and faithful church attendance. They had been involved in church ministry by helping to lead in ministry areas. The denominational streams that participants came from were Evangelical, Pentecostal, and Charismatic (EPC). The age range was between twenty and seventy-five years of age. Many of these individuals have reintegrated into a local church after their season of grief and disillusionment. Others have not reintegrated into a local church but have found ways to participate in Christian fellowship such as worship, sharing of Scripture, prayer, ministry to one another, and service in the surrounding community. Essentially, spiritual integrity has been reestablished in their lives.

A qualitative, open-ended questionnaire was developed to help assess each participant story and the facts involved in the situation in order to discern the major causes for each person's disillusionment and spiritual recovery. The minimum number of local participants required was ten; the final number was fifteen. Various reputable websites and blogs by people who frequently wrote about church issues were found. Participants were sought by posting the research topic with an appeal for participants on Internet websites. The minimum number required from Internet contacts was twenty; the final number was eighty-five. The insights gained from these participants have been compiled with the responses of the local participants in order to observe similarities in the accounts. These findings have been compared with what the literature has been indicating.

A second questionnaire was developed for pastors who had previously aided people who had experienced church distress. The minimum number of pastors needed was five; the total number participating was seven. The researcher attempted to avoid bias in designing the questionnaires, yet to totally exclude all bias is almost impossible.

The participants in this study brought a variety of experiences to consider. Biblical background, denominational background, spiritual maturity, age, length of time attending at their previous church, degree of involvement in previous church ministry, previous expectations of church leaders and church ministry, depth of personal injury, length of time they had been away from this particular fellowship, and other individual factors influenced the assessment process. People who responded from outside of North America came from similar denominational streams as those found in North America.

This study has not knowingly included congregants who had taken offense with a pastor regarding admonitions given while receiving spiritual guidance concerning moral failings, those who had taken offense at the ministry of godly discipline, or those who were antagonistic towards pastoral leadership without cause.

This study has not knowingly included congregants who have tried to generate heretical teachings contrary to the Gospel of Christ, who have been warned by leadership about this behavior, then have taken offense, and left. Paul's admonition to Titus was to warn those who were divisive and then have nothing further to do with them.[1] Paul further amplifies this thought when writing the Roman believers:

> I urge you, brothers, to watch out for those who cause divisions and put obstacles in your way that are contrary to the teaching you have learned. Keep away from them. For such people are not serving our Lord Christ, but their own appetites. By smooth talk and flattery they deceive the minds of naïve people.[2]

Although the term "divisive" may include people who oppose church leadership for any reason, using this term to describe those who have a difference of opinion with church leadership goes beyond the correct use of the term when dealing with general church issues and does not refer to those involved in this study.

This study has not dealt with every type of abusive hierarchical leadership structure or aberrant teaching that may be influencing church communities. This study has been selective and has tried to ascertain the main themes and trends that bring negative affects to the church and its attendees. It endeavored to find the elements which best aid individuals in the essential spiritual process of recovery.

Although individuals may perceive legitimate forms of spiritual direction at times as abuse, this is not the spiritual abuse that has been detected or will be addressed. This study will also provide preventative and constructive insights into the damaging affects of authoritarian and controlling leaders in order to recognize the harmful affects earlier on by denominational overseers, church consultants, and church networking or ministerial groups. This tool is a resource that can be adapted and adjusted as people with these needs identify themselves to church leadership.

ANALYSIS OF THE SURVEYS

As a researcher, I appreciated being allowed into an important yet personal area of people's spiritual journey—their emotional experience of church life. This was akin to being invited into each participant's living room. I have appreciated this unique opportunity to get to know people in this intimate way. As stated in chapter 1, since the author is not a

1. Titus 3:10.
2. Rom 16:17.

pastor, the insights given from the other side of the pulpit may have a distinct advantage in researching this rather sensitive topic.

When the completed surveys began to appear there was a need to remain objective in light of the many disheartening stories that were arriving via email over the period of many weeks. Although information was given mainly by a stranger to a researcher, the data still drew the researcher into a unique understanding of each participant's individual pain.

This study was based on self-report. No attempt has been made to hear the "other side" of the story. Although some may point out that the researcher did not check into the other side of the story and maybe some of these findings may appear to be unfair, the fact remains that this situation happened to this single person or to this married couple. This is how they perceived their circumstance, and eventually, this is how they recovered.

The questions in this survey were thoughtfully answered. The participants were articulate in narrating their experience. Some participants were concise while others crafted a longer response. The participant contributions showed that people had reflected on the issue with interest and intensity; that they were well informed about the issues through reading books and reading/interacting on the Internet; that they had compared ideas with a spouse, family, and friends; and that they were proactive in finding answers for themselves. The analysis procedure was qualitative—descriptive content in returned questionnaires was analyzed paying attention to categories and themes. Trends were recognized and recommendations made.

There were more than one hundred and ten people who took the time to complete a questionnaire.[3] One hundred participants, including forty-two men and fifty-eight women, fully fit the criteria. This represents ninety-eight stories regarding incidents which took place in the participant's home church and two stories which represent similar treatment by leadership of those involved in ministry in two separate parachurch organizations.

3. Although there were those who responded but could not be included in the final number because they did not fully fit the criteria, there were many elements which did fit the participant profile; the main one being that they were involved in a distressing situation with church leadership. Even though they did not qualify for the survey, they are still recognized as a valid number of people who are affected by this church malady and who had responded to this study.

The participants were from ten countries, including three expatriates who lived in three Middle Eastern countries.[4] The following are the countries where the participants were located: Canada[5] (twenty-five), United States[6] (sixty-four), United Kingdom (two), New Zealand (two), Australia (two), Malaysia (one), Philippines (one), Israel (one), Iraq (one), and Oman (one).

The age breakdown is as follows:

Age	20	30	40	50	60	70
	7	15	36	32	7	3

The primary age group was age forty to forty-nine, with the second group being the fifty to fifty-nine age range. Those representing the forty to fifty-nine age range compiled sixty-eight participants.

The following are the main categories used for analysis of the participant surveys, which include both quantitative and qualitative factors.

1. Participants were asked the length of time that they attended their previous home church, their ministry areas, their date of exiting, how long ago they left, the church Sunday attendance size, and the geographic location of the church (urban to rural). People's marital status was not one of the questions, but as participants described their situation, this factor was also discerned and added into the data.

2. Participants were asked what factors influenced their decision to leave their home church.

3. Participants were asked how these circumstances impacted them emotionally, how they coped, and how they processed their positive and negative emotions.

4. Participants were asked if they had learned anything from this experience and whether they felt that God had used this situation to mature them in their faith.

5. Participants were asked to describe what specific helps aided in their spiritual recovery.

4. The nationalities of the three expatriates were two American and one Canadian.
5. Four provinces.
6. Twenty-four states.

6. Participants were asked if they had found a church that they could call "home" and what criteria they now have for finding a church home.

7. Participants were asked if they felt personally disillusioned with their former church group and what advice they would give to others who find themselves in a similar circumstance.

8. Participants were asked if they had any shifts in their beliefs and if their view of God or his Word had been affected. They were asked if they felt that they were Pentecostal or Charismatic in experience. In the final question participants were asked to describe their journey with Christ today.

The following is the detailed quantitative and qualitative analysis of this project using these eight organizing categories.

Category 1

Participants were asked the length of time that they attended their previous home church, their ministry areas, the date of exiting, and how long ago they left, the church Sunday attendance size, and the geographic location of the church (urban to rural). (Question nos. 2–5.)

Attendance of the participants at the offending church was divided into five-year groupings. Those attending one to five years was thirty-seven. Those attending six to ten years was thirty. Those attending eleven to fifteen years was thirteen, along with thirteen who attended their church for over sixteen years. There were seven who indicated that they had attended their home church for over twenty-five years, with the longest attendance at one home church being forty-two years. See Figure 1.

A number of people recorded that they had attended two or three different churches with similar negative outcomes.[7] The number of those

---

7. A question may arise about people who have attended two or three churches. Could this indicate that these people may be predisposed to feel abused, which may indicate a personal problem rather than a systemic church/leadership problem? First, if a few people have had prior hurts and/or family dysfunction and may be predisposed to unhealthy thinking and behavior, isn't their need to be in a place that is safe, where they can hear the Word, and where they can grow in community even greater? Is the church helping to meet an emotional and relational need among these folk and allow the Holy Spirit to heal/transform them over time or are some in leadership using/abusing such people and making their situation so much worse—devastating, in fact? This seems to be the case. It comes down to the primary issue—abuse by church leadership—

FIGURE 1: Years of Attendance

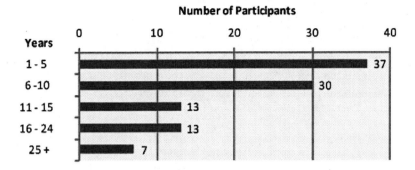

who attended two churches was ten. The number who attended three churches was four and one person indicated that they had attended five churches within the same denomination that generated similar problems. This makes a total of fifteen who attended two or more abusive churches. If people attended two or more churches, the attendance at the one with the greater number of years was counted.

The following are the decades in which these participants exited from their local church. For those who attended more than one church, the most recent church was noted.

2000–2008	65
1990–1999	20
1980–1989	12
1970–1979	3

Since the year 2000 (to 2007), there were sixty-five people who indicated leaving their previous and offending church. Christians who left their home church between the years of 2000–2005 were thirty-seven.

---

whatever the degree of vulnerability that people find themselves in. Second, is it the people who act in patterned ways that generate a response they consider abusive or is it those in church leadership who initiate the disconcerting patterned behavior that ends in devastating the people? Again, the author would like to point out that these participants were regular attenders and were involved in the serving and ministry of their churches. How could these people be in positions of leadership and even be on core leadership teams if they appeared to be so emotionally disconnected? Would this not reflect poorly on the ministry of that church or the denomination if the dedicated, long-attending congregants were so inclined?

Christians who left their local church between the years of 2006–2007, including one in January 2008, totaled twenty-eight.

Questions did not ask about people's marital status, but if participants mentioned this, it was added into the data. The number of participants in the final count was one hundred. Adding to that number was the spouse number[8] of approximately sixty-eight people, which represents a total of about 168 people who were significantly affected.

100	Total Participants
+ 68	Spouse Number (approx.)
168	Total Number Affected

Other members of a family and/or close friends are also part of the number of those significantly adversely affected. Here is one participant comment that uniquely demonstrates this:

> I confided in my husband, who also suffered, my father and a friend who endured worse than I at the hands of this leader. It was life saving to hear others that knew me and loved me say that I was not losing my mind.[9]

The church size demonstrated that most people attend churches in the 60–150 or the 151 to 300 Sunday attendance size. The number attending churches of 60 to 150 was twenty-nine and the number attending churches of 151 to 300 was twenty-two. These two sizes tallied to fifty-one. The church size of 301–600 had twenty-four; the church size of 601–1,000 had ten; the church size of 1,001–2,000 had four; and a church size of above 2,000 had five.[10] A few people indicated that they attended a church smaller in number than sixty.[11] This participant number was six. See Figure 2.

8. The marital status of each participant was not one of the questions on the survey. For this reason, this figure is approximate. It was observed that participants commented on their spouse regarding the same church situation. This confirmed that this participant's comments represented a couple's experience.

9. Participant no. 84.

10. If participants attended two or more churches the most recent church size/location was noted.

11. A question may arise if there is greater potential for abuse among groups that have sixty members or less. There may be an assumption that people who attend churches under sixty people might be prone to leadership control and abuse, yet there

FIGURE 2: Size of Churches

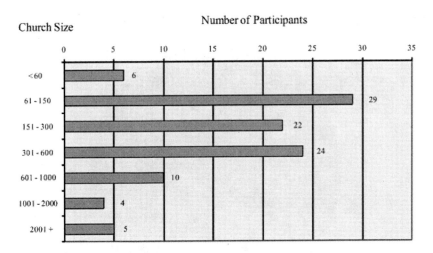

There were five geographical designations for the location of one's church. These were: urban, suburban, town, village, and rural. The majority of participants—forty-one—went to suburban churches, followed by urban churches (twenty-five); town (twenty-five); rural (eight); and village (one).[12] See Figure 3.

Adding the total number of participant years of devoted service revealed that there had been a significant investment of time, money, and energy by all of these participants in each of their home churches. Regrettably this investment turned out to be disappointing; it resulted in personal pain, and amounted to great loss all around in the Kingdom of God. As previously noted, the number of those participating in this study, about one hundred, along with adding in the spouse number of approximately sixty-eight people, represents about 168 people affected. This number does not include the number of children and teenagers affected when parents are put in a position of having to leave their home church. The stress and emotional fallout directly affects children and

---

does not appear to be enough data to clearly state this as fact. Some participants felt that house churches were problematic and would allow for authoritarian leadership behaviors. Others were quite content to promote house churches. There may be a tendency for some smaller churches with minimum networking to become ingrown. The issue goes back to the leadership of these groups. Is the leadership healthy or not? Is the corporate expectation of this church healthy or not?

12. Note that these geographic designations are approximate.

Figure 3: Church Location

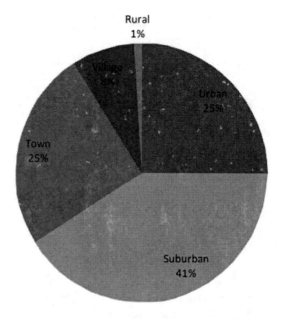

youth. It is assumed that other family members were impacted as well as the participant's friends and acquaintances.

When people are distressed by what is going on in their home church, it is likely that they are impaired in ministry to others, and efforts to share the Gospel may also be reduced or curtailed altogether. There is no doubt that people's daily workload is also affected by emotional turmoil, as is the overall health of those involved. Indeed, stress takes a toll on the physical body.[13] Related factors of stress and grief create recurring affects in the body. During times of grief, people's vitality is sapped and their energies are only involved in the minimum essentials of life. People often need medications and/or time off from work in order to cope with stressful situations. Some married couples find mutual comfort in sharing their positive and negative feelings with each other. For others the stress level is raised in the home as partners rehearse their perception of the pain of their situation. Couples and their children are

---

13. The researcher had occasion to discuss the topic of this doctoral research with two local medical doctors who confirmed that this factor has been observable in their practice. This has also been confirmed by the comments of the participants in the questionnaire. Cudmore's research, "Victim Suffering," supports this observation as well.

directly affected by the elevated stress levels in the home. The related implications for such a stressful condition are multiple.

Category 2

Participants were asked what factors influenced their decision to leave their home church. (Question no. 6.)

Participants described a number of reasons for leaving their home church. The main reason for leaving their local fellowship revolved around authoritarian and controlling pastors and/or the leadership team. The following are the common terms and themes that were recorded by participants. Thirty-two participants used the following terms to describe the leadership style at the church that they left: authoritarian, controlling, manipulation, and abusive.

There were twelve people who were asked to leave their church by the pastor and/or the leadership team. Since these participants had been deemed as regular attenders, fairly mature in their faith, involved in voluntary service in the church, the notion that they were excommunicated because of some moral sin is not reasonable to consider. Another factor that influenced people to leave was the fact that they perceived that the leader seemed to be accountable to no one (four).

Selected excerpts from the participant questionnaires will be included in each category to illustrate the point. Comments have been edited only for the purposes of clarity, spelling, punctuation, and spacing. The following participant comments describe the reasons why they left their home church:

> Yes. There was a tremendous dichotomy between what was said by leadership, and the message they actually conveyed. They often spoke of the freedom we have as believers, as well as our individual value in God's eyes. But any attempt to think or act with any degree of freedom was quickly and firmly labeled as unsubmissiveness to leadership. An overarching theme in most of the subtle messages was that only a few were actually spiritual enough to hear and follow God for themselves, and that everyone else must follow them.[14]

> The main problem stemmed from the fact that the leader was not submitted to anyone and yet wanted submission. His doctrine

14. Participant no. 7.

was off and his tactics were abusive and the church showed no fruit.[15]

It was clear that the pastor was never going to address any problems: present or future. . . . I was told that the Lord spoke to my pastor, so if I disagreed, I was in error.[16]

Deception, manipulation by a pastor who was absolutely accountable to no person. . . . Negative feelings were mostly the fact that there was nothing we could do to stop the misbehavior of the pastor, and the natural feelings of failure in such a situation. We had invested greatly in this congregation. It was also hard to understand how people in leadership positions could "put up" and even enable this kind of behavior by the pastor. . . . Leadership and authority exercised by one person in a congregation is not only unbiblical, but is inherently abusive and destructive.[17]

Previously I was taught I must not speak against a leader, either to voice concerns or disagree—that was the teaching, "Touch not the Lord's anointed," you were not allowed to say anything that didn't agree with the leader.[18]

He [the pastor] had left such a trail of hurting and damaged people, and I felt that I could no longer be a part of that type of destruction.[19]

We were falsely accused by the senior pastor of being rebellious and unsubmitted. . . . The church that we left is still being destroyed by authoritarian leadership, control, and abuse. It was a wonderful community of people that was ruined by false spiritual leadership.[20]

I learned that if a man is truly led to be the shepherd of a group of believers that he will be in among them and teach truth from his heart and not be a controlling, manipulating, and dominating person—lording his position over them.[21]

15. Participant no. 1. Similar comment by no. 26 of leadership control and no accountability.

16. From this point on, "participant" will be assumed, thus, no. 76.

17. No. 77.

18. No. 81.

19. No. 82.

20. No. 16.

21. No. 30.

We had felt like something was wrong over the years, but always "stuffed it" thinking it was "just us." Whenever we went to the pastor with grievances, it was denied or turned around on us. We finally realized that we had major doctrinal differences (they taught a harsh gospel lacking grace and mercy), along with the fact that we felt stifled, controlled, and intimidated. . . .

Yes. I believed so much of what they said. I towed the lines they put up. You need to understand something: these people (the leaders) were my life. I took care of their children for them. I put my own interests last and served them for years. I made it possible both physically and financially for them to exist. As far as the rest of the group, I really thought they would know our hearts and at least come to talk. Only one couple did.[22]

Our eyes were opened to seeing that our church was run by a manipulative and oppressively controlling pastor who had just enough charisma and mountain charm to bamboozle the masses into believing and following him as "God's anointed," appointed for this church and the surrounding area of the county. Adding to his ruling hand is an Elder Board of "Yes Men" of which the pastor was chairman.[23]

The following are six accounts of those who were asked to leave by their church leadership. Some of them made an effort to meet and communicate with the leadership and seek some type of understanding and/or resolve.

Couple 1 (This couple had been involved and served at this church for seven years.)

When I declined the opportunity from the pastor to be on staff my husband and I sensed a change in relationships from the pastor and staff members. We were no longer invited to social functions with the staff. I no longer received support in the church sponsored ministry work I was doing. Staff hindered opportunities for me to serve in other areas of the church. I stopped attending church sponsored events outside of the Sunday service because I did not feel welcome. I approached the pastor's wife and explained the events that were happening and feelings of not belonging and the pastor's wife said, "at the risk of further alienating you, maybe you should leave the church." My husband and I

22. No. 10.
23. No. 84.

experienced passive aggressive behavior toward us and our work in the home group we were leading.

Meeting with the pastor to discuss issues was nonproductive, passive aggressive, overly authoritative, and extremely controlling. I began to notice that the size of the church congregation had dropped from one thousand to six hundred in the past seven years. I discreetly sought out a few people who had left the church and learned of the same root causes as to why they left.[24]

Couple 2 (This couple was involved and served in this church for over ten years.)

After the first excommunication we applied to the courts to have our membership reinstated—the elders immediately agreed to the mediation we had originally requested. The Christian mediator found the elders at fault and had our membership reinstated—a process that took six months due to delays by the elders. Although the elders apologized in writing we were subjected to shunning and stalking by the elders and most ministry leaders. We were put under incredible pressure to leave.

Six months after returning we were once again excommunicated—virtually no reason given for the decision other than we seemed to make the leadership uncomfortable. Although the church membership held meetings to discuss our situation we were not allowed to attend to defend ourselves.[25]

Couple 3 (This couple was involved and served in their church for fifteen years. They were involved in this denomination for sixty-seven years.)

We were asked to leave by leadership. . . . I was charged for having a hard heart, by someone. My first response was to go to the Lord to check from Scripture what that means. . . . After I did a lot of soul searching before the Lord, I knew that the accusation was not true because the Scripture seems to indicate that when someone's heart becomes hard they cannot turn to God, and that was not my experience, but it took several days for me to come to that realization.[26]

Couple 4 (This couple was involved and served in this church for over ten years.)

24. No. 46.
25. No. 35.
26. No. 65.

> The hireling [the pastor] telling us to get out was why we left—we were so into the cult that we were trying to stay after all of the abuse we suffered. We were trying to communicate our problems with him and his wife, and their treatment of my wife and I, when the end came.[27]

Couple 5 (This couple attended this church for one year and six months.)

> The first church was totally under the control of the pastor and when we became aware of the lack of accountability, we spoke with the pastor, who kicked us out for questioning him.[28]

A single person (This person attended this church for eighteen years and was involved in the core ministry leadership of the church. The participant describes their response to a comment made by the pastor.)

> "You must be 100 percent loyal to the Senior Pastor or you can't be in leadership. I'm cleaning house—you must be enthusiastic about the church. You are not enthusiastic or happy and everybody knows it. I'm going to have to ask you to leave [the church]." I was totally devastated, spinning in confusion and disbelief.[29]

Twelve participants referenced legalism as their reason for leaving. Other reasons included: public rebuke, shunning, or being falsely accused (five); private rebuke by leadership in the church office or a home (three); or extreme church discipline (two). Questionable doctrines and beliefs that were deemed unhealthy were reasons given by nine.

The following are some of the descriptions given by the participants on this topic:

> Legalism, discipleship over evangelism, family of believers over "unsaved/un-churched/lost," Sunday attendance and tithing pressures and judgment, kept too busy doing things for the church to live much as a Christ follower among my neighbors, *most of all:* Lack of focus on the cross of Jesus Christ and prayer.[30]

> The leadership had become cult-like in its leadership. Two or three men, including the preacher, decided what happened in the lives of everyone else; this included who one could marry, wheth-

27. No. 30.

28. No. 95.

29. No. 17.

30. No. 15.

er one could look for another job and, if offered one, whether one could take it, whether one could buy a house, etc. The teaching on submission to authority was taken to ridiculous extremes.[31]

After the following participant had left, they described their thinking this way:

I viewed every decision and action through that legalistic lens. Realized I had a hard time thinking and making decisions on my own. Lost quite a few "friends" who ceased to associate with me once they realized I wasn't of the same ilk any more. I was free to think and yet at the same time, afraid to do so.[32]

A number of people defined the concept of carnal treatment of God's people by the lead pastor or church leadership (twelve). (This often influenced the shunning behavior of the congregants towards the participant.) Some commented on the pastor or the leadership's lack of integrity (five). Others noted either the pastor's impropriety (two) or the pastor's outright moral failure (two).

Gender hierarchy was a factor for men and women alike. A lack of biblical understanding of the place of women in the Church and women treated without respect was evident for a number (nine).

The following are examples of how participants perceived this issue:

First church held that women had to be submitted to the overseeing of men in anything they did. Even held that a woman had to check with a man to see if what she believed was correct. Second church was not that extreme. However, women's input was not welcomed.[33]

Women were not allowed to serve in areas where they felt called to serve. In this particular church women were not even allowed to read Scripture from the pulpit during the Sunday morning worship service.[34]

The following are a few comments from those who felt that they had to leave a position or were asked to leave (were fired) from a church

31. No. 39.
32. No. 74.
33. No. 23.
34. No. 24.

position (seven), or those who found no room to use their gifting in service (four).

> I got fired from the Assistant Pastor position for questioning the authority. Hardest part, for me, was to forgive myself for being duped by a pastor who I should have seen through much earlier on in the fourteen years I spent under his ministry. Second part of the pain was working through my anger with God at letting it happen to all the wonderful people who had dedicated their lives to such spiritual fraud.[35]

> The Senior Pastor while able to be quite charming to the congregation and others in the community, was emotionally abusive to his staff in general and had become increasingly abusive to me my last year on staff. The dynamics in the office were often hard for me to understand, but in the last months working there I saw the Senior Pastor's behavior as deceptive, grandiose, and highly manipulative . . . It was the denomination on the district and even national level that we believed could have come to our aid, but they chose to ignore the situation. Their behavior leads one to conclude that they don't believe a pastor should be held accountable by a lay person because they were upholding and employing a pastor who sued a parishioner for taking a concern in private to the elders.[36]

> The realization that there was no hope for most of us in ever following what God put in our heart; the fatigue with lots of hype but no real change; the growing disillusionment with the traditional church pattern; and the realization that it had little connection to the life that Jesus and his followers exhibited.[37]

Disagreement with the pastor or the church leadership regarding church governance was commented on by five participants. The fact that there was no dispute resolution process in place was noted by four. Although the term "elitism" was referenced only once to refer to leadership, this descriptor could be validated by similar terms used.

> I was disappointed with the leadership because I perceived that I did not get a fair hearing and opportunity to dialogue. I went into meetings where decisions had already been made and any listening was really only waiting for their turn to lower the boom. My

35. No. 20.
36. No. 55.
37. No. 7.

hope had been that as a minimum, we would clarify our differing
views and come to an understanding of each other's positions before agreeing to disagree, accommodating each other, and getting
on with ministry. If the views were differing enough, we could
painfully, but at least amiably, separate. Unfortunately, the leaders
just couldn't survive the "fog" of life, differing ideas, and had to
believe they had God's will and as such had to stick up for God by
booting us out the door.[38]

Those disillusioned with all organized religion or the institutional
church, not just their particular church or denomination, was referenced
by two.

Based upon the surveys, these participants indicated that they
had come from churches with a significant level of authoritarian and
controlling behavior from the lead pastor and/or the leadership team.
This leadership style was the expected ministry style and seemed to
go unquestioned among the congregation until a certain point, which
involved these congregants. After this point, for many of these participants, this accepted behavior took on greater vigor and simply got
worse. Participants were faced with the realization that any hope of
change in behavior or restoration of fellowship was unattainable at this
time, if ever.

Legalism was another main reason for leaving. An apparent faulty
view of the grace of God provided grounds for leaders to place heavy
loads or theological burdens on people. This corruption of the Gospel
of grace placed participants in a vulnerable position to be manipulated
by leaders.[39] Public or private rebuke, shunning, or being falsely accused
by leadership in the church office or a home seemed to be a form of
extreme church discipline to intimidate congregants and seemed to be
unwarranted in nearly every case. Furthermore, the entire concept of
biblical church discipline seemed to be a topic that was misunderstood
and misapplied and needed to be revisited by the local church as well as
by denominational overseers.

38. No. 98.

39. The idea of "manipulation" by a pastor among a group of congregants may at
first appear to be a rather extreme designation. Unfortunately, the participants in this
study have found this to be the case. It is a negative practice among other negative
behaviors that has been identified and it seems to be one of the ways some pastors have
regrettably handled their flocks.

The mar factors referenced in chapter 3, which had been recognized in the majority of participants, demonstrated that these damaging teachings and the hurtful actions manifested by church leaders were evident among them at that time. It pointed to the fact that participants were lacking a secure and reliable theological foundation. Distortions in understanding the Christian faith included the following: not fully understanding salvation and sanctification by the Holy Spirit by grace; having poorly developed skills for interpreting God's Word; inability to fully discern whether teachings were biblical truth or not; blindly trusting leadership without exercising discernment; not fully grasping how God's people actually should be treated by Christian leadership; and not fully understanding how to experience authentic Christian community. Specific areas of Christian belief are often distorted in abused people—these misbeliefs need to be discerned and set straight so that their spiritual life can be restored. The distortions in these basic beliefs and the personal impairment they created were evident among the majority of participants. A renewed biblical understanding in these areas helped people to be restored and to establish balance in their spiritual walk.

Category 3

Participants were asked how these circumstances impacted them emotionally, how they coped, how they processed their positive and negative emotions, and if they considered leaving the Church. (Question nos. 7–10.)

1. The following are insights into how people coped after making the decision to leave (Question no. 7):

    We found it a massive relief, but also a hugely traumatic experience. Our connections to the church meant we weren't sure how to process our various feelings. Ultimately though we knew it was for our good that we got out.[40]

    In some ways [we coped] well. In other ways, leaving a missionary position, in a place you have waited five years to get to, was very difficult. It made us question everything we believed about ourselves, our calling, how God was using us. It brought everything we had done to get to [the mission field] into question. Did we miss God in the midst of things? Did we make our

---

40. No. 59.

own way instead of God's way? We both went into a level of depression and rejection during the aftermath of that time. We both needed time away from all work and ministry in order to get our lives back on track. Our coping became getting through each day with a hope for future missions work.[41]

By the second church, I was resigned that this was just the way things are when you leave the church. When you're in there, you're like family, but it's an illusion, and a shallow one. The illusion will shatter once you leave the confines of the church building and system. Then you realize you don't really have anyone.[42]

2. The participants were asked to describe some of the positive and negative feelings they experienced during their time of exiting from their home church. (Question no. 8.) The following captures some of the pervading negative emotions experienced by participants during this time.

The descriptive words used by the participants are in related groupings:

1. Anger—at pastor, at self, at God; upset; resentment; bitterness; betrayal (forty-three).

2. Disillusioned; devastating; disappointment; shock; disbelief (twenty-nine).

3. Grief; pain; cried a lot; soul bleeding (twenty-eight).

4. Isolated; loneliness; disconnected (eighteen).

5. Guilt for not sharing reasons for leaving; sense of shame/condemnation (sixteen).

6. Abused; taken advantage of; hurt; wounded (fifteen).

7. Depression (fourteen).

8. Rejection; abandonment; not accepted; ostracized (fourteen).

9. Confusion; anxiety; conflicting acceptance/rejection of church people (thirteen).

41. No. 60.
42. No. 88.

10. Hard to trust other church leaders in the future (nine).

11. Helplessness; powerlessness to do anything (eight).

12. Embarrassed; aghast at one's thinking; remorse; despair; humiliated (seven).

13. Sorrow for those left behind (five).

14. Loss of community (four).

15. Thought I was/we were going crazy (three).

16. Felt betrayed by those still attending; awkward; frustrated with family or friends still there (three).

17. Feeling like my arms had been ripped off and I was bleeding constantly; feeling post traumatic shock; nightmares (three).

18. Regretted the waste of those years (three).

19. Keeping quiet; the "no talk"/silence stance made it appear that there was something to hide (two).

20. Anguish regarding the decision to leave and the affect on children and extended family (one).

21. Desperation for an answer to the problems that the Church is facing (one).

22. Some who had been abused as children found that leadership abuse hooked into old wounds (making them feel helpless) (one).

The following are some of the positive emotions and insights described by participants during and after their time of exiting from their home church:

1. Relief; release; burdens lifted; starting fresh (twenty-seven).

2. Freedom; freedom to now choose; escape; exiting was a positive thing (twenty).

3. A deepening experience of Christ; trust in God; have grown spiritually (thirteen).

4. Recognizing others who have had the same church experience brought joy, comfort, peace, hope—they felt that they were not alone (ten).

5. Now thinking theologically (nine).

6. After leaving it was easier to forgive; no feelings of anger or bitterness (four).

7. Realized that they were not crazy, backslidden, or rebellious (three).

8. New friends; new community (three).

9. Purified by fire—felt closer to some of the Bible characters (one).

10. Felt empowered when others heard their story (one).

11. Growing self-confidence and sense of well-being (one).

12. Wholeness (one).

13. Hope (one).

3. The following comments are examples of answers given to the question: How did you process the negative and positive feelings after you left? (Question no. 9.)

> I spent months going over things, over and over and over, trying to figure out how they went wrong, what we could have done differently, examining my own heart, trying to see if I was blind to the things they accused me of. That basically led me to a search to understand how and why something like this could happen. I began reading a lot about systemic, governmental, and relational issues in church, especially things related to the use and misuse of authority by leadership. Being able to understand what was wrong about our situation helped me to accept and deal with it.[43]

> At times it was very painful, but I found that pain would drive me deeper into Father's arms, where I would find His love and His peace which resulted in transformation (rather than conformity to principles or rules).[44]

43. No. 16.
44. No. 5.

I believe that God also showed me very clearly that it was not my job to change the system or the mindset of those in it. I was also able to see that even the leaders were victims who were trapped worse than we were. By the grace of God alone, I was able to start having compassion for them.[45]

4. In Question no. 10, participants were asked to mark an "X" beside each of the following actions that they considered relevant to them after their negative church experience. These included: not going to church at all; not going to church for a period of time; going to a house church; going to another fellowship context; or other.

The responses were as follows. The initial reaction of over half of the participants was that not going to church at all was a reasonable option (51 percent). Half also felt that they would not attend any church for a period of time (50 percent). Some got involved in a house church as a reasonable alternative (30 percent) while the majority answered that over time they got involved in another Christian church context (59 percent). There were a variety of answers under "other": helped a friend start a ministry; started our own church; changed denomination; fellowship with other believers; got involved in an Emergent Church; found other places to minister; used websites; got involved in a small women's group; did not want to be associated with organized church.

A few participants added comments to this question. Here are two comments:

> I am currently part of a launch team for a church plant. Currently I am meeting in a home.[46]

> I go to a house church every other Sunday at a friend's home. It is more of a Bible study group and does not function in other churchy ways, except we do have communion together at times. I appreciate this the most.[47]

The level of emotional turmoil described by participants was great. The high trust level among congregants towards their pastor and leadership team, and that this trust had been dishonored, was a primary issue

45. No. 7.

46. No. 26.

47. No. 27.

that deeply wounded the majority of people. The fact that the participants were loyal and active in this church yet were now emotionally and physically disconnected, as well as abruptly and apparently unjustly disfellowshiped, added to the depth of distress.

Going from active involvement, with hearts and minds fully committed to supporting the goals of this church and being willingly submitted to the leadership, these participants abruptly experienced disconnection and turmoil. This realization shocks one's core belief of the local church being a microcosm of the Kingdom of God on earth.

It is therefore not surprising that some of the participants prefer not to be connected with the institutional church. Others, although reconnected, hesitate to be as committed as they had been in the past. Many are in a hopeful, yet somewhat of a holding pattern as they take on a *wait and see* stance. For a majority, there has been fairly quick reintegration into a healthy community, yet the lessons learned provide a significant reference point for present and future ecclesiological reflection.

Category 4

Participants were asked if they had learned anything from this experience and, if so, what, and did they feel that God had used this situation to mature them in their faith? (Question nos. 12 and 17.)

Participants felt that they had learned much through this unique experience. Participants gained a keen sensitivity surrounding ecclesiological issues. Many participants were professionals and/or had graduate degrees. This harmful church experience propelled a number to seek biblical and theological training in some way. They were motivated to go to seminary, Bible college, or take courses at various institutions. A number of women and men were taking courses or had completed a Master of Divinity or other master's degree, such as counseling. Two women felt called to complete a Doctor of Ministry degree. One man already had a doctoral degree in science. In reflection upon his church situation he identified the fact that a number of people in his church had attained a PhD degree. Unlike a biblical and theological degree, this degree level did not prevent them from seeing the theological weaknesses and discerning their church leadership situation with clarity. The overall education level of the participants in this study has been noted.

Reflecting on and researching the issues that had directly affected them heightened their ability to articulate their observations of the situation. Participants concisely described what they had learned through their experience. The main themes recognized by participants were: godly leadership, biblical community, spiritual growth, the need for discernment, being proactive around abusive situations, giving and receiving forgiveness, and recognizing the depth and intensity of this learning context. Salient comments will be included in each of the following groupings.

1. What people had learned regarding leadership includes: the role and task of pastors; the heart and integrity of a leader; the need for healthy leaders; being aware of hurtful and unprofitable practices in leadership; the need for healthier leadership models; the need to guard the flock against heresy; and the need for help from governing and denominational oversight. Twenty-two participants commented on these leadership issues.

   There is tremendous potential for abuse in the church. Church leaders who have no accountability are very dangerous and should be avoided. It is my responsibility to act, if I encounter leaders who are abusive.[48]

   That many people shouldn't be pastors, but are. That you can't expect people older than you (even older in the Lord) to necessarily be more spiritually mature.[49]

   Pastors who profess love for the brotherhood are not necessarily sincere. Friendships based on a forced association do not last when a crisis occurs.[50]

   A better understanding for what godly leadership looks like. Because I am a leader, and I have seen some really bad ways of discipleship, I have had to go on a search to answer the question: So, what does real godly leadership look like? What does godly correction in love look like?[51]

   Yes, I learned that not every church body or church leader that calls themselves "Christian" understands the responsibilities of that descriptor, and that a group of church leaders can be profoundly and distressingly undiscerning, self-centered, and

48. No. 53.
49. No. 50.
50. No. 52.
51. No. 45.

self-serving while still claiming to be following Christ. I also learned that there isn't much a single person can do to change people's minds or to change a bad system to a better one.[52]

2. The topic of church and community include: The role of the church to teach the Scriptures and to help encourage opportunities for authentic community; the importance of biblical truth, biblical scholarship, and hermeneutics; the need to personally search the Scriptures to find answers for oneself regarding a topic of interest; the need to guard against heresy; and the need to test and discern. Fifteen participants commented on the topic of church and community.

I've learned tons of things about biblical scholarship, exegesis, and hermeneutics; how to deal with disagreements; how to teach what I have learned; grace, forgiveness, and patience; many, many other things . . . [53]

Oh My! I thank God for it now that I'm on the other side! There is a huge and growing number of people who have been hurt by the Church and left. The ministry I am with now ministers to these folks as well as women who just cannot find what they need in their own church. I am qualified to listen and to teach so much more effectively now! Since the wounds have healed, they no longer need to find voice with me . . . and I am free to spend 100 percent helping others get through their hurt and find their passion for Christ. We all have equal access to God—He does not play favorites.[54]

It has made me examine the whole idea of the institutional church, and what happens when you give pastors authority and control, over their staff, over entire ministries. Who is the Church? Isn't it us? . . . It has also made me value support groups more. The belief of these senior pastors is that more Bible study is all we need. Well it isn't. We need to be in relationships where we can begin to experience relationship with others, where authenticity and honesty are valued, where grace can be experienced.[55]

52. No. 58.

53. No. 33.

54. No. 75.

55. No. 31. Many authors affirmed this need of being connected and participating in healthy relationships.

3. The topic of spiritual growth includes: the process of learning about the grace of God in salvation and in sanctification (twelve); learning how to recognize the work of the Holy Spirit in sanctification in the believer's life (ten); learning how to trust God more (twelve); and basically learning how to live the Christian life better.

After the main topics of leadership, church, and community were identified, the next most noteworthy theme identified was the need to take personal responsibility for one's own faith (twenty-two). A number of participants expressed their regret that they had thought it was the custom to leave their spiritual growth up to their leaders. This immature view had now become an impetus to replace faulty concepts with biblical foundational truths and to aim to keep on a path of rediscovering truths that they had missed along the way. In fact, the practice of examining all teachings in light of the Scriptures has grown to be a more mature dimension in their Christian life.

> God's love—this whole thing propelled me on a search to trust in and believe in the love God has for me as I am. It has moved me out of a very insecure place of being dependent on what others think of me, and has moved me closer to believing and relying on what God says of me.[56]

> Yes, many things. First, that "God works all things together for good." Through this painful experience, I have learned to be compassionate and understanding toward others. I have also learned the tremendous value of salvation by grace through faith.[57]

> Yes—more than I can put in a short response, but the summary is that I am not only saved by grace, but I live by grace. Living by grace does not imply antinomian license, rather it fosters freedom that comes from Christ living in and through me as my true hope—not me struggling, striving, or performing. The distinction is comparable to the difference between marching and dancing.[58]

56. No. 45.
57. No. 32.
58. No. 25.

The positive aspect would be that I have a tremendously deeper relationship with God today, due to the painful experience. I've come to learn a great deal about His Kingdom in a very healthy manner and have actually come to thank Him for the whole ordeal.[59]

4. Growth in discernment includes: learning to test and question everything and how to more quickly recognize the signs of spiritual abuse (fourteen); learning to trust one's instincts (eleven); learning to trust God and not to blindly trust man or put one's total focus on the local church or a denomination (eleven).

We need to question everything that is taught to us, by going to the Bible.[60]

To recognize poor or abusive leadership, sometimes even when others don't see it. To strive, personally, to never be that kind of leader. To never put the opinion of a human being above the words of my Creator.[61]

Yes! Jesus loves me! I have a sensitivity for strugglers and a radar for fakers. I guard against heresy, always checking Bible references that speakers just throw out there to back up their opinions. I question practices and teachings that set off my warning lights. I have a heightened sense of discernment. I am very aware of the potential for the abuse of power in any setting, even my own. I am more candid and honest. I am less of a people-pleaser.[62]

5. Learning to take action when a problem arises includes the need to allow a place for differences of opinion and not to fear confrontation with leaders (seven).

I examine people carefully; choose only those I consider safe and helpful in my life. I no longer feel obligated to give my time to people who harm me, but I choose a few people and consciously build deep and intimate friendships with them, and I am better able now to communicate and build close friendships. . . . I now have a wide variety of friends from dif-

59. No. 20.
60. No. 26.
61. No. 64.
62. No. 73.

ferent settings. I no longer have friends only in my church, but I maintain friendships with non-Christians and Christians from different churches; and if something happens that I find distressing I make a point of telling several people and I listen to their reactions and thoughts. I no longer allow myself to be isolated and silenced. I tell church leaders straight, though I do it with grace, I hope. I do not allow leaders to be gurus or popes. I see them as one of the sheep who needs to be put in their place sometimes and I'm happy to stand against them now and rebuke them, something I would never have done before.[63]

6. The topic of learning about how to give and receive forgiveness was expressed (six). Since forgiveness is one of the core dimensions or spiritual disciplines of the Christian life, this factor needed to be wrestled with by each participant if they were going to go forward in Christ and in ministry in a Christian community. Although the general response to this question was not as marked, it was evident that each participant had to seriously reckon with this issue at some point in the process. Inevitably they also had to make forgiveness a recurring action when negative memories crowded back into their thinking. Since their future spiritual health depended on this action, it became a natural part of the healing process through the help of the Scriptures, the model of Christ, the prompting of the Holy Spirit, and the comfort and encouragement of Christian community.

It was important that wrongs needed to be faced and not simply excused. Forgiveness is a work of grace by the power of the Spirit in one's life. Only when the depth of injustice was conscientiously reckoned with could the basis for forgiveness through the work of Christ be willfully extended. Although difficult, this became the repeated experience among the participants.

> Forgiveness and trust are not synonymous. Letting go of hurts does not automatically require us to drop our boundaries on people who have abused the trust we invested in them.[64]

63. No. 81.
64. No. 56.

I learned how difficult it is to forgive everyone who hurt me, gossiped about me, made false presumptions about my character, and accused me of things I didn't do.[65]

7. Two participants summarized the perceived depth and intensity of this learning context by saying: "I could write a book." Others indicated in various ways that they had learned an enormous amount.

I could write a book on what I have learned.[66]

I feel I could write a book. I question much of what I thought was a legitimate part of living out my faith: institutional church, pastor-laity divide, attending Sunday morning services, the rituals of religion. I believe the system is very broken.... On the positive side, my marriage is better, my communication with my kids is better; I understand myself and my own dysfunctional way of relating to others better than ever before.[67]

8. Fewer in number, but noteworthy comments, include the following: learning what not to do regarding leadership malpractices (four); recognizing that their marriage and other relationships were now better (four); learning about the plight of women in church and how women can have a biblical foundation in order to minister in the church (two). Again, it was evident that participants gained a heightened sensitivity to many situations.

Personal stewardship of where we invest ourselves in our life circumstances, spiritual gifts, and relationships are more important than I realized before.[68]

Those experiences made me begin to research and study what God's will for women really is. It changed my feelings towards God once I learned there is a scriptural basis for the equality of women.[69]

I believe that many pastors are afraid of strong and talented women. They enjoy the position of power and adoration within

65. No. 58.
66. No. 10.
67. No. 55.
68. No. 56.
69. No. 68.

their congregations and want nothing to interfere with that position. I believe that many Christian women are emotionally depressed because of the indoctrination of inequality and that they may not even realize the source of their depression. I believe that many people in the Church are bigots. And, I believe that most think that they are faithful to Scripture when, in fact, they have ignored the Scriptures that do not agree with what they have been taught.[70]

Individual comments included: learning that spiritual growth can come from being wounded; understanding human frailty better, theirs and others; learning that there is not much that an individual person (or a couple) can do to change people's minds or change a bad system; people will choose what they want regardless of the facts; learning about the spiritual dimension behind the situation; learning about the hurt in the Church and the need to minister to those who are hurt; learning to be careful who you can or cannot trust among Christians; learning not about a new religion, but about a new relationship [with God] without guilt.

> Don't fear confrontation, I also learned telling the whole truth is not always good; you have to take into account who you are dealing with and what they will do with it. Are they trustworthy?[71]

It was hypothesized that subjects would need to take time to reflect on their circumstance so that they would grow deeper spiritually. Again, there was evidence of the mar factors found in participants. As they initially worked through their grief they were in a position to investigate personal beliefs and consider if they indeed were valid biblical beliefs or if they were simply misbeliefs that needed to be jettisoned. Participants confirmed that they had been impelled to think deeply about the Church and its leadership and to aim to get answers for themselves. As they researched on their own or were coached by spiritual advisors, a number of theological truths, which had apparently been obscured from their view, increasingly came into focus. Theological foundations were reestablished, especially their ecclesiological paradigm. They were enabled to analyze and reconfigure their view of biblical leadership with a greater desire to be godly leaders themselves.

---

70. No. 70.

71. No. 44.

It was hypothesized that subjects had not fully understood the grace of God toward them. They had relied on the ingrained teaching that the Christian faith was works-based rather than grace-based. Many people's theological understanding of the grace of God was marred. This significant mar factor was confirmed. This lack distorted the potential for a victorious spiritual life. Believers needed to understand that the gift of salvation is by God's grace and one's spiritual identity is to be found solely "in Christ."[72] Becoming enlarged in the entire concept of God's grace initiated a greater measure of giving and receiving of the love which God had given them, through faith in Christ, at conversion. Grasping what the Apostle John had written to believers in the early Church was essential to their spiritual growth.[73] Now that these believers had reconnected to the love they had received at salvation, their Christian life was deeper and fuller. They were now able to dispense this love to others with greater sensitivity and new found zeal.

Category 5

Participants were asked: What have you found to be most helpful regarding your spiritual recovery from a negative church experience? Basically, what types of help did you find both necessary and helpful to move you forward in Christ after your harmful church experience? They were given a choice of selections and asked to comment on the ones that were most helpful to them. These included: a) someone to confide in; b) help from friends; c) comfort from certain Scripture passages; d) help from a minister; e) involvement in a small support group; f) participation on blogs (websites); g) reading books (please give titles); and h) other. (Question no. 18.)

Since this was the primary enquiry, participants were most helpful in identifying the main elements that helped them to recover. The first selection, "someone to confide in," was identified as the principal source of help that worked for the majority of participants (74 percent). It would appear that when people face severe trials, with various levels of personal grief and emotional pain, having a trusted confidant is essential to allow verbal processing of these events and to receive consolation from others. Being able to consider all aspects of one's pain in a safe

---

72. Eph 2; "It is for freedom that Christ has set us free. Stand firm, then, and do not let yourselves be burdened again by a yoke of slavery" (Gal 5:1).

73. See 1 John.

place, receiving thoughtful and wise feedback to bolster one's faith and identity in Christ, and helping to recognize the fact that God had been with them through this trial has been a primary method for people to process their disheartening situation. The dedication of those who were available to listen, to affirm, to offer helpful perspectives, and to gently point the way to a better path at such a time has been the single most aid to those who have regained spiritual harmony after this type of circumstance. Cudmore's research also confirms this finding.[74]

Someone to confide in included professional counselors as well as pastors.[75] Many people referenced how important their spouse and family was in allowing them to talk through issues. For the majority, sharing with a confidant involved processing the main elements of one's story with one trusted friend. This included someone that they could unload on without judgment, someone that they could cry with, and someone who would give them other ways to look at their situation. For the majority of those who participated in this study, having one person or a married couple that participants could trust and safely confide in was the single most helpful factor in their recovery.

Along with a trusted confidant, help from friends greatly assisted those in need. Sixty-one percent of respondents referenced help from friends. Knowing that they had close friends who would listen, empathize, and grieve along with them, and offer hope for the future, was both helpful and necessary. Along with the opportunity to articulate and share their pain, enjoying activities with friends helped take their mind off their circumstance and recreate normalcy.[76] This was also an essential

74. Cudmore, "Victim Suffering," 102. Cudmore's research confirmed four major areas of significant support among her participants. These included: support from a Christian friend; support from a non-Christian friend; spousal and family support; and psychological, medical, or counseling support. Four participants found help through a Christian who was not involved in their church or Christian organization. Three found help from more than one Christian. One participant stated: "You didn't need a whole lot of friends when you have a couple of friends like that," 102. These friends prayed, loved, and cried with them.

75. Enroth, in *Recovering from Churches*, offers a comment on how some victims approach professional counseling with reluctance; a speculation confirmed by this researcher. "Some victims of spiritual abuse are reluctant to pursue professional counseling because they are wary of allowing another authority figure into their lives," 30. He also states: "Learning to trust others in authority without creating a new codependent relationship is one of the first issues that victims of spiritual abuse confront," 31.

76. A helpful insight confirmed by no. 56.

part of the help that friends could provide for a hurting companion. As previously indicated, many supportive friends were those who had gone through a similar experience at the same church or a different one. Various other friends were able to support participants with love and care. Some found that non-Christian friends were also sympathetic and helpful. The fact that people found someone to confide in and/or had friends to share their story with was complementary in ministering to people's social and spiritual need for companionship and to help them process their thoughts and feelings in a positive way.

Second, 66 percent of the participants found that reading books on these topics fortified their understanding of these issues. Books confirmed that they were not alone in their struggle since many of the authors and those referenced in case studies had walked this path before them. Timely information gave a broader understanding of these complex church problems and provided them with answers for themselves and for others who find themselves in a similar dilemma. Many stated that they had read books "without number"—too many to name.

The primary books which were identified as helpful were: *The Subtle Power of Spiritual Abuse* (fourteen), *Healing Spiritual Abuse* (ten), *Toxic Faith* (five), *Twisted Scriptures* (five), *So You Don't Want to Go to Church Anymore* (five), *The Tale of Three Kings* (five), *Tired of Trying to Measure Up* (four), *Why Not Women?* (three), *Churches That Abuse* (three), and *What's So Amazing About Grace?* (three). Henri Nouwen was cited three times as an author. Other book titles referenced by participants addressed these main subjects as well.

Third, 64 percent found comfort in certain Scripture passages. Passages of comfort as well as Scriptures that provided relevant teaching about leadership and/or the Church were most helpful.

The fourth item named was that it was essential to participate on blogs. This broadly included access to Internet information. Thirty-six percent specifically referenced this. Participants found immediate help by reading Internet websites that had articles on the topics of spiritual abuse, healthy and unhealthy leadership and church life, cults and cult-like beliefs and behavior, as well as sites that offered the opportunity to participate on blogs or forums. Many participants were delighted to find such a welcome resource via the Internet at this critical time in their lives.

The fifth item was involvement in a small support group. This was identified by 31 percent as being helpful for them. Small groups included those who had left the same church about the same time and became a support for one another to process their mutual grief, along with times to eat and share life together. Other participants joined small groups in new church settings that were developed for Bible study and/or fellowship. Some met with believers outside of a church setting. These small groups were formed to help participants to process their situation in a safe place with others on a similar path. Other small groups provided an opportunity for healthy fellowship, which introduced people to a more wholesome outlook on life. Although a few churches provide grief support groups, among this group of participants, a support group specifically designed for those wounded through a devastating church situation was not available. No such focused support groups,[77] which met within or outside of the church, were identified.

The sixth item was getting help from a minister. Although pastors or other church leaders had personally hurt many people, 18 percent found help from ministers who were sensitive and empathetic to their devastating situation. Having a caring pastor who listened with sensitivity to their recent difficult church experience helped individuals and couples to cope. Being accepted, loved, and affirmed by this pastor helped them to process their pain and losses and reinforced the fact that the leadership behavior they had previously experienced was outside the parameters of pastoral care for the flock. They were also encouraged by the fact that the Body of Christ was still a place for them to find fellowship, theological and emotional safety, and hope for the future.

The seventh item, identified as "other," provided a place to share particular helps that worked for certain individuals. Participants identified prayer (nine), journaling (five), and music (two) as being helpful during this time.

77. Spirited Exchanges, in New Zealand and now in the United Kingdom is specifically geared for people who have come through negative church experiences. They describe their group this way: "Spirited Exchanges is an umbrella name for a variety of initiatives for people grappling with issues related to faith and church. Many of these people have left the institutional church while others continue but have a less than comfortable alliance with it. Many have felt marginalised and misunderstood; others have felt controlled and disrespected. And for most it has led to considerable upheaval in their Christian understanding and practise and has often meant the loss of previous valued community." Information about this group can be accessed through: http://www.churchlessfaith.org. See also Jamieson et al, *Church Leavers.*

The following are some of the varied comments made by participants:

> The absolute key for me has been the friends I could honestly,
> openly confide in. I could cry with them, rant about my frus-
> trations, share my epiphanies, dissect each experience, view and
> review our pastor, analyze his personality, feel safe with them, get
> angry at the whole mess with them, let pieces go with them, cry
> with them, laugh with them at the idiocy of it all, and then cry
> with them some more. I am so deeply blessed that God gave me
> friends to help me live through this with. I am convinced that the
> presence of these loving, godly people is the reason I came out
> of this sane.[78]

> Someone to confide in. It helped to be able to vent the experience.
> It was traumatic and I did a lot of processing through speech.[79]

> Help from friends. But without these people I would not have
> moved on.[80]

> Help from friends. Internet buddies who had also been there and
> done that were my sanity savers.[81]

> Help from a minister. It took awhile before I trusted leaders again.
> I guess I was just afraid that they were going to do the same thing.
> So I didn't openly talk to my pastor about this, instead when oth-
> ers from my church ran into trouble with this group as well, I was
> called in to meet my pastor and elders. They wanted more infor-
> mation about my own experience. I then experienced something
> from my pastor that was really helpful: he became my advocate
> and defender. He went after this group and was one of the initial
> ones that brought into question what had happened.[82]

> I have to say that God has worked with me in an amazingly car-
> ing method to eradicate all my anger, my questions, my argu-
> ments, and my disillusionment with Him and churches by means
> of His tender guiding and explaining in my life. There have been
> many years now of experiences where God has shown me that
> I can trust Him, and know His love in manners that were so

78. No. 41.
79. No. 51.
80. No. 3.
81. No. 15.
82. No. 45.

damaged by my negative experience. His ability to encourage me to continue to seek Him has been my spiritual life's blood.[83]

I was actually amazed at the many sources on the Internet that have helped me out—namely blogs, Internet websites such as Bleatinglambs.org and Batteredsheep.com—as it shows that such negative experiences are widespread and that the organized church has clearly swept this whole topic under the rug.[84]

Finding like-minded individuals who could reveal the truth of Scripture on this subject. There are so many books. I've read a lot from the CBE [Christians For Biblical Equality] website.[85]

Many things are factoring into my ongoing recovery. Embracing the *process*—spiritually abusive environments do not tolerate processes. Yet, the renewal of one's mind to the truth of Christ "in them" as his/her hope, is a process. As I have accepted and embraced that process, my healing has progressed.[86]

Supportive relationships were the most helpful for me. I received help from a minister. She was able to bring a lot of wisdom, and ministered inner healing prayer that was very effective. But the thing that helped me the most (which isn't on the list here) is asking God questions about what happened. He taught me about abdication, about misuse of authority. He taught me about forgiveness. He spoke to me about the lies the devil had told me (as a result of the abuse) and told me the truth about things, replacing those lies with His truth. That was the most healing for me. I appreciated the support, the counsel, and the teaching from people that I received. But listening to the Holy Spirit was the key for me in having my questions answered and my wounds healed. This was a process, not overnight.[87]

Be willing to seek professional help and find a way to tell your story and experience in a public manner. Have a circle of Christian friends that you can count on and that they can count on you.[88]

Christian counseling was helpful to process my anger, although I did hear later that at the time my counselor didn't really believe

83. No. 20.
84. No. 21.
85. No. 23.
86. No. 25.
87. No. 14.
88. No. 35.

in spiritual abuse! (What did he think he was dealing with?!) I hear his thinking has developed since; and I had, and still have, huge respect.[89]

When we've been so deeply wounded, we need more than just people to confide in and process with. As important as working things through is, they are constant reminders of the destructive experiences. So, we desperately need friends who can help restore a sense of normalcy and balance to life and be with us to break depression, isolation, addictive acting out, and other potentially self-destructive cycles that piggyback onto spiritual abuse. My friends and I would go out for coffee, shopping, a movie, etc.—activities that had absolutely nothing to do directly with the horrible circumstances I was dealing with. These visits and outings offered a breath of fresh air in an otherwise sulfurous environment.[90]

Help from a minister. In the aftermath of each of the three toxic church situations, I talked with at least one pastor or minister. I have come to believe this is a critical part of the healing process. Since it was pastors/ministers/church leaders who inflicted the damage, only a pastor, minister, or church leader can serve as a representative agent of healing. . . . If we do not at some point receive from a church leader the acknowledgment of the wrong done to us by another of their kind, I'm not sure we will find the healing we hope for. It may also be in the presence of a minister that we can speak our commitment to forgive those ministers who perpetrated evil upon us.[91]

Having someone to confide in, especially without judgment or condemnation, was necessary for me to clear my mind through the situation. The debrief/renewal was so helpful in clarifying feelings, being able to understand why we felt certain ways. It helped us distinguish between the stress of being a missionary, the stress of normal life, and what was the stress of the abusive situation. Each type of stress has a different way of healing and lowering the stress. Being able to understand the source and how to begin the change was very helpful.[92]

89. No. 78.

90. No. 56.

91. Ibid.

92. No. 60.

Subjects needed confidants and mature friends to help them through this upsetting time. Finding friends who participants could trust, in order to comfortably share their story and take refuge and strength among those who had also been through a similar distressing church situation helped participants to process the range of emotions from such an unsettling circumstance.

Many participants accessed relevant Internet sites. They found immediate and essential help by interacting with website hosts and others who described their similar negative experience through the Church. This reinforced the idea that they were not alone. This realization brought direct comfort along with insights that enabled them to process their circumstances and get a broader perspective on what had just happened to them. Participants were grateful that they could find and benefit from the support provided through Internet websites, blogs, and forums.

It has been confirmed that subjects found reassurance through books that addressed the definition and nature of spiritual abuse and suggested the factors that contribute to abusive leadership styles. Although help through church support groups was also presented as a potential help, this means to recovery was not the experience of these participants. Although some participants benefited from a small group in a new church context, groups which specifically dealt with the topic of wounding from exiting distressing church situations was apparently unavailable.[93] This was not a viable option for the majority of the participants in this study. Possibly in the future, some churches or groups will take this on as a ministry.

Subjects needed to realize that they would need time to heal spiritually and emotionally. Allowing time to heal and to grow deeper in their relationship to their Lord has been verified by almost every participant. Although the passing of time was a key factor in the grief process, there was a need for the support of others and the access to knowledge during the recovery time that ensured full benefit of the recovery process. It was these combined elements, working together over time, which validated that participants had fully recovered from this spiritual and emotional trauma.

---

93. As mentioned earlier in this section, a support group started in Wellington, New Zealand, by Alan Jamieson, was developed to help people at various stages of faith as well as to help those who had hurtful church experiences. This group, called Spirited Exchanges, is described in the book *Church Leavers*.

For some, there was also a felt need to take their time in finding a new church fellowship. Their plan was not to hurry with this important task and to seriously consider the essentials of their personal criteria for finding a new church. For others, finding a new church home quite quickly, or sooner than they might have expected, brought consolation and peace. The majority of participants found that they needed to take the time to reassess their ecclesiological paradigm.

For a number of participants, this time of reflection served to affirm that they needed to meet with Christians outside of the institutional church setting. This reorientation of how they envisage church is based on their redesigned criteria for Christian fellowship and service—which has been forged through this disheartening experience. Alan Jamieson used the term "post-church" to describe these individuals or groups. Post-church indicates that their previous participation in an established church context has ceased. Post-church needs to be distinguished from the terms post-Christian or post-faith.[94] Jamieson observed that when people had left an EPC church they were unlikely to rejoin one.[95] He noted that, "Many who are apparently on the edge of leaving an EPC church may in fact not leave."[96] All of his respondents expressed reservations, concerns, or clear aversion to established churches. For most, the conclusion was that, for them, church was simply irrelevant to their faith and life.[97] He concluded that:

> Considering the deep and long term commitment these people had previously made to their churches (on average being adult committed members for 15.8 years) this must raise serious concerns for those responsible for shaping churches today.[98]

The final observation regarding participant connections with established churches centered on their significant concerns with leadership in faith and church groups.[99]

94. Jamieson et al, *Church Leavers*, 12–13.

95. Ibid., 79.

96. Ibid., 80.

97. Ibid.

98. Ibid., 80–81.

99. "Universally, the leavers looked primarily for 'character' strengths including integrity, vulnerability, and willingness to express weakness. The Wayfinders [those mature in faith] especially pointed to the need for theological and pastoral training, spiritual and psychological maturity, and the deep personal skills of empathy and listening," ibid., 81. This finding concurs with the findings of this study.

Participants verified that understanding God's grace in vital new ways propelled them forward in their recovery. In securing a biblical understanding of God's grace, participants were able to develop a deeper relationship with God and a greater trust in His plan for their life. Although most people may still require a reminder of the great measure of grace that they have received, periodic reflection on their spiritual progress in light of this fact will prove rewarding. The mar factors that were initially recognized among the majority of participants at the beginning of this pivotal experience have slowly been ministered to in various ways. For the majority of participants the mar factors have been replaced. Participants have legitimately been renewed in body, mind, and spirit and are now in a position to minister to others who may come across their path. As participants become acquainted with those who are struggling with similar circumstances they ought to be able to humbly offer their insights with grace and compassion that they have learned through their personal trial by fire.

Category 6

Participants were asked if they had found a church that they could call "home" and what criteria they now have for finding a church home. (Question no. 14.)

The number of people who found a suitable local church to attend was 67 percent and those who did not was 33 percent. This ratio is two thirds to one third. See Figure 4.

Many of the yes and no answers were qualified as "Yes, but . . ." or "No, but . . ." Those who said no[100] had found various ways to fellowship with other believers, to share the Word together, to share in community life, and to have a missional focus among family, friends, and coworkers. There was interest in finding ways to serve in the local community through street ministry, feeding the hungry, working with teens and children, and welcoming the stranger. Their engagement with the world was primarily based on a growing relationship to each other in Christian community life activities. For those who said yes, these identical elements were also a priority for them when looking for a new church community. Some had not found all of the elements in their new fellowships that they currently valued, but for now, they felt theologically safe

---

100. Many of those who said no would now consider themselves post-church and have no intention of trying to reintegrate into a traditional/institutional church.

Figure 4: Church Reintegration

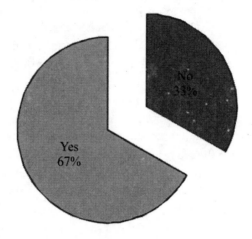

and were developing new relationships with a renewed ecclesiological expectation. Some had switched denominations while others had found a healthier church within their denomination.

The following are the seven priority elements identified by participants when looking for a potential church home. These criteria were articulated in individual ways yet the corporate expression was almost singularly of one accord. It is also relevant to note that "what the participants had learned" through this process (as stated by their answers for Question no. 12), has demonstrated a heightened sensitivity, which directly influenced what factors they value as criteria for choosing a new church. These insights, therefore, ran along parallel lines. The prioritized criteria for the majority of people included the following: God's Word, caring community, pastors/leadership, motivation by the Spirit, ministry to those in need, the role/place of women in the church, and the priority of worship in a Christian community.

1. Their expectation of the place of God's Word. Almost half of the participants strongly referenced the need for a place of honor for God's Word in the church (48 percent).

Is it doctrinally sound? Is the teaching grace-based? What principles are used to interpret the Scriptures? How do individuals and a community understand God's will? Participants were clear as they articulated their desire for accurate expositional biblical preaching and teaching based on sound hermeneutical principles. Equally, esteeming God's grace and the believer's identity in Christ were foundational and must be taught and lived. Questions to ask when looking for a new home church are: Is God's Word interpreted and taught well? Does doctrine flow out of who Christ is? Are people taught how to read and study the Bible on their own? What is the place of biblical scholarship?

2. Their expectation of participating in a dedicated Christian community. This factor also included almost half of the participants (48 percent).

Another equally valued expectation was the hope of finding and participating in a genuine caring Christian community; those who have their individual and corporate identity in the Risen Christ. Participants wanted to be among Christians who expressed love to God, who followed Christ, and who desired to serve as a Christian community together. They were interested in a place where people lived out the grace given. Questions to ask when looking for a new home church are: Do people hunger to know God? Are they living for Christ? Is the Spirit of God evident in the people?

3. Their expectation of leadership with integrity (42 percent).

Humble, honest, teachable, sincere, servant-hearted pastors who were Spirit led and biblically competent—ministering in a context of shared leadership and genuine leadership accountability—encapsulate this mutual priority.[101] A number expressed the desire for denominational and/or outside ways to ensure accountability (six). Questions to ask when looking for a new home church are: Does the leader know how to wisely interpret the Scriptures? Would spiritual abuse be understood and stopped? How do the leaders handle conflict? How does this leadership handle church discipline? Is there a plurality of leaders? Who are the leaders accountable to?

4. Their expectation that the leadership and community be motivated in ministry by the Holy Spirit (21 percent).

---

101. In Alan Jamieson's follow-up study, participants developed a similar list. Participants placed openness and humility in church leaders at the top of their list. There was also more agreement on leadership than any other follow up question. See Jamieson et al, *Church Leavers*, 64–69.

Participants were looking for a church community where they could use their gifts and be a part of the shared ministry among believers in their extended community. They looked for a church that demonstrated that ministry was motivated by the Holy Spirit rather than by man. People valued the place of spiritual gifts (charismata) (three) and longed for a place that encouraged creativity (three). Questions to ask when looking for a new home church are: Can I find a place of ministry through this fellowship? Does this fellowship value the charismata defined by the Apostle Paul? Is there a place for creativity and for the arts in this group? Is there evidence that the Holy Spirit motivates this community?

5. Their expectation for social awareness outside the church community (17 percent).

Being among those who were serious-minded disciples of Christ, who were motivated by the Holy Spirit, would naturally cause these believers to seek to love and serve the surrounding community as Christ's representatives. Participants expressed the need to be involved in a church that was focused outward rather than inward. They were anxious to participate in a church that was socially aware, was interested in mission, and desired to minister to the lost and the needy. Questions to ask: Does morality and social ethics flow out of who Christ is? Does this church minister outside its walls? How can this church be missional in a postmodern and post-Christian society? Does this church have a vision/plan to minister to the least and the lost in the neighboring community?

6. Their expectation of an equal place for women to minister in the church (8 percent).

Finding a place for women to serve in the local church was a priority for many. Since many women and men were concerned about the place of women in the church, it was important to find a church that values women as co-laborers in the church as modeled by the New Testament. In order to effectively minister as a church in the surrounding community it was important to know that women could serve Christ according to their gift set and not according to a gender hierarchical view. Questions to ask when looking for a new home church are: Where do women fit in this church? What is their interpretation of biblical teaching regarding women in ministry? Are women honored and respected as co-laborers in the church?

7. The priority of vibrant spiritual worship of God by his people (7 percent).

Participants expressed their desire for meaningful worship which was Spirit led. Some preferred contemporary liturgy while others found meaning in formal liturgy. The common denominator was that the church they could call "home" would make worship a priority. They valued the fact that God could speak to them during times of corporate worship. Questions to ask: What does this church believe about the Triune God? How do they express their love and devotion to God through worship? Could I be involved in the worship ministry at this church and use my gifting or is it only for a select few?

Some of the fewer identified elements by the majority of participants were nevertheless important for a few. These included: a place for children and youth in the church, that the church must engage people, that the church be geographically close to their home, that it be smaller in size so that they could participate in ministry, churches that valued everyone and were intergenerational, a place where the wounded would feel safe, those that preferred a house church setting, and that members have a say in how the funds are distributed.

The following are comments by participants indicating whether they had found a local church fellowship or not, along with their prioritized criteria for finding a church or a Christian fellowship group that they could call "home."

> No. I am not currently attending anywhere. However, I would allow God to lead me to whatever "church" He wanted me to be at. He has done that for me. God brought me to a "home" church that nurtured and taught me for a season. That is an amazing story itself. Now He has led me to other places and right now I'm in no group at all. I still have many relationships with the people I met through the journey. It was priceless.[102]

> No. I no longer define church as a group of people who meet regularly in a building. But I do fellowship very often. Those I meet with tend to be: 1. Those who have a hunger to know God much better. 2. Those who place more value on our relationship than

102. No. 5.

on strict agreement with what "church" should look like. This includes people both inside and outside of traditional structures.[103]

Yes. Liturgical emphasis where the Word is central. Plurality of
leadership. Emphasis on communion ("Eucharist" if you will).
Elder oversight instead of congregational rule (i.e. I'll never attend another church business meeting).[104]

Yes. Plurality of elders. Elders who are approachable and humble.
A church where everyone has input. Finally, a church that models
one of the New Testament.[105]

No. We have decided to take a break for a year or two—maybe
longer. Servant leadership, openness, grace given and received,
and no program.[106]

House church. We participate in fellowships within homes without designated leaders; the body of Christ is my home on earth.[107]

Is the Spirit of God evident in the people? (Not just in the service.) Is there an "in group"? Are there people who are left out? Is
this church interested in developing the people intellectually and
spiritually? Is God's Word taught and are people taught how to
read and study on their own? Is there evidence of lives being invested in others inside and outside the church? Does their money
go to a good performance on Sunday or to minister to people?
Are they actually involved in the lives of the poor, the widows,
and the orphans?[108]

A significant correlation can be noted regarding the responses to
Questions no. 12 and no. 14. Participants had basically identified that they
had learned the value of Christian responsibility, described as "accountability" or simply, "dependability." Responsibility infers accountability to
the Lord, to others, and to one's conscience. This type of responsibility affects three interconnecting dimensions of church life: the responsibility
of leadership, the corporate church responsibility, and the responsibility
of the individual Christian.

---

103. No. 7.
104. No. 8.
105. No. 9.
106. No. 10.
107. No. 11.
108. No. 75.

First, the responsibility of pastor/leadership included: role and task of the pastor, the heart and integrity of the pastor, and the absence of the tendency for spiritual abuse among leadership, the need to interpret and teach the Scriptures well, and the need to guard the flock against heresy. Second, the corporate church responsibility included: the role of the church community to teach the Scriptures, to value biblical truth and biblical scholarship, to value hermeneutical principles, to maintain watchfulness in order to guard against heresy, to test/discern any teaching, and to value authentic, caring Christian community. Third, individual responsibility included: being accountable for one's spiritual life and not leaving the task solely up to the leaders. Taking responsibility for one's beliefs and practices was an important core belief that was recognized as no longer optional but mandatory. Learning how to read the Bible and interpret the text with a measure of skill in order to be formed spiritually and not to be vulnerable to false teachings, paying attention to how God's Spirit was leading them, and being able to give an informed answer to everyone who may ask them, were essentials for individuals to cultivate in their personal lives.

Growth towards spiritual formation and discernment were each deemed as corporate and individual responsibilities. Tolerance for diverse opinions, especially by leaders, was regarded an individual, leadership, and corporate responsibility. Learning to give and receive forgiveness as a spiritual discipline begins with the individual, but there is need for leadership and community support with this spiritual discipline. Learning about the intensity of this type of trial is usually an individual experience, but leadership and community need to be understanding of those who are going through or have gone through this type of circumstance.

When participants considered their personal criteria for a church that they could call "home," seven priorities rose in significance. These top priorities parallel what the participants acknowledged that they *had learned* through this experience. The first priority identified by participants was the need for God's Word to be honored and taught with clarity. This complemented the idea that the corporate church responsibility included the role of the church community to teach the Scriptures faithfully, to value biblical truth and biblical scholarship, to value hermeneutical principles, to be on guard against heresy, and to test/discern any teaching.

The second priority for a home church was the desire to participate in an authentic caring Christian community. The place for spiritual growth among community places an emphasis on learning about the grace of God in salvation and in sanctification, learning how to recognize the work of the Holy Spirit in sanctification in the believer's life, learning how to better live the Christian life, and learning how to trust God more. Growing in a community also requires that both the leadership and the people are motivated by the Holy Spirit. This spiritual motivation will undoubtedly lead believers to minister to the needs outside of their walls with a God-given desire to care for those in the local community as well as the world.

The third priority was church leadership. What people had learned about leadership was a broader understanding of the role and task of pastors, the heart and integrity of a leader, the need for healthy leaders, recognizing hurtful and unprofitable practices by leadership, the need for healthier leadership models, and the need for good denominational and governing oversight. This complemented how participants expressed their criteria for leaders in a new church context. They valued servant-hearted pastors who were Spirit led, biblically competent, and who ministered in a context of shared leadership and had the dynamics of genuine leadership accountability in place. There was equal interest in the desire for denominational and/or outside structures to ensure accountability. The remaining two priorities included the place of women in leadership in the local church and the place of vibrant worship among the community.

These first three priorities, God's Word, Christian community, and godly leadership, have been isolated as the main concerns of participants—through what they had learned and what they now look for in a potential church home. It was suggested earlier that these subjects of concern were among the mar factors that remained unrecognized or were dormant among many Christians in their previous church experience. Basically, Christians lacked a full biblical understanding and experience of these essentials.

After the distressing encounter with leadership in their former churches, which resulted in feelings of devastation, grief, and disillusionment, what would it take to bring these Christians to a place of recovery—from this situation in their life as well as the inherent recovery from the mar factors in their spiritual life? Would these individuals and couples be among those who would be a statistic of those hurt by church leadership and therefore leave the Church or would there be hope for recovery and eventual reintegration of these participants among those who loved and served Christ?

Thankfully, the process of recovery brought about significant healing and restoration for these individuals. This restoration came in the form of biblical knowledge, which replaced faulty understandings with biblical correction. Restoration also came in the form of healthy relationships, which allowed an individual to process their grief and losses in a safe and compassionate atmosphere. Wise and caring confidants and supportive friends helped participants during this time of heightened reflection. This time of introspection helped many people to face up with the reality that they had acquired faulty and invalid beliefs over time. This reflection also helped participants to slowly replace faulty beliefs with beliefs that were in alignment with the Scriptures. Their "theological closet" was basically aired out and light was shone onto garments that were no longer "fitting" to wear. They had the courage to extricate these items and replace them with new theological garments worthy of their calling. They were enabled to move forward in a healthier way from this point.

Category 7

Participants were asked if they were personally disillusioned with this group and what advice they would give to others who find themselves in a similar circumstance. (Question nos. 11 and 13.) Question no. 11 was phrased this way: Do you feel personally disillusioned with this church group? Please describe.

People were disillusioned with their church group in two main ways—either very much so (76 percent) or not much at all (17 percent). The majority response was that participants were quite disillusioned with their previous church group. The comments under this question identified disillusionment in four main areas which were prioritized this way: pastor and leadership behavior (controlling and abusive) (54 percent); the church community's behavior (lack of love, care, or support) (26 percent); the spiritual danger in accepting untested erroneous teachings (those that did not reflect solid biblical teachings) (23 percent); and disappointment with denominational leadership behavior (13 percent).

The following are comments regarding participant disillusionment with leadership, church community, faulty beliefs, and lack of denominational support:

> It is seldom the group as such—the problems for us were mostly leadership that operated outside of New Testament design—trying to be something for which there was no biblical warrant. I have never been able to blindly follow anyone without asking questions.[109]

> No I do not feel disillusioned. I feel justified, because I have felt for a long time that something wasn't right in church. I am thankful for their self-exposure. It helped me sort out and put into words what I have felt for so long. It gave me the freedom to move on.[110]

> Yes. I see specific errors, particularly in the leadership, the lack of accountability and oversight, the lack of training, the mistakes in how leaders are chosen, the power and authority they wield, the immorality in the leaders, and the authoritarian teaching and cult-like demands on the congregation.[111]

> Yes. Friends of ours abandoned us without ever asking our side. The local church maintained the "no talk" rule that was encouraged by the denomination. The local church recognized that the denomination failed them and failed us, but they still bow to the district superintendent and the denomination. They have chosen to pretend nothing happened and act like that means the church is healed. They seem afraid to just sit down and talk to us or others hurt in the experience. Their idea of community seems to be that everyone will just pretend there isn't anything wrong.[112]

> I was terribly disillusioned with the first church group, primarily because the denominational leadership was very aware of the difficulties and did nothing to intervene.[113]

It was recognized that the main areas highlighted again were primarily how participants were treated by leadership, how participants were treated by their former church community, how the leadership and community absorbed and promoted faulty beliefs, and how the denomi-

---

109. No. 6.
110. No. 57.
111. No. 81.
112. No. 55.
113. No. 90.

nation did not provide help for these congregants, especially at a time when they needed their support. This fact points out that a significant number of participants named the problems in the local church as being rooted broadly in the denomination's beliefs and practices. Rather than solely being disillusioned with the pastor (and the pastor's wife) and/or the leadership team, or being disappointed with the church community, disillusionment with the denomination ranked high among many of the participants. A number of people identified their particular denomination in their answers and stated that they would no longer be attending churches of that denomination.

Question no. 13 was phrased this way: What advice would you give to others who find themselves in emotionally distressful or abusive spiritual contexts?

The response to this question compiled a variety of fitting counsel for those facing this situation. The following is an overview of the composite wisdom provided by participants. Many stated emphatically that their advice to others would be to simply leave ("get out" of) their local church if it had abusive leanings and/or favored destructive aberrant teachings (26 percent). If some really felt that they still needed to stay in a difficult church situation then they were admonished to have outside help—people that they could confide in and count on for support. This was a must if they considered staying. Some stated that an attempt should be made to find some resolve with leaders, but many observed that they didn't feel that one person or one couple had very much influence in toxic systems.

People were exhorted not to tolerate abuse in any form. It was important to participants to consider one's spouse, children, and family when making the determination to stay or leave one's home church. People were encouraged to allow sufficient time to grieve, to allow time to heal, and to even take a break before seeking to join another church fellowship too quickly. It was important to recognize that the healing process would inevitably be painful. They confirmed that although people could see problems in their church they needed to be aware that many still at their church would not comprehend their concerns, even though these may be serious issues that need attention. Some learned from their own circumstance that when they began to notice problems those in their church branded them as troublemakers and this insight was also given as a caution.

People were admonished to find support and counsel by seeking out others who had a similar experience or those who understood the issues. They were cautioned to find someone who they could fully trust before sharing their church problems and emotions. Many commented that there might be minimum or no help from denominational overseers when they shared their church or leadership concerns. People were encouraged to look outside of their context for help in understanding various destructive church issues, such as church governance, spiritual abuse, and the need for biblical leadership. Many participants suggested professional counseling to help process their situation or use the Internet to glean information.

The following are some examples of advice offered to others. Some offered terse advice while others elaborated, offering detailed and thorough recommendations.

> Get out of the situation immediately and find someone who will support you emotionally and spiritually. Speak to a healthy pastor or go to a counselor or spiritual director. Depending on the person and the situation, I would encourage reporting the problem to someone in authority, otherwise you're just leaving a spot open for the next unsuspecting victim.[114]

> If possible, get out. But either way, find some people who will believe you, pray with you and for you, and help you make wise decisions. If needed, seek professional counsel. In time, begin to address whether there is anything about you that drew you to that situation.[115]

> I'd say get out, surround yourself by others who have either gone through something like this and who have healed, and/or are positive about it. Not negative people. It's easy to complain or gossip about a big bad church. Pray for them all. And it's okay to be hurt and angry and sad. They had no right to do this to you. It was mean. Forgive them and move on, but it doesn't mean you have to go back and/or trust them again with your own personal spirituality![116]

> Church shouldn't hurt.[117]

114. No. 61.
115. No. 64.
116. No. 63.
117. No. 51.

People's initial shock and confusion about their church circumstance brought them into a period of spiraling grief. Concurrent with their feelings of grief, reflection on their pain usually led them to feelings of disillusionment. At this time some people slipped into cynicism regarding their church's beliefs and/or their leadership's marred practices. Some people went as far as being totally disillusioned with their denomination.[118] Some became disillusioned with the whole way of doing church and were not happy to continue. Their view of participating in any local church setting was no longer an option for them. Since basic trust in leadership had been tarnished; distrust in leadership ran high among the majority of participants.

Participants suggested a correlation between faulty beliefs and distressing leadership behaviors. Denominations that carry these two theological weaknesses will most frequently produce the distressing behaviors confirmed by these participants.

Category 8

There are four questions in this category. Participants were asked if they had any shifts in their beliefs and if their view of God or his Word had been affected. They were asked if they considered themselves to be Pentecostal or Charismatic in their experience. In the final question, participants were asked to describe their journey with Christ today. (These questions will be considered in this order: Question no. 16, 19, 15, and 20.)

1. What shifts in your beliefs have you recognized since this experience? (Question no. 16.)

Participants had a range of answers from not much change to a great number of shifts in their beliefs. For many, their theological underpinnings were given an overhaul, yet the changes have been mainly positive. The number of those who stated that they had minimum shifts or none at all was about 12 percent. The majority, over 85 percent, registered major shifts in their beliefs. Some expressed the thought that it wasn't so much a change in beliefs but a basic change in the practice of those beliefs that impacted them.

---

118. As stated earlier, many participants exited from their denomination and found fellowship in another denominational grouping.

The following comments are a sampling from the 12 percent who did not recognize any major shifts in their beliefs:

> My beliefs have not changed fundamentally. I am more convinced that we have an obligation as Christians to test everything by the Scriptures, even what is spoken by our church leaders.[119]

> I'm not sure I'd call it a "shift" but I believe it solidified what I already believed; it strengthened my faith and loyalty to Christ and His Word.[120]

> I don't know that my beliefs have shifted as much as they have been strengthened.[121]

> My belief in the goodness of God and His care for me has been strengthened. I believe I'm precious in His sight and that He loves me.[122]

> It has been more of a shifting in practice and growth in understanding than a shift in beliefs.[123]

For those who recognized major shifts in their beliefs (85 percent) here is a succinct example of the two common themes which came under renovation: "A paradigmatic shift, especially in terms of the purpose and function of 'church' and 'leadership.'"[124]

A change for many was the deepening love for God and Christ through this experience. Many participants' theological views expanded to see God in all of life not just confined to their church context. As their devotion and thanksgiving to God deepened, their understanding of how to express God's Kingdom on earth through meaningful and caring relationships multiplied. Many expressed the extent of the alteration in core beliefs in the following ways:

> The biggest shifts in my beliefs have been concerning church and religion, realizing that we have great freedom in our expression

119. No. 40.
120. No. 42.
121. No. 50.
122. No. 53.
123. No. 98.
124. No. 77.

of community. I also have changed many of my former beliefs about spiritual authority.[125]

What didn't shift?! From anti-charismatic to open to the idea, from traditional sex roles to committed egalitarian, from KJV only to collector of Bible translations, no longer separatist, banned from my home . . . you name it, it shifted. Most importantly, my faith is relationship-focused and not rules-focused. There's a big picture now, and I can test new beliefs in part by whether they fit into it. I love knowing that Jesus Christ has set me free and not condemned me to live under rule upon rule.[126]

2. After this experience how was your view of God's Word changed or affected? (Question no. 19.)

Although this question received a similar response to Question no. 16, there were different expressions to this question since the main emphasis was their view of God's Word being changed or affected through this experience. Many people stated that their view of God's Word had not been greatly affected while others qualified how there was change and to what degree. There was a greater appreciation for God's Word and an emphasis placed on the value of hermeneutical principles to aid in wisely interpreting the Scriptures and the dangers inherent in the observed practice of taking the Bible out of context. There was renewed hope for spiritual growth in new and vibrant ways.

The following comments are a sampling regarding this section:

Oh yeah! One word, hermeneutics. You can't just make up doctrine.[127]

I actually started studying the Word for myself, instead of letting a pastor dictate it to me.[128]

My view of God's Word has changed a lot. I realize that you can twist it to say anything, and that a wise person will seek a witness of two or three in the Scriptures before making a call. That one cannot believe it just because it says it. That we have to work hard

125. No. 16.
126. No. 13.
127. No. 1.
128. No. 2.

to see it in context and in the original meaning. And this is hard because we bring our own agenda to it all the time.[129]

3. Question no. 15 was phrased this way: Would you consider your-self a Pentecostal/Charismatic in experience? Please describe.

About 31 percent answered no. People who answered yes include those who believe that the charismata are for today, yet may not have experienced any of these gifts, and those who have had personal experi-ence in using charismatic gifts. This number was about 58 percent. The answers covered a broad range of experience defined by the participants as well as variations in personal experiences. There were a variety of de-nominations represented among both the no and yes answers.

Participants responded from many different church denomination-al settings along with those from independent groups. These responses suggested that this was the common experience among believers from a wide range of denominational heritages. This research has suggested that there is a greater correlation among those with Pentecostal and Charismatic traditions, but it is not limited to them.

The following are examples of how participants answered this question:

> No, but yes. Pentecostalism has some very negative connotations for me, because the church we left was ultra Pentecostal. However I do believe in God's Spirit working here and now, as God always works. . . . I find that I am a bit cynical about a lot of P/C things, and that they are shallow and emotionally driven leaving people washed up at the end of the day.[130]

> No. Though my experiences were in a Charismatic Pentecostal church.[131]

> I would not consider myself Pentecostal/Charismatic, but I am open to it. My childhood church was highly cessationist in prac-tice. I am no longer cessationist and enjoy visiting the xx church whenever I get the chance. I would join a Charismatic church if the need arises in the future and if the right church is available.[132]

129. No. 3.
130. Ibid.
131. No. 9.
132. No. 13.

Yes. I believe fully in the power and gifts of the Holy Spirit in the personal life of the believer and in corporate gatherings of believers. I am not in a situation now where I experience this corporately, but I still believe in it.[133]

I do believe that the gifts of the Spirit are operational today, but I don't consider myself either Pentecostal or Charismatic.[134]

No. I come from a very conservative, fundamental xx Christian background.[135]

4. How would you describe your journey with Christ today? (Question no. 20.)

Nearly every participant had positive comments regarding their trust in Christ and their faith in God today. Although some stated that they still had various struggles, their spiritual life was ultimately moving forward in the strength of Christ. It was hugely rewarding to read the range of responses for this question. Some expressed their thoughts in brief one-line statements while others described their situation in a fuller way.

Better than ever! Although there are ups and downs, I finally feel that I am beginning to know God personally. Although I know I have only scratched the surface in this respect, I have a hunger to know him more that is not driven by fear or obligation. I feel far more rooted in grace now, not performance. And I firmly believe that performance and perfection is not what he wants in me either, but only that I would know how totally I am loved.[136]

Light-years and 180 degrees from then. I'm less dogmatic than before, less confident that I have things figured out, more cynical and less trusting of others, fearful of intimacy. All this translates into a rollercoaster ride of faith, but I'm still on the train with my hands in the air.[137]

A journey that began with a bunch of aches and pains, but one that has shaped me into someone confident in God's love through His Son's death, and one that is fruitful for ministry and helping

133. No. 16.
134. No. 80.
135. No. 100.
136. No. 7.
137. No. 8.

others understand the Gospel and what Christ desires of our lives (the call to repent and trust in His work on the cross, not man, or institutions).[138]

Making a change to live what I now believe. I love Jesus more than ever. I understand that I have a Father that loves me. More alone, more alive, more expectant, but not with crazy expectancies. More expectant to see God love others through me. More expectant that He loves me more than I will ever know, and wanting to see my life through those lenses.[139]

The following are a few of the author's personal favorites:

Woohoo! It is not I who lives but Christ who lives in me![140]

Abiding, loving, peaceful as the daughter of the King of Kings—a princess in His royal court, not the maid in the palace who can never rise above being called what I was before I was saved—a dirty rotten sinner deserving of Hell.[141]

I am loved and cherished by Him and I feel it. I used to feel like I was his "problem child." Now I know I am his Joseph and he has made me a coat of many colors. He revels in who I am. His favor is on me, not his hand of wrath.[142]

My home is in His bosom.[143]

It had been hypothesized that participants would need time to heal and grow deeper in the Lord; that they would grow spiritually through this trial; that they would experience giving and receiving forgiveness in more meaningful ways; and that they would grow spiritually healthier through the recovery process. The evidence seems to demonstrate that this is indeed the case. The recognized mar factors were significantly impacted and replaced by biblical beliefs and practices. The depth of the participant's relationship to Christ has been noted and their restored emotional state has been evidenced by greater love, joy, and peace as part of this new phase in their Christian life. Many are being renewed in their trust level with caring leadership and loving communities, while

138. No. 9.
139. No. 10.
140. No. 1.
141. No. 92.
142. No. 43.
143. No. 84.

some still struggle with this factor. There is renewed ecclesiological expectation and a willingness to work with other believers in seeing the Kingdom of God advanced in the earth in whatever Christian context that they now find themselves.

ANALYSIS OF THE PASTOR SURVEYS

The following is an analysis of the ten-question survey completed by pastors who gave spiritual guidance to those who had been in this type of church circumstance before. There were seven pastors. Five of those were male; the other two were female. Three were local, one from another location in British Columbia, and three were located in the United States. The age range of the pastors was from twenty-nine to seventy-four years.

Pastors confirmed that they had met and counseled people who had suffered under authoritarian and controlling pastors. Two pastors described their contacts with such people this way:

> Most are angry that they have worked so hard yet had been "rejected" or "used" by the leaders. I found it best to allow them to let off steam and then slowly encourage them to get on their feet spiritually—often by reading appropriate books and by regular times of sharing with them.[144]

> Many times: People who were browbeaten for disagreeing with leaders. People who were forbidden to leave a church or community because to do so would be "rebellion" against the leadership. People who had their own children physically disciplined by leaders (pastors). People who were warned that God would punish them if they left the church. People who were told they were demonized because they were sick. People who were coerced into giving more money or possessions to leaders. People who had counseling confidences betrayed. People who were criticized for being sick. The list goes on and on. All of the above I have dealt with personally.[145]

Pastors also confirmed that in their pastoral experience they had met and counseled with people who had experienced emotional and spiritual distress from being exposed to aberrant teachings. They noted that abuses have their roots in false teaching. Many pastors also

144. No. P3. (The letter "P" designates a pastor survey.)
145. No. P2.

confirmed that the mar factors were recognized in those who came to them. They were able to be part of the solution for the mar factors in many individuals. When people realized that they were exposed to false teachings that were devoid of God's love and grace, they turned to a pastor who they thought could help them to process this distress.

One pastor stated that an apparent church discipline situation had been based on passages such as 1 Corinthians 5.[146] Further details in this pastor's account suggested that the lead pastor had apparently overreacted and the situation was not handled in an appropriate manner nor based on the actual facts. Consequently, the situation became devastating to the individual and his family and their interest in going to any church in the future was suppressed.

The pastor participating in this study also noted that it is very hard for pastors and board leaders to back down from an escalating situation of discipline. Other church members are often on notice to fall in line behind the pastor and leadership board.[147] This appears to be a recurring pattern among some leadership when dealing with perceived spiritual disciplinary issues in an inappropriate way. The individual is not only grievously affected by their willful moral choices but they are also now overwhelmed by the way the church has handled the situation. The situation is now geared for devastation rather than restoration. Any hope of a changed and repentant heart and the hope of restitution through the ministry of the church have now been lost. The only recourse left for such an individual and their family is to exit the church in shame.

The fact that the Corinth church initially missed it on both counts is an example of how church leaders today have poorly dealt with various church problems and church discipline issues. The church in Corinth did not at first practice any church discipline with this wayward individual. When there was a genuine change of heart and behavior recognized by the entire community, they did not follow through with full restoration.[148] Paul exhorted that the sinning brother was to be welcomed back into the church fellowship and that they were to forgive and comfort him. The Corinth church eventually got it right and demonstrated a mutually beneficial way to bring about restorative church discipline even though dealing with a very difficult moral issue.

146. No. P5.

147. Ibid.

148. 2 Cor 2:5–11.

Church discipline is often indiscriminately used as a methodology to deal with many issues that do not legitimately qualify as those needing such discipline. Action such as public shunning or excommunication is heavy handed with the sole purpose of control by leaders. Even in extreme moral lapses among individuals, there should be a gracious view among leadership with the aim to restore a sinning brother or sister. The ministry of restoration is a biblical principle that was eventually grasped and modeled in the Corinthian setting.

Two pastors who completed the survey suggested that abusive leadership is a manifestation of insecurity.[149] One pastor reflected: "Most abusive leaders are victims themselves."[150] A pastoral observation regarding how people might react under controlling leadership with aberrant teachings is that people do not thrive in authoritarian situations. They will eventually feel the need to disagree or oppose their leaders with potentially devastating results. The end result is that this outcome engenders a cynical view of the Church or it may take some people further away from Christianity.[151]

As pastors considered how they personally processed such circumstances, they offered the following insights. One priority is to protect oneself from becoming an abusive leader.[152] There is a caution to avoid two innate negative tendencies: getting "caught up in the lament" or "trying to force people back to a place of balance." On the other hand, it is important to help people to carefully walk through the process of healing with the emphasis being on getting them through it.[153] Another way of processing such circumstances is to be proactive. This would include: finding and exposing the error, getting people into healthy relationships, being patient with people, modeling health, being clear over the pulpit, and allowing opportunity to talk about these issues—to the pastor and among the congregation.[154]

When pastors were asked how this type of encounter impacted their teaching and energized their efforts to warn the flock under their care to better understand such issues, it was clear that the need to expose error

149. No. P2 and P5.
150. No. P2.
151. No. P7.
152. No. P1.
153. No. P7.
154. No. P2.

and warn the flock against false shepherds is part of the job description for a pastor.[155] The need, as a church leader, is to constantly point people to God, rather than man. This thought was expressed this way: "Most typically, I will find that the victim has a deeper relationship (or fearful respect) with the leader than they have with God."[156]

One pastor strongly suggested that when these incidents occur, it was a reminder to continue telling his congregants that their relationship with God is their primary responsibility. He confirmed a correlation with this research finding that many times congregants want someone to tell them what to do rather than to look to God. That is, people often have this expectation placed on their leaders when they should instead have an intimate and growing relationship with God. Developing a deeper relationship with God should be the aim of a disciple of Christ. Therefore, the pastor(s) should avoid being an intermediary between the congregant and God but instead encourage and model Christian disciplines that develop confidence in God through prayer and Bible study.[157]

In reflecting on the strategies used to assist recovery for those needing help, there were a number of relevant suggestions offered. It is important for church leaders to develop a safe atmosphere where people can share in community. This can be done by allowing each person to share without shutting them down.[158] During a home visit or prearranged session at the church office, pastors need to allow people the opportunity to vent and share their distress with them. A word of caution was that pastors need to avoid counsel beyond their competency and to make efforts to refer people to trained counselors when the need arises.[159] People need to be encouraged to set aside time for Scripture reading and for prayer on their own. There is also need for corporate times of worship, prayer, and for sharing life narratives. One pastor placed a high value on worship as a tool that can have positive affects on victims. Worship gives God the opportunity to heal the victim personally in a meaningful corporate worship setting.[160] Another pastor offered that it is important to remind people of the undeniable fact that humans are

155. Ibid.
156. No. P4.
157. No. P6.
158. No. P7.
159. No. P1.
160. No. P4.

fallible and that no one is perfect. This helps people to give themselves a break, to know that God is there for them, and to process the fact that leaders are not always right.[161]

One of the greatest problems with the authoritarian leader is that they convey the idea that nothing anyone else thinks or believes is important. Therefore, a strategy to help people would be to intentionally listen to individuals when they speak. This ensures that they are respected and that their opinions are valued. Since this pastor also had gone through a long healing process, the principle learned was that it is important to never try to push people.[162] A pastor can encourage the importance to forgive others who feel differently than you do and it is equally important to seek to move on with God no matter what.[163] It is important for people to risk participation in community again. Although it may be difficult, in one pastor's experience, those who do, thrive.[164]

Through this situation pastors expressed a number of things that they had learned. Recognizing one's own fallibility,[165] being reminded that God will not share his glory with a man/pastor, and everyone needs their own relationship with God, independent of any leader. It is important to seek God for your own understanding of His will in your life and not to let anyone (even church leaders) impose what they think God's will for them might be.[166] Although the task of the pastor to encourage and affirm individuals may seem to take a long period of time, eventually "people learn to like themselves and are empowered to rise up above the past unhealthy people and ways they had embraced."[167] A couple of pastors expressed that they, too, had experienced leadership abuse. This personal insight has helped them to overcome the former feelings of being overwhelmed and helpless and to rely on God's grace, which is sufficient, and to filter all things through love.[168]

The questions about what pastors wished they had known before this encounter and what they might have done differently did not

161. No. P6.
162. No. P4.
163. No. P5.
164. No. P7.
165. No. P3.
166. No. P4.
167. No. P6.
168. No. P7.

provide many comments. One pastor combined the two into one answer that expressed the wish of knowing progressive community leaders to network with as sometimes it feels very lonely.[169]

The thoughtful insights of these pastors who took the time to complete this survey are appreciated. Both requests for participants for this study were posted simultaneously, yet there was a limited response from pastors. The possible reasons could be that pastors did not read any of the websites that had this information posted, many pastors have not encountered people with this type of wound, and/or pastors are quite involved in ministry and needed to guard their time.

SUMMARY AND CONCLUSIONS

This chapter has detailed the responses of participants in this ministry research project. It has been confirmed that participants needed confidants—a person that they could trust and discuss personal and upsetting church matters with in a safe and caring setting. It was confirmed that confidants would be found among two categories of people—those who were mature in their faith and had been in this type of church experience themselves or those who could empathize with the participant's unsettling situation. That confidants were mature Christians, such as good friends, relatives, professional counselors, or church ministry leaders from other fellowships, was essential to help them process their negative experience. Along with a single trusted confidant, help from friends greatly assisted those in need. Although many people had been personally hurt through pastors or other church leaders, a number of participants found help from ministers who were sensitive and empathetic to their devastating situation.

Subjects discovered a range of resources that helped to give them practical insights. These resources included use of the Internet to connect with people via websites or blog interactions to give immediate support and feedback; it included finding books that addressed spiritual abuse and the factors that contribute to abusive leadership styles; it also included the resource of a small group offered by some churches that would provide support through this season.

Participants were enabled by the Spirit to grow deeper in the Lord through this crisis as he provided comfort, gave wisdom, renewed,

169. Ibid.

refreshed, stirred up the need to forgive, created compassion for those caught up in error, and finally, guided them in a renewed and healthier spiritual direction. Essentially, the majority of participants have legitimately been renewed in body, mind, and spirit. They are now in a position to minister to others facing similar circumstances. Since they have been healed in this area, they will have developed sensitivities to minister to those in need in other areas and with greater compassion. Where participants had previously felt marred and inadequate in their Christian faith, they have now been rehabilitated and fortified in their faith. The majority of participants would affirm that they are more devoted to Christ and the Christian community through this pivotal circumstance in their Christian lives.

I was hugely impressed and energized by the good response from so many participants from so many locations. This distressing and pivotal church experience has been considered, the emotions have been documented, and the devastation registered among this host of participants. They have recognized the stages of grief and the ultimate stages of personal renewal and recovery.

The majority of participants are now able to provide suitable help and caring ministry to others found in this circumstance. These participants would welcome being called upon by church leaders to reflect on their trial by fire in their previous church and would seek to help leadership to understand the complex aspects of this problem. Their spiritual growth in God with a renewed love for the Church has enriched them further in their Christian life. Their more wholesome view of godly leadership and caring community has enriched them as individuals and has made them able ministers of the grace of God in the community of Christ and in the world.

5

What Can We Do About It?

THIS CHAPTER SUMMARIZES AND attempts to discern the implications of the research findings for current church and leadership
practice. Many pastors may not have had encounters with Christians
who have had negative church experiences and may not be familiar with
this complex issue. When seeking pastors to complete a survey for this
research it was noted that there were very few pastors who responded
to the invitation to participate. Therefore, this study has aimed to be redemptive and to provide awareness of this ministry problem as well as
possible solutions.

This research considered the question: How have Christians recovered after experiencing perceived spiritual abuse in a local congregation?
Participants in this study confirmed that they needed confidants—a
person that they could trust and discuss personal and upsetting church
matters with in a safe and caring setting. These confidants were found
among two categories of people—those who were in this type of church
experience themselves and had come through it wisely, or those who
understood God's grace, had a mature understanding of the Scriptures,
and could empathize with the participant's unsettling situation. That
confidants were mature Christians, such as good friends, relatives, or
church ministry leaders from other fellowships, was essential to help
people process their negative experience. Having someone they could
trust and talk to about their upsetting situation was identified as a basic
need. The fact that people required time to tell and process the details of
their story was also recognized.

Someone to confide in also included professional counselors as well
as pastors. Many people referenced how important their spouse and family members were in allowing them to talk through the issues. Along with
a single trusted confidant, knowing that participants had close friends

who would listen, empathize, and grieve along with them, and offer hope for the future, was both helpful and necessary. Having friends that one could share life together by enjoying common activities helped take the participant's mind off their circumstance and recreate normalcy.[1] This was an essential part of the help that friends could provide for a hurting companion. The need for relationships in a healthy community is one of the primary needs of those affected.[2] Some found that non-Christian friends were also sympathetic. In regard to the importance of help from friends, many participants might strongly agree with this participant's bold declaration: "Without these people I would not have moved on."[3]

Although many people had been personally wounded through pastors and other church leaders, a number of participants found help from ministers who were sensitive and empathetic.[4] Having a caring pastor who listened well helped individuals and couples to cope. Being accepted, loved, and affirmed by this pastor helped them to process their pain and losses. They were also encouraged by the fact that the Church was still a place for them to be involved and find fellowship, to find theological and emotional safety, and to be assured of hope for the future.

Confidants are indispensable when people face severe trials and various levels of personal grief and emotional pain. They allow verbal processing of events and offer consolation. Being able to consider all aspects of one's pain in a safe place, receiving thoughtful and wise feedback to bolster one's faith and identity in Christ, and the recognition that God had been with them through this trial helped people process their disheartening situation. The dedication of those who were available to listen, affirm, offer helpful perspectives, and gently point the way to a better path at such a time was the single most aid to those who have regained spiritual harmony.[5]

1. A helpful insight confirmed by no. 56.

2. See chapter 2.

3. No. 3.

4. This number was 18 percent.

5. Cudmore's research confirmed four major areas of significant support among her participants. These included: support from a Christian friend; a non-Christian friend; spousal and family support; and psychological, medical, or counseling support. Four participants found help through a Christian who was not involved in the church or Christian organization. Three found help from more than one Christian.

One participant stated: "You didn't need a whole lot of friends when you have a couple of friends like that." They prayed, loved, and cried with them. Cudmore, "Victim Suffering," 102.

Progression of Recovery

→ People Leave   (their church)

→ People Grieve   (their losses)

→ People Cleave   (to caring others)

→ People Achieve Renewed Spiritual Harmony

Subjects discovered a range of resources that provided practical insights. These resources included use of the Internet to connect with people via websites or blogs, which allowed them to gain immediate support and feedback. Internet resources also listed participant support groups and recommended books about spiritual abuse, including how to recognize abusive leadership behaviors.

Through connecting with websites, many participants were encouraged to discover that they were not alone, that others had also experienced this type of abusive leadership, and that there were resources they could read to help them further understand and process their situation. The insights gained in this way gave them a broader understanding and renewed hope. When the avenues for Christian fellowship among their local church family had been extinguished, Internet connections that enabled participants to share or ask questions provided a link to the Body of Christ in a way that was crucial for keeping the flame of faith alive and steady. Participants were able to thank God for this oasis of help in the desert of their church experience.

CHURCH		Welcoming
Door Shuts //	→ INTERNET →	Virtual
Ministry Ends //		Christian
Fellowship Ends //		Community

Participants became avid readers and found that their personal research fortified them with an enhanced understanding of these issues. They were also exposed to many books and articles through the online community. These books also confirmed that they were not alone in their struggle since many of the authors and the case studies they included verified that many others had gone this way before them. This timely information gave them a fuller understanding of this Church problem and provided immediate answers for themselves and for others.

Although assistance through specified church support groups was also presented as a potential help, this means to aid recovery was not the experience of these participants. Although some benefited from a small group in a new church context, focus groups that specifically dealt with the topic of grief from exiting distressing church situations was not apparently available or perhaps not even needed. This was simply not a viable option for the majority. It may be difficult to predict if they would have found the availability of such a group appealing or not. Possibly in the future some churches or groups will take this on as a ministry. For this group it was confirmed that the use of the Internet and books that addressed spiritual abuse provided much needed understanding and support.

Participants were propelled forward in their desire to get closer to God through a deepening faith experience. They were enabled by the Spirit to grow deeper in the Lord through this crisis as he provided comfort, gave wisdom, refreshed, stirred up the need to forgive, created compassion for those caught up in error, and finally, guided them in a renewed and healthier spiritual direction. By the Spirit, participants were enabled to experience God's grace in fresh and revitalizing ways and to be renewed in body, mind, and spirit in order to understand the Kingdom of God in new ways. A depth of spiritual formation was experienced in their lives.

Participants confirmed that although difficult at first, their faith grew in ways they had not expected. Participants took comfort when reading certain Scripture passages. This brought immediate support to those who searched for passages of comfort as well as Scriptures that provided pertinent teaching about leadership and/or the Church.[6] They needed time to heal and grow deeper in the Lord; they grew spiritually through this trial; they experienced giving and receiving forgiveness in more meaningful ways; and they grew spiritually healthier through the recovery process.

Allowing time to heal and to grow deeper spiritually has been verified by almost every participant. Although the passing of time was a key factor in the grief process, there was a need for the support of others and the access to knowledge during the recovery time that ensured full

6. This number was 64 percent.

benefit of the recovery process. It was each of these elements, working together over time, which validated that participants had fully recovered from this spiritual and emotional trauma.

Support of Others + The Passing of Time + Access to Knowledge

= RECOVERY

There was a need for some to take their time in finding a new church fellowship. Their plan was not to hurry with this important task but to seriously consider the essentials of their personal criteria for finding a new church. For others, finding a new church home happened quite quickly, or sooner than they had expected. The majority of participants needed to take the time to reassess their ecclesiological paradigm. For a number of participants this time of reflection served to affirm that they ought to meet with Christians outside of the institutional church setting. Some now consider themselves to be post-church. How participants now envisage church is based on their redesigned criteria for Christian fellowship and service that has been forged through this disheartening experience.

Two Trajectories for "Doing Church" Again

Group 1	Found a New Church Home	} Continual
		} Reflection
Group 2	Meet Outside the Institutional Church	} on the Church

Understanding God's grace in vital new ways propelled them forward in their recovery. In securing a biblical understanding of God's grace, participants were able to develop a deeper relationship with God and a greater trust in his plan for their life.

A Solid Biblical Foundation

GOD'S GRACE   → For Salvation   → For Sanctification

Essentially, the majority of participants have legitimately been renewed in body, mind, and spirit and they are now in a position to minister to others. As participants become acquainted with those who struggle with similar circumstances, they can humbly offer their insights with compassion. The Spirit of God has helped and supported participants from their point of devastation to this new place in their Christian lives. They have increased in knowledge and understanding and have experienced a renewed outlook on God's Word, community, and godly leadership. Where participants had previously felt marred and inadequate in their Christian faith, they rehabilitated and fortified their faith. The majority would affirm that they are more devoted to Christ and his Church through this pivotal circumstance in their Christian lives.

Personal Renewal Has Come In These Five Main Areas:

1. Understanding God's Word
2. Experiencing Christian Community
3. Understanding and Experiencing Godly Leadership
4. Greater Devotion to Christ
5. Greater Devotion to the Body of Christ

IMPLICATIONS FOR THE CHURCH

What are the implications for the Church and for church leadership practices that can be gleaned from these study participants? Reflections shared in this section have been inspired by the harvest of insights gained. The following topics will be reviewed: church leadership, the need to recognize dysfunction in the Body of Christ; the need to learn from the corporate wisdom of God's people; the need for compassion for abusive leaders; the need to revisit leadership styles in our churches; the need to teach God's grace and assure Christians of their identity in Christ; the need to rely on the Spirit to develop Christian community; the need to develop discernment skills in the church community; the need to value the place of women in church ministry; and the need to reexamine the teachings and practice of church discipline. Throughout this summary the role that denominational overseers can play will be referenced.

There is an array of topics that Christian communities need to examine together so that they are grounded theologically. Leadership plays a huge role in this. There has been increased attention in literature on dysfunctional leaders in the last decade.[7] Plainly, some Christian leaders, either intentionally or unintentionally, distort what the Bible says. It has been added to, subtracted from, and made to say things that were never intended.[8] Devious leaders use the Scriptures in ways that suit their purposes and consequently people are brought into spiritual bondage. The Scriptures become unknowingly misrepresented and people simply follow without question or without discerning the dangers resident in those belief systems.

Those with pastor-teacher giftings have a mandate to instruct and care well for God's people. Pastors are at the forefront and are called to be active in building up the people of God in his grace and defending them from error. In the primary function of a pastor-teacher, there are foundational teachings to ground Christians in biblical truths, fortify them spiritually, and help to provide a defense against misbeliefs.

Chapter 3 considered that the teaching, or rather, the misbelief of legalism, shows how the various mar factors could be easily intertwined. First, how one interprets the Word of God, how one essentially understands their salvation, and how one discerns truth from error are simultaneously negatively affected. Furthermore, a stifled understanding of the sanctification process, a lack of experiencing authentic community, and a lack of experiencing caring leadership take their toll in the life of believers. Many Christians are spiritually defenseless in places where control and manipulation are exercised. Therefore, the vital teaching on God's grace is foundational to a Christian's spiritual walk and is a defense against legalism.

A leader's task is to show how grace seeks out the lost soul, reawakens the spiritually demoralized, and brings forth spiritual growth.[9] The purpose of caregiving is to make the truth of grace a reality in the inner life of the individual. "The purpose of preaching is to attest the history of grace effectively at work amid the history of sin."[10] Since much in our cultural environment goes directly against the stream of the Christian teaching of grace, believers who remain ignorant of this history of grace are not apt to take deep root spiritually.[11] The teaching of grace stands as

7. Cudmore, "Victim Suffering," 47.

8. See chapter 2 for insights from Cudmore's thesis.

9. Oden, *Transforming Power*, 15.

10. Ibid.

11. Ibid., 17.

a penetrating challenge to all pretensions of self-sufficiency.[12] It would appear that "Only that which is enabled by divine grace will endure in the Church. All plays and maneuvers circumventing grace will atrophy."[13] To reiterate, many recurring distortions of the faith might have been averted if more effort had been expended to ground the people of God in the biblical teaching of grace.[14] This research has suggested this correlation. Comprehending the teaching of God's grace is foundational to spiritual formation and the believer's daily walk with Christ and how well a Christian community can journey together as an eschatological community.

Instruction on God's grace and the empowerment of the Holy Spirit help the believer to live a spiritual life that is pleasing to God. Being grounded in dependence on the Spirit is the only way for people of God to know what is pleasing to him.[15] It is important to fully grasp what the Spirit intends the Church to be.[16] Instead of giving believers in the early churches rules to live by, Paul gave them the Spirit.[17] This is a far superior way of Christian discipleship.

Spiritual principles and beliefs flow out of who Christ is. Since Christ modeled his dependence upon the Spirit, relying totally on the Spirit is what the Christian life is all about.[18] Leaders need to understand this for themselves and then teach and model it. They need to follow the Apostle Paul's example of not giving Christians rules to live by but giving them the Spirit.[19] Since it is only by a renewed mind that Christians discover how best to love and that the renewing of a believer's mind is the direct work of the Holy Spirit,[20] creating loving communities is also the work of the Spirit and they will not happen any other way.

12. Ibid., 38.

13. Ibid., 21.

14. Ibid.

15. Fee, *Paul*, 95.

16. See chapter 2 where insights from Fee, *Paul*, shed light on what the Church should be.

17. Fee, *Paul*, 106.

18. Ibid., 95.

19. Ibid., 106.

20. Ibid., 105, 67.

| PASTORS | Build Up God's People in His Grace |
| | Alert God's People to False Beliefs |

The entire idea of personal holiness has so often been works-based. When considering personal holiness in the context of community, Christian ethics is not primarily an individualistic one-on-one-with-God kind of holiness. Rather, it has to do with living the life of the Spirit in Christian community and in the world. Christian ethics also has to do with corporate life in the Spirit whereby God has created an eschatological people who live the life of the future in the present. This life reflects the character of God. It is the Spirit who now leads God's children in paths of righteousness for his name's sake.[21] Therefore, it is the Spirit, and the Spirit alone, who not only gets believers on their way in Christ, but also is what Christian life is finally all about.[22]

How can pastors ensure that their flocks are spiritually strong and that they have eliminated the debilitating effects of the mar factors? Since the teaching-pastor's responsibility is to teach sound doctrine and to confront error, this task has two components: teachings that elaborate on the spiritual riches that the Church has received through the finished work of Christ—those that encourage confidence in God and spiritual vitality—and those beliefs that must be exposed as error since they debilitate and weaken people's faith. Christian discipleship needs to include the following topics as part of a believer's theological understanding: God's grace (the antidote for legalism), an understanding of how to read and interpret the Bible (the antidote for a faulty hermeneutic), instruction in sound doctrine and practice (the underpinnings for discerning truth from error), and biblical teaching and modeling of godly leadership (the antidote for faulty leadership models).

---

21. Ibid., 98–99. Fee notes that "Even though it was God's presence that distinguished Israel as God's own people, their identity as that people was bound up with their obedience to the Torah, the law. Itinerant Jewish Christians were forever dogging Paul's heels, entering his churches and arguing that for believers in Christ to be identified with God's people they must also observe Torah. On the contrary, Paul argues, the Spirit, and the Spirit alone, identifies the people of God under the new covenant," 100.

22. Ibid., 95.

God's Grace	Antidote for Legalism
How to Read and Interpret the Bible	Antidote for a Faulty Hermeneutic
Instruction in Sound Doctrine and Practice	Underpinnings for Discerning Truth from Error
Teaching and Modeling Godly Leadership	Antidote for Faulty Leadership Models

One primary implication derived from this research was to recognize that this data represents a sampling of the dysfunction which can be found in the Church today, mainly in the United States and Canada, but not limited by the Church culture found there. One crucial factor in dealing with dysfunctional families is to recognize that there is dysfunction and that it is harming those who are part of it. If there is dysfunction in the Church, then the least we can do is recognize it. Not to recognize dysfunction will portray an unrealistic understanding of the Church and add to the problem. Clergy maltreatment will continue to allow harm among Christians. Some participants strongly believe that a "code of silence" needs to be broken and that the voice of those affected needs to be heard.

Not all churches have an environment that is conducive to healing and there are many "toxic" churches today. These are communities where guilt, manipulation, fear, and shame reign. The inevitable fact is that the spiritual atmosphere is poisoned and healing is all but impossible.[23] According to a number of authors, the belief is that in most cases distressing leadership behavior is consistently premeditated. Improper understanding of biblical leadership, ingrained habits, poor modeling, and a feeling of insecurity within an individual and/or in the leadership task may contribute to unwarranted leadership behaviors. It is suggested that these findings need to draw the attention of denominational overseers.

23. See chapter 2.

Just doing things the way they have always been done is a large part of the problem. It would be prudent to evaluate why certain behaviors continue. If they prove to have a negative outcome rather than a positive outcome then appropriate action should be initiated in order to remedy such patterns. There is a specific challenge for older leaders to intentionally question their assumptions about leadership and adopt new attitudes and learn new skills.[24] Leadership roles and styles must change because it is a necessity not an option. Churches need to move from a hierarchical and highly controlling style of leadership to a decentralized relational model because "leadership is about connecting, not controlling."[25]

Younger evangelicals have gone back to the servant leader model of Christ and are considering "a much older faith and practice, more tested by time, more rooted in the traditions of the ancient Church rather than a perpetuation of twentieth-century traditional evangelical-ism."[26] The leadership ministry style of the younger evangelical will be distinctly different from that of the twentieth-century evangelical.

> It will be biblically informed by the *Missio Dei* to rescue the entire created order; it will be theological, rooted in the Trinitarian and Christological purposes of God to restore the fullness of his image in us and to bring all creation to its redemption and reconciliation to God; and it will be conscious in its action in and to the world of the new cultural situation in which we live, taking into consideration the new realities of the twenty-first century.[27]

The people of God are the Body of Christ on the earth and his Spirit resides within them. I have always been impressed with the corporate wisdom of the people of God. In working through the many answers of the survey questions, this was evident again and again. This body of wisdom, which was gained through personal pain, is presented as a testimony to the spirit and conviction of those who have suffered in the Church. The potential remedies they offer to those who would hear their corporate voice can assist in dealing successfully with this complex ministry problem.

It is important to consider the seven criteria that would enable participants to call a particular church "home." They include the follow-

24. Gibbs, *Leadership Next*, 16.

25. Ibid., 106.

26. Webber, *Younger Evangelicals*, 239.

27. Ibid., 253.

ing: God's Word is primary, people are loved and able to participate in a dedicated Christian community, the church is led with integrity, leadership and the community is motivated by the Holy Spirit, there is social awareness outside the church community, women can minister in the church, and vibrant spiritual worship of God is the priority.

Participant Criteria For Finding a Church Home

1. The primary place of God's Word in Christian Community.

2. Being loved and participating in a dedicated Christian community.

3. Integrity of Christian leadership.

4. Leadership and community motivated in ministry by the Holy Spirit.

5. Social awareness outside of the church community.

6. An equal place for women to minister in the church.

7. The priority of vibrant spiritual worship of God by His people.

The writer is confident that if pastors asked the core families of their church what they valued in a church community that they would likely come up with a similar list of criteria. These criteria appear to be the essentials needed for Christians to continue to grow spiritually so that they can minister effectively as a Christian community.

The church home that participants are looking for could be stated this way:

The Church that I Am Looking for
Is a Christian Community that:

- Loves God and reverences His Word
- Follows the example of Christ
- Is motivated by the Holy Spirit
- Encourages participation by everyone
- Includes ministry by both genders
- Includes ministry by all age groups
- Includes ministry by all ethnicities
- Ministers outside of its own community

There is a need to have compassion for those church leaders who have followed a faulty paradigm of leadership. Somehow in their training, in their study of the Scriptures, as well as in the modeling that they have observed, they missed out on the fuller view of godly, Christ-like leadership. A pastor's insecurities, along with his or her hopes and aspirations of being a good leader, may have been clouded over by the human element that also longs for conspicuous importance and control. The tendency to value power over relationship and to hold the reins of authority tightly ranks high among many leaders and thus, the wounding continues. Many of those who have been influenced or marred by this type of leadership feel that there is little that they, as an individual, a couple, or even as a small representative group, can do. It is difficult for those who have been hurt to take action and express that this leadership bent does not work, that it brings spiritual and emotional pain, and that it provides no avenue for resolve among those who have been under this type of pastoral regime.

Compliant governing boards often protect pastors and associate church leaders in these systems. From the vantage point of denominational leaders who oversee a large number of churches, this ministry problem may remain undetected. In some places, the denominational oversight may be part of the dysfunctional leadership bent of this group. This factor may further enable or excuse this type of behavior. It is difficult for those who have been harmed to alert the attention of church leaders at the denominational level or those in sister churches in order to get help and/or a measure of resolve in these situations. It is important that others in the Church awaken to this situation in order to be involved and take any appropriate action.

It is vital for church and denominational leaders to consider the insights and warnings offered by various authors. These research findings could motivate church and denominational leaders to consider their group's priorities and see if they may need to make minor adjustments or more strategic changes in theology or practice. The potential for greater authenticity in Christian communities and greater dependence on the Spirit can be the outcome.

Should denominational overseers, church consultants, or seminary professors encourage pastors to take on more authority in their churches? First, this idea needs to be unpacked as to what is meant by this admonition. Although initially this may seem like a reasonable plan, there is much more that needs to be considered and brought into the equation. This admonition may prove to be unprofitable since the implications may not be thought through well enough. It also may exacerbate an existing problem.

NEW LEADERSHIP STYLES

It is imperative to consider leadership styles in the Christian Church. Do the ones that are suggested, encouraged, and modeled bear fruit among the flock? Are they biblical? The whole issue of a viable leadership model in the Church needs to be periodically revisited. The questions to be reckoned with are: Why change my leadership style? And, if there is need for change: How can I change? The biblical model for leadership encourages dependence upon the Holy Spirit as modeled by Christ. As church leaders comprehend that the leader's role is to depend on the Spirit in order to model the character of Christ, they can reexamine their own life and seek the Spirit's help to continue to aid them in ministry. Any mixed or corroded model of leadership that does not measure up to the model that Jesus taught and demonstrated will be ineffective and consequently in need of renewal. The question that the disciples asked: "Who could become the greatest in the Kingdom?" needs to be rephrased, as Christ earnestly enquired: "Who will be the servant of all?"[28]

Since the concept of servant leadership is not only a New Testament concept but was also recorded in the Old Testament, church leaders can be encouraged that this would be the best paradigm for leadership for any season of Church history. According to biblical design, servant leadership can only be attained by the enabling power of the Holy Spirit. The ideal would be to scrutinize one's leadership beliefs and practices and see if there is need for adjustment and change. The season of momentous change that the Church is now experiencing consistently requires that leaders are fortified by the Word of God with total dependence upon the Holy Spirit in order to minister well in the Kingdom.

A healing community is a place where the broken can find help and where the disconnected can find connection. It is a place where people can go from the point of initial salvation in Christ to a place of discipleship and journeying together with others by the enabling power of the Spirit of Christ. Leaders who minister to Christians in the basic theo-

28. Mark 9:33–35.

logical concepts of God's immeasurable grace, their identity in Christ, and vibrant biblical community pave the way for healthier spiritual communities.[29]

The importance of the grace of God as an essential teaching for new Christians and a refresher for those further along in their faith needs to be the energizing motivation of godly leaders. Where grace is taught, distortions in the Christian faith are minimized.[30] There is a need to step up the pace regarding the primary teaching of God's grace since there has been so much teaching to the contrary and the lack of comprehension of this essential teaching abounds. The heart of a community could then center on looking for opportunities to be dispensers of grace accompanied by wisdom.[31] On this foundation, the teachings of one's identity in Christ and vibrant community can be securely built.

Leadership Goals to Aim for in the Local Church

→   Foundational Teaching on God's Grace
    and the Finished Work of Christ

→   This Establishes the Believer's Identity in Christ

→   This Helps to Establish a Vibrant Biblical Community

In order to establish spiritual communities, leaders must rely on the fact that it is the Holy Spirit who initiates eternal salvation as well as spiritual formation and Christian mission. The Spirit's aim is to develop the image of Christ in individual Christians and corporately in the spiritual community. Christians need to be frequently reminded that "God is not just saving individuals and preparing them for heaven; rather, he is creating a people among whom he can live and who in their life together will reproduce God's life and character."[32] Believers in Christ need to understand and often be reminded that: "The community of God's people owe their life together as a body to their common, lavish experience of the Spirit."[33]

---

29. See chapter 2.
30. Oden, *Transforming Power*, 21.
31. See chapter 2.
32. Fee, *Paul*, 66.
33. Ibid.

GOD is Creating a People
Among whom He can Live
And who in their Life Together
Will reproduce God's Life and Character.[34]

The Apostle John, in his First Epistle, points out that it is the work of the Spirit to move individuals and Christian communities closer to the will of God and into total obedience to him. The dependence on the leader to hear what the Spirit is saying to the community is vitally important, but it is not solely his or her responsibility. It is the mutual responsibility of all those who have come together as a believing community. The dependence of the leader upon the guidance of the Spirit can be a safeguard against trying to shape people according to the leader's design. Equally, the dependence of the community upon the Spirit can safeguard it against being shaped into the leader's design and not the Holy Spirit's. Honoring the role of the leader by the congregants and mutually valuing the principle of the priesthood of all believers strikes a better harmony for journeying together as the people of God.

THE CHURCH AS A HEALING COMMUNITY

The Church is a healing community characterized by the fact that as individuals connect in small healing communities they can go out to connect even more deeply and invite others to enjoy that same intimacy.[35] Simply put, "Maybe the center of Christian community is connecting with a few."[36] This is an uncomplicated yet effective way to disciple others well and to grow deeper in Christ together. A healing community, therefore, would be a people who place connecting at the center of their purpose and passion—connecting with God (worship), others (loving service), and self (personal wholeness). Loving God and loving others lie at the core of God's intention for his people.[37]

---

34. Ibid.
35. Crabb, *Connecting*, xiv.
36. Ibid., xiii.
37. Ibid., 206.

	GOD
CONNECTING WITH	SELF
	OTHERS

Being involved in a church that does not connect is not where these participants are interested in fellowshiping or ministering. Making connecting a priority is important to Christians who have come through this recovery process. Connecting authentically with others lends itself to a purposeful and caring community. Everything becomes deeper and more meaningful when Christians start to use their faith in a manner than reaches out and helps others.

Seeing those who appear to be "invisible" would be a community goal to aim for. Many people feel that although they are among a crowd of Christians in a church, they actually feel invisible. They wonder if anyone really cares for them. They are equally perplexed as to how they can truly love God's people and connect with them in certain Christian contexts since it seems like a difficult task among an apparently unwelcoming crowd. They question if there are others who struggle with their faith as well as with life in general like they do. A community that is touched by the unsearchable love of God can reflect this love to those who seek purpose and have the innate desire to belong.

Developing a culture of hospitality to the stranger is one that has been modeled by God himself. God reached out and demonstrated hospitality to those foreign to his house. He continues to inspire his people how to demonstrate his kind of hospitality in a general culture of self-centered aloneness and independence. Human beings everywhere need to be continually exposed to the kindness and generosity of God. This begins among those who have tasted and experienced his lavish generosity.

People Everywhere Need to be Exposed to The Kindness and Generosity of God

It is difficult to grow an emotionally healthy church if the leaders do not address issues beneath the surface of their lives.[38] It is foundational to recognize that emotional health and spiritual health are inseparable.

38. Ibid., 45.

"It is not possible for a Christian to be spiritually mature while remaining emotionally immature."[39] Since the ultimate purpose of the Gospel is to transform Christians, the end result ought to be that Christians are better lovers of God and other people.[40]

In order for individuals to explore some of the disturbing and dark aspects of who they are, it is crucial that they are grounded in God's grace and that they confidently stand before God as his beloved. It is the revelation of God's free grace that gives his people the courage to face the painful truth about themselves. As all of God's children, not just the leaders, step out onto the tightrope of discovering the unpleasant things about themselves, they realize that they have a safety net below—the Gospel of Jesus Christ.[41] As leaders continue to be healed and transformed by the penetrating power of the Gospel, the effect will be felt among the believing community.

Since people can only change by the direct intervention of God, it is important to cultivate a safe and healing atmosphere—a place where deep emotional and spiritual healing is the norm. Many authors, along with the message of the New Testament, confirm that it is hard to imagine living out healthy family life apart from the context of a healthy church life.[42] It is important to look to God's Spirit to initiate and build meaningful relationships among a spiritual community. A Christian community needs to realize that becoming a Christian, although giving someone a new identity for the future and forgiveness for the past, does not automatically erase the past. Such a community needs to incarnate the fact that God desires to heal brokenness and to patch up wounds. Therefore, people inside and outside of Christian communities can begin to recognize that the local church is a spiritual family where hurting children can be truly reparented.[43]

As a community learns to absorb and grow through pain, it will bear the fruit of Godlike compassion toward others. Churches can steward their corporate experience of pain and minister God's grace to the hurting.[44] The ability to embrace grief and losses together will equip a com-

---

39. Ibid., 50.
40. Ibid., 78.
41. Ibid., 83.
42. Ibid., 99.
43. Ibid.
44. Murren, *Churches That Heal*, 251.

munity to love others as Jesus did. This leads to making incarnation the model for loving well. Making incarnation a priority ought to strengthen the core of a community. People don't need to belong to church to be fixed, they need to receive and experience love and forgiveness in Christ. Together, Christians can grow in genuine love as the New Testament has plainly exhorted is the pattern for authentic Christian experience.[45]

There are two unfulfilled needs among some participants that healing churches and their leaders could consider. The first idea would be to have a focus group specifically designed for those previously wounded by church leaders.[46] In the future, some churches or groups may take this on as a ministry. Those in their fellowship who have gone through such a trial may be the ones who could minister to those with this need. Second would be to stimulate an interest among church leaders who could develop practical care among those who may now be classed as "wandering sheep." Wandering sheep are defined as those who carry the affects of personal pain in their lives but don't yet feel comfortable reintegrating into one healthy church. They instead wander from place to place in hopes of finding a community that they can call home. One local ministerial has taken this assignment on as a shared interdenominational ministry task. Both of these ideas can be small but meaningful contributions to this complex situation.

Mistaken concepts regarding the place of women as co-laborers in the Church need to be carefully reconsidered by church leaders. Women and men, daughters and sons, need to be undergirded by an egalitarian view of ministry inside and outside of the church setting. As many authors have noted, the biblical view of the place of women in the Church has been distorted. The fallout in the Church, along with the Christian influence lost in the secular world, continues to throw a negative spin on the ministry of the Church in society. Since the place of women in the

45. Jesus confirmed that the two greatest commandments are to love God and to love one's neighbor.

46. As stated earlier: Although some churches provide grief support groups, among this group of participants a support group specifically designed for those wounded through a devastating church situation was not available. No such focused support group within a church or meeting outside of a church setting was identified. Although some participants were benefited by a small group in a new church context, groups that specifically dealt with the topic of grief from exiting distressing church situations was not apparently available. This was not a viable option for the majority of the participants in this study.

Church does not solely affect women but affects men as well, this theological issue needs to be tackled in order to have greater breakthroughs on the Christian landscape.

IN CLOSING

Most Christians would freely agree with James's statement regarding how they would develop perseverance in their faith through various trials.[47] What Christians often haven't been able to fathom is the depth of the trial by fire that they have had to endure in the Church and under their own church leadership. Furthermore, many have proven the admonition to ask God for wisdom. Over time, people have received insightful theological answers to explain what has happened to them. This has been confirmed by the accounts of others who have gone through the same ordeal.

A number of participants expressed the fact that they hoped that their contribution would do some good; that their insights would be helpful; and that church leaders might pay attention to their experience and to the "emotionally expensive lessons" learned through it. They hoped that those who could do something about it would take note in order to prevent a multitude of others from experiencing the same type of devastation that they have gone through.

As pastors and other church leaders reflect on the survey comments it is hoped that they will better understand the emotional toll on this representative group alone as well as attempt to understand the magnitude of these effects in the lives of many others. It is hoped that as church leaders consider the elements described in the process of recovery that there will be a greater appreciation for the work of God's immeasurable grace experienced in these lives. The fact that these participants are willing and ready to minister to others, as opportunities arise, should cause thanksgiving to God. It is hoped that the renewed corporate passion for the things of God among these participants will be recognized and celebrated.

The entire topic of corrective church discipline[48] has been only moderately developed in this study. Participants have experienced harsh and unloving forms of church discipline that was neither corrective

47. James 1:2.

48. White and Blue's book *Healing The Wounded* may be a helpful tool.

nor restorative. Leaders in the Church who had used a faulty model of church discipline have brought great pain on a multitude of people. The accounts of these participants verify that this unfruitful methodology continues to bring devastating results among those who claim to be followers of Christ. The statistics continue to mount of those who have faced the "spiritual guns" of the Christian "firing squads" in the local church setting. The entire concept of biblical corrective church discipline seems to be a topic that has been misunderstood and misapplied and needs to be revisited by the local church as well as by denominational representatives. There needs to be a stronger New Testament model for the local church to emulate. All aspects of corrective church discipline need to be reconsidered theologically in order for a more reasonable biblical pattern to be practiced. The main goal should be restoration, not just shunning or expulsion. These questions arise: What is corrective church discipline and why and how does it need to be applied? How was corrective church discipline administered in the New Testament? What can be learned in order to avoid the pitfalls of extreme and unfruitful church discipline? When and how could restoration be applied?

The following are suggested topics for further research: 1. Corrective church discipline and the ministry of restoration; 2. Impact on second generation people who have experienced the devastating effects of spiritual abuse as children of parents who went through this upsetting family situation; 3. Emotional consequences encountered by church leavers;[49] 4. Correlation between local church denominations and the patterns of spiritual abuse encountered by their congregants; and 5. The relation between legalism (dogmatism) and pastoral abuse.

In conclusion, this chapter has reviewed the outcomes of this study. The implications for the Church and church leadership have been discussed. There are many more topics that could be developed from this complex Church ministry situation. How church leaders have been enlightened through reading about this research will be manifested in how they take on afresh the challenge of ministry in their congregations and how the Church as a whole responds to the needs that have been identified by this study. The Church is in a season of momentous change. There are many needs in the Church today and there is much work to do. The issue of spiritual abuse in the Church is one area that needs serious at-

49. These two ideas for research were suggested by one of the participants.

tention. Only by the grace-full power of the Holy Spirit can these issues be sensibly tackled and conscientiously solved.

* * *

May the God of peace, who through the blood of the eternal covenant brought back from the dead our Lord Jesus, that great Shepherd of the sheep, equip you with everything good for doing his will, and may he work in us what is pleasing to him, through Jesus Christ, to whom be glory for ever and ever. Amen.

—Hebrews 13:20–21

Bibliography

à Kempis, Thomas. *Of the Imitation of Christ.* Burlington, ON: Inspirational Promotions, 1970.

Achtemeier, Elizabeth. *Preaching from the Old Testament.* Louisville: Westminster John Knox, 1989.

Adams, Jay E. *Shepherding God's Flock.* Philipsburg, NJ: Presbyterian and Reformed Publishing, 1980.

Adam, Peter. *Speaking God's Words: A Practical Theology of Expository Preaching.* Downers Grove, IL: InterVarsity, 1996.

Anderson, Neil T. *Bondage Breaker.* Eugene, OR: Harvest House, 1993.

————. *Helping Others Find Freedom in Christ.* Ventura, CA: Regal Books, 1995.

————. *Living Free in Christ.* Ventura, CA: Regal Books, 1993.

————. *Victory Over the Darkness.* Ventura, CA: Regal Books, 1990.

————. Freedom in Christ Ministries. Online: http://www.ficm.org.

Anderson, Neil T., et al. *Breaking the Bondage of Legalism.* Eugene, OR: Harvest House, 2003.

————, et al. *Christ-Centered Therapy.* Grand Rapids, MI: Zondervan, 2000.

Anderson, Neil T., and Charles Mylander. *Setting Your Church Free.* Ventura, CA: Regal Books, 1994.

Anderson, Neil T., and David Park. *Overcoming Negative Self-image.* Ventura, CA: Regal Books, 2003.

Apologetics Index. Online: http://www.apologeticsindex.org.

Apologetics Resource Center. No pages. Online: http://www.arcapologetics.org.

Arterburn, Stephen. *Faith that Hurts Faith that Heals.* Nashville: Thomas Nelson, 1991.

Arterburn, Stephen, and Jack Felton. *Toxic Faith.* Colorado Springs: Waterbrook, 1991.

Assemblies of God. Online: http://www.ag.org.

Backus, William. *Telling Each Other the Truth.* Minneapolis: Bethany House, 1985.

————. *Telling the Truth to Troubled People.* Minneapolis: Bethany House, 1985.

Backus, William, and Marie Chapian. *Telling Yourself the Truth.* Minneapolis: Bethany House, 1980.

Bakke, Ray. *The Urban Christian.* Downers Grove, IL: InterVarsity, 1987.

Banks, Robert, and Bernice M. Ledbetter. *Reviewing Leadership.* Grand Rapids, MI: Baker Academic, 2004.

Barna, George. *Finding A Church You Can Call Home.* Ventura, CA: Regal Books, 1992.

————. *Leaders On Leadership.* Ventura, CA: Regal Books, 1997.

The Barna Group. "Women Are the Backbone of the Christian Congregations in America." March 6, 2000. Online: http://www.barna.org/FlexPage.aspx?Page=BarnaUpdate&BarnaUpdateID=47.

Beasley-Murray, Paul. *Power for God's Sake.* Carlisle, United Kingdom: Paternoster Press, 1998.

Beverley, James A. *Holy Laughter and the Toronto Blessing.* Grand Rapids, MI: Zondervan, 1995.

Bierly, Steve R. *How to Thrive as a Small-Church Pastor.* Grand Rapids, MI: Zondervan, 1998.

Bilezikian, Gilbert. *Community 101.* Grand Rapids, MI: Zondervan, 1997.

Blackaby, Henry T. *Created To Be God's Friends.* Nashville: Thomas Nelson, 1999.

Block, Daniel I. "The Burden of Leadership: The Mosaic Paradigm of Kingship (Deut 17:14–20)." *Bibliotheca Sacra* 162 (2005) 259–78.

———. "The Grace of Torah: The Mosaic Prescription for Life (Deut 4:1–8; 6:20–25)." *Bibliotheca Sacra* 162 (2005) 3–22.

———. "The Joy of Worship: The Mosaic Intervention to the Presence of God (Deut 12:1–14)." *Bibliotheca Sacra* 162 (2005) 131–49.

———. "Preaching Old Testament Law to New Testament Christians." Paper presented to Lutheran pastors in Copenhagen, May 6, 2005.

Blue, Ken. *Healing Spiritual Abuse.* Downers Grove, IL: InterVarsity, 1993.

Bower, Tim, and Jason Loftis. Letters From Leavers. Online: http://lettersfromleavers .com.

Bredfeldt, Gary. *Great Leader Great Teacher.* Chicago: Moody, 2006.

Bridge, Donald, and David Phypers. *Spiritual Gifts and the Church.* London: InterVarsity, 1973.

Brown, Michael L. *What Happened to the Power of God?* Shippensburg, PA: Destiny Image Publishers, 1991.

Burchett, Dave. *When Bad Christians Happen to Good People.* Colorado Springs: Waterbrook, 2002.

Burgess, Stanley M., and Gary B. McGee, eds. *Dictionary of Pentecostal and Charismatic Movements.* Grand Rapids, MI: Zondervan, 1988.

Burks, Ron, and Vicki Burks. *Damaged Disciples.* Grand Rapids, MI: Zondervan, 1992.

Cairns, Earle E. *Christianity Through the Centuries.* Grand Rapids, MI: Academie Books, 1954.

Calian, Carnegie Samuel. *Survival or Revival.* Louisville: Westminster John Knox, 1998.

Christian Research Institute. Online: http://www.equip.org.

Christianity Today Library. Online: http://www.ctlibrary.com.

Christians For Biblical Equality. Online: http://www.cbeinternational.org.

Chrnalogar, Mary Alice. *Twisted Scriptures.* Grand Rapids, MI: Zondervan, 1997.

ChurchAbuse.com. Online: http://www.churchabuse.com.

Clinebell, Howard. *Basic Types of Pastoral Care and Counseling.* Nashville: Abingdon, 1966.

———. *Counseling for Spiritually Empowered Wholeness.* New York: Haworth Pastoral Press, 1995.

Clinton, J. Robert. *The Making of a Leader.* Colorado Springs: NavPress, 1988.

Cloud, Henry. *Changes That Heal.* Grand Rapids, MI: Zondervan, 1990.

Clowney, Edmund P. *The Church.* Downers Grove, IL: InterVarsity, 1995.

Cordeiro, Wayne. *Doing Church As a Team.* Ventura, CA: Regal Books, 2001.

Couture, Pamela D., and Rodney J. Hunter, eds. *Pastoral Care and Social Conflict.* Nashville: Abingdon, 1995.

Crabb, Larry. *Connecting.* Nashville: Word Publishing, 1997.

———. *Inside Out.* Colorado Springs: NavPress, 1988.

Cudmore, Marilyn J. "The Experience of Victim Suffering and Perception of Leadership Abuse in Christian Organizations." MA thesis, Trinity Western University, 2002.

Cult Awareness and Information Center. Online: http://www.caic.com.au.

Cult Awareness Network. Online: http://www.cultawarenessnetwork.org.

Cunningham, Loren, and David Joel Hamilton. *Why Not Women?* Seattle: YWAM Publishing, 2000.

Dayringer, Richard. *The Heart of Pastoral Counseling.* New York: Haworth Pastoral Press, 1998.

Dodd, Brian J. *Empowered Church Leadership: Ministry in the Spirit According to Paul.* Downers Grove, IL: InterVarsity, 2003.

Douglas, J. D., org. ed. *New Bible Dictionary,* 2nd ed. Wheaton, IL: Tyndale, 1982.

Dudley, Carl S. *Making the Small Church Effective.* Nashville: Abingdon, 1978.

Dupont, Marc A. *Walking Out of Spiritual Abuse.* Tonbridge, England: Sovereign World, 1997.

Easum, Bill. *Leadership on the Other Side.* Nashville: Abingdon, 2000.

Eichel, Steve K. D. RETIRN (Re-entry Therapy, Information and Referral Network). Online: http://www.retirn.com.

Emergent Village. Online: http://www.emergentvillage.com/Site/index.htm.

Enroth, Ronald. *Churches That Abuse.* Grand Rapids, MI: Zondervan, 1992. Also available online at: http://www.ccel.us/churches.toc.html.

———. *Recovering from Churches That Abuse.* Grand Rapids, MI: Zondervan, 1994. Also available online at: http://www.ccel.us/churchesrec.toc.html.

Enroth, Ronald, and J. Gordon Melton. *Why Cults Succeed Where the Church Fails.* Elgin, IL: Brethren Press, 1985.

Erickson, Millard J. *Christian Theology.* Grand Rapids, MI: Baker Books, 1983.

Estrada, Nelson P. *From Followers to Leaders.* New York: T. & T. Clark, 2004.

Farnsworth, Kirk E. *Wounded Workers.* Mukilteo, WA: WinePress, 1998.

Fee, Gordon D. *The First Epistle to the Corinthians.* Grand Rapids, MI: William B. Eerdmans, 1987.

———. *Gospel and Spirit.* Peabody, MA: Hendrickson Publishers, 1991.

———. *Listening to the Spirit in the Text.* Vancouver, BC: Regent College Publishing, 2000.

———. *Paul, the Spirit, and the People of God.* Peabody, MA: Hendrickson Publishers, 1996.

Fee, Gordon D., and Douglas Stuart. *How to Read the Bible for All Its Worth.* Grand Rapids, MI: Zondervan, 1981.

Forman, Rowland, et al. *The Leadership Baton.* Grand Rapids, MI: Zondervan, 2004.

Frazee, Randy. *The Connecting Church.* Grand Rapids, MI: Zondervan, 2001.

———. *Making Room For Life.* Grand Rapids, MI: Zondervan, 2003.

Frick, Don M. *Robert K. Greenleaf.* San Francisco: Berrett-Koehler Publishers, 2004.

Fromont, Paul. *Prodigal Kiwis.* Online: http://prodigal.typepad.com.

Frost, Michael, and Alan Hirsch. *The Shaping of Things to Come.* Peabody, MA: Hendrickson Publishers, 2003.

Gangel, Kenneth O. *Feeding & Leading.* Grand Rapids, MI: Baker Books, 1989.

George, Carl F., and Robert E. Logan. *Leading and Managing Your Church.* Old Tappen, NJ: Fleming H. Revell, 1987.

Gibbs, Eddie. *Church Next.* Downers Grove, IL: InterVarsity, 2000.

———. *Leadership Next.* Downers Grove, IL: InterVarsity, 2005.

Gibbs, Eddie, and Ryan K. Bolger. *Emerging Churches.* Grand Rapids, MI: Baker Academic, 2005.

Goldsworthy, Graeme. *Preaching the Whole Bible as Christian Scripture.* Grand Rapids, MI: William B. Eerdmans, 2000.

Gowan, Donald E. *Reclaiming the Old Testament for the Christian Pulpit.* Atlanta: John Knox, 1980.

Grady, J. Lee. *What Happened to the Fire?* Grand Rapids, MI: Chosen Books, 1994.

Gratton, Carolyn. *The Art of Spiritual Guidance.* New York: Crossroad Publishing, 1999.

Greenleaf, Robert K. *Servant Leadership.* New York: Paulist Press, 1977.

Greidanus, Sidney. *The Modern Preacher And The Ancient Text.* Grand Rapids, MI: William B. Eerdmans, 1988.

———. *Preaching Christ from the Old Testament.* Grand Rapids, MI: William B. Eerdmans, 1999.

Grenz, Stanley J. *Created For Community.* Grand Rapids, MI: Baker Books, 1996.

———. *A Primer on Postmodernism.* Grand Rapids, MI: William B. Eerdmans, 1996.

———. *What Christians Really Believe and Why.* Louisville: Westminster John Knox, 1998.

———. *Women in the Church.* Downers Grove, IL: InterVarsity, 1995.

Grenz, Stanley J., and Roger E. Olson. *Who Needs Theology?* Downers Grove, IL: InterVarsity, 1996.

Guder, Darrell L., ed. *Missional Church.* Grand Rapids, MI: William B. Eerdmans, 1998.

Guralnik, David B., ed. *Webster's New World Dictionary, Second College Edition.* Toronto: Nelson, Foster & Scott, 1970.

Hadaway, C. Kirk. *What Can We Do About Church Dropouts?* Nashville: Abingdon, 1990.

Hammond, Mary Tuomi. *The Church and the Dechurched: Mending a Damaged Faith.* St. Louis, MO: Chalice Press, 2001.

Hanks, Jr., Billie, and William A. Shell, eds. *Discipleship.* Grand Rapids, MI: Zondervan, 1981.

Harney, Kevin G., and Sherry Harney. *Finding a Church You Can Love and Loving the Church You've Found.* Grand Rapids, MI: Zondervan, 2003.

Hassan, Steven. *Combatting Cult Mind Control.* Rochester, VT: Park Street Press, 1988.

Hirsch, Alan. *Forgotten Ways.* Grand Rapids, MI: Brazos Press, 2006.

———. The Forgotten Ways. Online: http://www.TheForgottenWays.org.

Hjalmarson, Len. Next Reformation. Online: http://www.nextreformation.com/html/postmodern.htm.

Honig, Duncan, and Marilyn Honig. Dunmars Journey. "10 Earmarks of a Spiritually Abusive Church." August 18, 2007. Online: http://dunmarsjourney.blogspot.com/2007/08/10-earmarks-of-spiritually-abusive.html.

Jacobs, Janet. "Deconversion from Religious Movements: An Analysis of Charismatic Bonding and Spiritual Commitment." *Journal for the Scientific Study of Religion.* 26:3 (1987) 294–308.

Jamieson, Alan. *A Churchless Faith.* London: SPCK Publishing, 2002.

———. "A Churchless Faith." PhD thesis, University of Canterbury, 1998.

Jamieson, Alan, et al. *Church Leavers.* London: SPCK, 2006.

Johnson, David, and Jeff VanVonderen. *The Subtle Power of Spiritual Abuse.* Minneapolis: Bethany House, 1991.

Johnston, Graham. *Preaching to a Postmodern World.* Grand Rapids, MI: Baker Books, 2001.

Kaiser, Walter C. *Preaching and Teaching from the Old Testament.* Grand Rapids, MI: Baker Academic, 2003.

Karkkainen, Veli-Matti. *An Introduction to Ecclesiology.* Downers Grove, IL: InterVarsity, 2002.

Kinnaman, David. The Barna Group. Online: http://www.barna.org.

Kingdom Grace. Online: http://kingdomgrace.wordpress.com.

Kinnon, Bill. Achievable Ends. Online: http://www.kinnon.tv.

Kouzes, James M., and Barry Z. Posner. *The Leadership Challenge.* San Francisco: Jossey-Bass, 1987.

Kreider, Eleanor. *Communion Shapes Character.* Scottsdale, PA: Herald Press, 1997.

Lalich, Janja. "Repairing The Soul After a Cult." *CSNetwork Magazine,* Spring (1996) 30–33.

Larson, Craig Brian, and Haddon Robinson, eds. *The Art and Craft of Biblical Preaching: A Comprehensive Resource for Today's Communicators.* Grand Rapids, MI: Zondervan, 2005.

Lawless, Chuck. *Discipled Warriors.* Grand Rapids, MI: Kregel Publications, 2002.

Lawrenz, Mel. *The Dynamics of Spiritual Formation.* Grand Rapids, MI: Baker Books, 2002.

Linn, Dennis, and Matthew Linn. *Healing Life's Hurts.* New York: Paulist Press, 1978.

Littauer, Fred. *The Promise of Restoration.* San Bernardino, CA: Here's Life Publishers, 1990.

Macchia, Stephen A. *Becoming a Healthy Church.* Grand Rapids, MI: Baker Books, 1999.

MacNair, Donald J. *The Practices of a Healthy Church.* With Esther Meek. Philipsburg, NJ: P. & R. Publishing, 1999.

Mallory, Sue. *The Equipping Church.* Grand Rapids, MI: Zondervan, 2001.

Mallory, Sue, and Brad Smith. *The Equipping Church Guidebook.* Grand Rapids, MI: Zondervan, 200l.

Malphurs, Aubrey. *The Dynamics of Church Leadership.* Grand Rapids, MI: Baker Books, 1999.

Malphurs, Aubrey, and Will Mancini. *Building Leaders.* Grand Rapids, MI: Baker Books, 2004.

Maxwell, L. E. *Born Crucified.* Chicago: Moody Bible Institute, 1945.

Maynard, Brother. Subversive Influence. Online: http://subversiveinfluence.com.

McAlpine, Rob. *Post Charismatic?* London: Kingsway Communications, 2008.

———. Post Charismatics. Online: http://www.PostCharismatics.com (site now discontinued).

———. Robbymac. Online: http://www.Robbymac.org (site now discontinued).

McConnell, D. R. *A Different Gospel.* Peabody, MA: Hendrickson Publishers, 1988.

McDonnell, Kilian. *The Other Hand of God.* Collegeville, MN: Liturgical Press, 2003.

McLaren, Brian D. *The Church on the Other Side.* Grand Rapids, MI: Zondervan, 1998.

———. A New Kind of Christian. Online: http://www.anewkindofchristian.com/articles.html.

McNeal, Reggie. *A Work of Heart: Understanding How God Shapes Spiritual Leaders.* San Francisco: Jossey-Bass, 2000.

Menzies, William W., and Robert P. Menzies. *Spirit and Power.* Grand Rapids, MI: Zondervan, 2000.

Morris, Danny E., and Charles M. Olsen. *Discerning God's Will Together.* Nashville: Upper Room, 1997.

Mountford, Roxanne. *The Gendered Pulpit.* Carbondale: Southern Illinois University Press, 2003.

Mulholland, Robert, Jr. *Shaped by the Word: The Power of Scripture in Spiritual Formation.* Nashville: Upper Room, 1985.

Murren, Doug. *Churches That Heal.* West Monroe, LA: Howard Publishing, 1999.

Myers, Joseph R. *The Search to Belong.* Grand Rapids, MI: Zondervan, 2003.

Nathan, Rich, and Ken Wilson. *Empowered Evangelicals.* Ann Arbor, MI: Vine Books, 1995.

Noll, Mark A. *America's God.* New York: University Press, 2002.

Nouwen, Henry J. M. *In the Name of Jesus.* New York: Crossroad Publishing, 1989.

—. *Reaching Out.* New York: Doubleday, 1986.

—. *The Wounded Healer.* New York: Doubleday, 1972.

Oak, John H. *Healthy Christians Make a Healthy Church.* Ross-shire, Scotland: Christian Focus Publications, 2003.

Oden, Thomas C. *The Transforming Power of Grace.* Nashville: Abingdon, 1993.

Olsen, Charles M. *Transforming Church Boards.* Herndon, VA: Alban Institute, 1995.

Oropeza, B. J. *A Time to Laugh.* Peabody, MA: Hendrickson Publishers, 1995.

Ortberg, John. *Everybody's Normal Till You Get to Know Them.* Grand Rapids, MI: Zondervan, 2003.

Osborne, Grant R. *The Hermeneutical Spiral.* Downers Grove, IL: InterVarsity, 1991.

Packer, J. I. *I Want to be a Christian.* Wheaton, IL: Tyndale, 1977.

Pagitt, Doug. *Reimagining Spiritual Formation.* Grand Rapids, MI: Zondervan, 2003.

Palmer, Parker. *To Know As We Are Known.* San Francisco: Harper & Row, 1983.

Pearlman, Myer. *Knowing the Doctrines of the Bible.* Springfield, MO: Gospel Publishing, 1995.

Pendergast, Barry, and Jennifer Pendergast. Bleating Lambs. Online: http://www.bleating lambs.org (site now discontinued).

Perkins, Larry. "Church Governance." Course notes DMIN 914, The Associated Canadian Theological Schools the Graduate School of Theological Studies of Trinity Western University, Langley, BC, Canada, October 2004.

Personal Freedom Outreach. Online: http//www.PersonalFreedomOutreach.org.

Peterson, Eugene H. *Reversed Thunder.* San Francisco: Harper & Row, 1988.

—. *Working the Angles.* Grand Rapids, MI: William B. Eerdmans, 1987.

Poloma, Margaret M. *Main Street Mystics.* Walnut Creek, CA: AltaMira Press, 2003.

Porter, Stanley E., and Philip J. Richter. *The Toronto Blessing or Is It?* London: Darton, Longman and Todd, 1995.

Priddy, Mark. Allelon. Missional leaders. Online: http://www.allelon.org.

Randall, Robert L. *What People Expect From Church.* Nashville: Abingdon, 1992.

Rice, Howard. *The Pastor as Spiritual Guide.* Nashville: Upper Room, 1998.

Robinson, Haddon W., and Torrey W. Robinson. *It's All in How You Tell It.* Grand Rapids, MI: Baker Books, 2003.

Ryan, Dale. Recovery from Abuse. Online: http://www.recoveryfromabuse.com.

Ryan, Dale, and Juanita Ryan. *Recovery from Distorted Images of God.* Downers Grove, IL: InterVarsity, 1990.

—. *Recovery from Spiritual Abuse.* Downers Grove, IL: InterVarsity, 1992.

————. The National Association For Christian Recovery. Online: http://www.nacron line.com.

Saffold, Guy. "Leadership." Course notes DMIN 913, The Associated Canadian Theological Schools the Graduate School of Theological Studies of Trinity Western University, Langley, BC, Canada, October 2004.

Sailhamer, John H. *The Pentateuch As Narrative*. Grand Rapids, MI: Zondervan, 1992.

Salter, Darius L. *Prophetical-Priestly Ministry*. Nappanee, IN: Evangel Publishing, 2002.

Sanders, J. Oswald. *Spiritual Leadership*. Chicago: Moody Bible Institute, 1967.

Sargent, Brad. Futurist Guy. Online: http://futuristguy.wordpress.com.

Scazzero, Peter. *The Emotionally Healthy Church*. Grand Rapids, MI: Zondervan, 2003.

Schaller, Lyle E. *44 Steps Up Off The Plateau*. Nashville: Abingdon, 1993.

————. *Growing Plans*. Nashville: Abingdon, 1983.

————. *Tattered Trust*. Nashville: Abingdon, 1996.

————. *21 Bridges to the 21st Century*. Nashville: Abingdon, 1994.

Schrotenboer, Paul, ed. *An Evangelical Response to Baptism, Eucharist, and Ministry*. Carlisle, United Kingdom: Paternoster Press, 1992.

Scotland, Nigel. *Charismatics and the Next Millennium*. London: Hodder & Stoughton, 1995.

Setser, John. Shattered Trust. Online: http://shatteredtrust.com.

Singer, Margaret Thaler. *Cults In Our Midst*. San Francisco: Jossey-Bass, 1995.

Smail, Tom, et al. *The Love of Power or the Power of Love*. Minneapolis: Bethany House, 1994.

Smart, James D. *The Teaching Ministry of the Church*. Philadelphia: Westminster, 1954.

Smith, Gordon T. *Beginning Well*. Downers Grove, IL: InterVarsity, 2001.

————. *The Voice of Jesus*. Downers Grove, IL: InterVarsity, 2003.

Smulo, John. "Missio Dei Book Review." Review of *Missio Dei*, by Fred Peatross. SmuloSpace, (August 10, 2007), http://johnsmulo.com/Books/missio-dei-book-review.html.

————. SmuloSpace. No pages. Online: http://johnsmulo.com.

Snyder, Howard A. *Decoding The Church*. With Daniel V. Runyon. Grand Rapids, MI: Baker Books, 2002.

Stanger, Frank Bateman. *Spiritual Formation In The Local Church*. Grand Rapids, MI: Francis Asbury Press, 1989.

Streib, Heinz. "The Bielefeld-Based Cross-Cultural Research on Deconversion: Quantitative Results." Final Report, vol. 1. Germany: University of Bielefeld, 2007.

————. "Biographies in Christian Fundamentalist Milieus and Organizations." Report to the Inquiry Commission of the 13th German Parliament on "So-called Sects and Psychogroups." Translated by Ella Brehm. Germany: University of Bielefeld, 2000.

Streib, Heinz, and Barbara Keller. "The Variety of Deconversion Experiences: Contours of a Concept in Respect to Empirical Research." *Archives for the Psychology of Religion* 26:1 (2004) 181–200.

Stronstad, Roger. *The Charismatic Theology of St. Luke*. Peabody, MA: Hendrickson Publishers, 1984.

Sue, Paul, and Alan Mack. Battered Sheep. Online: http://www.batteredsheep.com.

Sweet, Leonard. *AquaChurch*. Loveland, CO: Group Publishing, 1999.

————. *Postmodern Pilgrims*. Nashville: Broadman & Holman, 2000.

————. *Soul Salsa*. Grand Rapids, MI: Zondervan, 2000.

————. *Summoned to Lead*. Grand Rapids, MI: Zondervan, 2004.

Synan, Vinson. *Aspects of Pentecostal-Charismatic Origins.* Plainfield, NJ: Logos International, 1975.

———. *The Holiness-Pentecostal Tradition.* Grand Rapids, MI: William B. Eerdmans, 1971.

Towns, Elmer L. *10 of Today's Most Innovative Churches.* Ventura, CA: Regal Books, 1993.

Tozer, A. W. *The Pursuit of God.* Harrisburg, PA: Christian Publications, 1948.

Tucker, Ruth A., and Walter Liefeld. *Daughters of the Church.* Grand Rapids, MI: Zondervan, 1987.

VanVonderen, Jeff. *Tired of Trying to Measure Up.* Minneapolis: Bethany House, 1989.

———. *When God's People Let You Down.* Minneapolis: Bethany House, 1985.

———. Spiritual Abuse Recovery Resources. Online: http://www.spiritualabuse.com.

Ver Straten, Charles A. *A Caring Church.* Grand Rapids, MI: Baker Books, 1988.

Virkler, Henry A. *Hermeneutics.* Grand Rapids, MI: Baker Books, 1981.

Wagner, E. Glenn. *Escape from Church, Inc.: The Return of the Pastor-Shepherd.* Grand Rapids, MI: Zondervan, 1999.

Waters, Claire M. *Angels and Earthly Creatures.* Philadelphia: University of Pennsylvania Press, 2004.

Wear, Charlie. The Next Wave. Online: http://www.the-next-wave.org.

Webber, Robert E. *The Younger Evangelicals.* Grand Rapids, MI: Baker Books, 2002.

———. Ancient Future. Online: http://www.ancientfuture.blogspot.com.

Wells, C. Richard, and A. Boyd Luter. *Inspired Preaching: A Survey of Preaching Found in the New Testament.* Nashville: Broadman & Holman, 2002.

Wellspring Retreat and Resource Center. Online: http://www.wellspringretreat.org.

White, John, and Ken Blue. *Healing The Wounded.* Downers Grove, IL: InterVarsity, 1985.

Wikipedia. Spiritual abuse. Online: http://en.wikipedia.org/wiki/Spiritual_abuse.

Wilhoit, Jim, and Leland Ryken. *Effective Bible Teaching.* Grand Rapids, MI: Baker Books, 1988.

Wilkes, C. Gene. *Jesus on Leadership.* Wheaton, IL: Tyndale, 1998.

Willard, Dallas. *The Divine Conspiracy.* San Francisco: Harper SanFrancisco, 1998.

Williams, Benjamin E., and Michael T. McKibben. *Oriented Leadership.* Wayne, NJ: Orthodox Christian Publications, 1994.

Williams, J. Rodman. Charismatic Pentecostal Theology. Online: http://www.jrodman williams.net.

Wills, Dick. *Waking to God's Dream.* Nashville: Abingdon, 1999.

Woods, Richard. *Mysticism and Prophecy.* Maryknoll, NY: Orbis Books, 1998.

Yancey, Philip. *Church, Why Bother?* Grand Rapids, MI: Zondervan, 1998.

Yocum, Bruce T. *Prophecy.* Ann Arbor, MI: Servant Books, 1976.

Zoba, Wendy Murray. "Rediscovering the Holy Spirit." *Christianity Today.* 40:7 (1996) 18–24.